CLIFFS

S0-BNR-549

Graduate Management Admission Test

PREPARATION GUIDE

by

Jerry Bobrow, Ph.D.

and

William A. Covino, Ph.D.

Contributing Authors
Daniel C. Spencer, M.S.
Harold Nathan, Ph.D.
David A. Kay, M.S.
Dale Johnson, M.A.

Consultants
Peter Z Orton, M.Ed.
Polly Greist, M.A.
Merritt L. Weisinger, J.D.

Cliffs Notes
INCORPORATED
LINCOLN, NEBRASKA   68501

ACKNOWLEDGMENTS

I would like to thank the following people for their invaluable assistance in typing, proofreading, and editing the manuscript: my wife, Susan Bobrow; my coordinating assistant, Joy Mondragon; my typist, Lynne Turner; and my little daughter, Jennifer Bobrow (for comic relief).

I would also like to thank Michele Spence of Cliffs Notes for final editing and careful attention to the production process and Dr. Albert Upton for the use of excerpts from his outstanding book Design for Thinking.

CONTENTS

Preface vii

Study Guide Checklist viii

PART I: INTRODUCTION

COMMON FORMAT OF RECENT GMAT EXAMS 3

GENERAL DESCRIPTION 4

QUESTIONS COMMONLY ASKED ABOUT THE GMAT 5

TAKING THE GMAT: A SUCCESSFUL OVERALL APPROACH 7

PART II: ANALYSIS OF EXAM AREAS

INTRODUCTION TO READING COMPREHENSION 11
    Ability Tested • Basic Skills Necessary • Directions
    • Analysis • Suggested Approach with Samples
    A Patterned Plan of Attack 13

INTRODUCTION TO PROBLEM SOLVING 15
    Ability Tested • Basic Skills Necessary • Directions
    • Analysis • Suggested Approach with Samples
    A Patterned Plan of Attack 21

INTRODUCTION TO DATA SUFFICIENCY 22
    Ability Tested • Basic Skills Necessary • Directions
    • Analysis • Suggested Approach with Samples
    A Patterned Plan of Attack 27

IMPORTANT SYMBOLS, TERMINOLOGY, FORMULAS, AND GENERAL
MATHEMATICAL INFORMATION THAT YOU SHOULD BE FAMILIAR
WITH 28
    Common Math Symbols and Terms That You Should Be Familiar
    With 28

iii

Math Formulas That You Should Be Familiar With 28
Important Equivalents That Can Save You Time 29
Measures 29
Words and Phrases That Can Be Helpful in Solving Problems 31
Geometry Terms and Basic Information 31

INTRODUCTION TO SENTENCE CORRECTION 33
    Ability Tested • Basic Skills Necessary • Directions
    • Analysis • Suggested Approach with Samples
A Patterned Plan of Attack 37

INTRODUCTION TO CRITICAL REASONING... 38
    Ability Tested • Basic Skills Necessary • Directions •
    Analysis • Suggested Approach with Samples
A Patterned Plan of Attack 43
Critical Reasoning Practice Problems... 43
Answers for Critical Reasoning Practice Problems 48

INTRODUCTION TO DATA INTERPRETATION: A LESS COMMON
QUESTION TYPE.. 50
    Ability Tested • Basic Skills Necessary • Directions
    • Analysis • Suggested Approach with Samples
A Patterned Plan of Attack 56

PART III: PRACTICE-REVIEW-ANALYZE-PRACTICE
Three Full-Length Practice Tests

PRACTICE TEST 1
    Answer Sheet for Practice Test 1 61
    Section I: Reading Comprehension 63
    Section II: Problem Solving.. 74
    Section III: Sentence Correction 77
    Section IV: Data Sufficiency.. 85
    Section V: Critical Reasoning 90
    Section VI: Problem Solving.. 100
    Section VII: Data Sufficiency 104
    Answer Key for Practice Test I 109
    How to Score Your Exam.. 111
    Analyzing Your Test Results... 111
    Practice Test 1: Analysis Sheet 112
    Analysis-Tally Sheet for Problems Missed 113

COMPLETE ANSWERS AND EXPLANATIONS FOR PRACTICE TEST 1
Section I: Reading Comprehension 117
Section II: Problem Solving 120
Section III: Sentence Correction 126
Section IV: Data Sufficiency 129
Section V: Critical Reasoning 132
Section VI: Problem Solving 135
Section VII: Data Sufficiency 140

PRACTICE TEST 2
Answer Sheet for Practice Test 2 147
Section I: Reading Comprehension 149
Section II: Problem Solving 160
Section III: Data Sufficiency 164
Section IV: Sentence Correction 169
Section V: Problem Solving 178
Section VI: Problem Solving 183
Section VII: Sentence Correction 189
Answer Key for Practice Test 2 198
How to Score Your Exam 200
Analyzing Your Test Results 200
Practice Test 2: Analysis Sheet 201
Analysis-Tally Sheet for Problems Missed 202

COMPLETE ANSWERS AND EXPLANATIONS FOR PRACTICE TEST 2
Section I: Reading Comprehension 205
Section II: Problem Solving 208
Section III: Data Sufficiency 212
Section IV: Sentence Correction 215
Section V: Problem Solving 218
Section VI: Problem Solving 222
Section VII: Sentence Correction 225

PRACTICE TEST 3
Answer Sheet for Practice Test 3 231
Section I: Critical Reasoning 233
Section II: Problem Solving 243
Section III: Data Sufficiency 248
Section IV: Sentence Correction 252
Section V: Problem Solving 259
Section VI: Reading Comprehension 264
Section VII: Problem Solving 275

Answer Key for Practice Test 3 280
How to Score Your Exam 282
Analyzing Your Test Results 282
Practice Test 3: Analysis Sheet 283
Analysis-Tally Sheet for Problems Missed 284

COMPLETE ANSWERS AND EXPLANATIONS FOR PRACTICE TEST 3
Section I: Critical Reasoning 287
Section II: Problem Solving 290
Section III: Data Sufficiency 295
Section IV: Sentence Correction 298
Section V: Problem Solving 301
Section VI: Reading Comprehension 305
Section VII: Problem Solving 308

Final Preparation: "The Final Touches" 312

PREFACE

YOUR GMAT SCORES MAKE THE DIFFERENCE! And better scores result from thorough preparation. Therefore, your study time must be used most effectively. You need the most comprehensive test preparation guide that you can realistically complete in a reasonable time. It must be thorough, direct, precise, and easy to use, giving you all the information you need to do your best on the GMAT.

In keeping with the fine tradition of Cliffs Notes, this guide was developed by leading experts in the field of test preparation as part of a series to specifically meet these standards. The testing strategies, techniques, and materials have been researched, tested, and evaluated, and are presently used at GMAT preparation programs at many leading colleges and universities. This guide features the PATTERNED PLAN OF ATTACK for each section and emphasizes the BOBROW TEST PREPARATION SERVICES approach which focuses on six major areas:

1. The Ability Tested
2. The Basic Skills Necessary
3. Understanding Directions
4. Analysis of Directions
5. Suggested Approaches with Samples
6. Practice-Review-Analyze-Practice

These major areas include important mathematical symbols, terminology, and formulas, and a helpful list of prefixes, suffixes, and roots. THREE complete practice exams follow with answers and *in-depth* explanations.

This guide was written to give you the edge in doing your best by maximizing your effort in the minimum amount of time. If you take the time to follow the Study Guide Checklist in this book, you will get the best preparation possible.

STUDY GUIDE CHECKLIST

_____ 1. Read the GMAT Information Bulletin.

_____ 2. Become familiar with the Test Format, page 3.

_____ 3. Familiarize yourself with the answers to Questions Commonly Asked about the GMAT, page 5.

_____ 4. Learn the techniques of a Successful Overall Approach, page 7.

_____ 5. Carefully read Part II, Analysis of Exam Areas, beginning on page 11.

_____ 6. Review math Symbols, Terminology, Formulas, and General Information, page 28.

_____ 7. Strictly observing time allotments, take Practice Test 1, section-by-section (review answers after each section), page 61.

_____ 8. Check your answers and analyze your results, page 109.

_____ 9. Fill out the Tally Sheet for Problems Missed to pinpoint your mistakes, page 113.

_____ 10. While referring to each item of Practice Test 1, study ALL the Answers and Explanations that begin on page 117.

_____ 11. Review as necessary Basic Skills, Symbols, Terminology, Formulas, and General Information given in Part II of this book.

_____ 12. Strictly observing time allotments, take Practice Test 2, page 147.

_____ 13. Check your answers and analyze your results, page 198.

_____ 14. Fill out the Tally Sheet for Problems Missed to pinpoint your mistakes, page 202.

_____ 15. While referring to each item of Practice Test 2, study ALL the Answers and Explanations that begin on page 205.

_____ 16. Again, selectively review materials as needed.

_____ 17. Strictly observing time allotments, selectively take sections of Practice Test 3 (those sections in which you want extra practice), page 231.

_____ 18. Check your answers and analyze your results, page 280.

_____ 19. Fill out the Tally Sheet for Problems Missed to pinpoint your mistakes, page 284.

_____ 20. While referring to each item of Practice Test 3, study ALL the Answers and Explanations that begin on page 287.

_____ 21. Carefully reread Part II, Analysis of Exam Areas, beginning on page 11.

_____ 22. Go over "FINAL PREPARATION" on page 312.

Part I: Introduction

COMMON FORMAT OF RECENT GMAT EXAMS

Section	Subject Area	Time	Number of Questions
I	Reading Comprehension	30 Minutes	25 Questions
II	Problem Solving	30 Minutes	20 Questions
III	Data Sufficiency	30 Minutes	25 Questions
IV	Sentence Correction	30 Minutes	25 Questions
V	Critical Reasoning	30 Minutes	25 Questions
VI	Last 2 sections are repeats of one or more of the	30 Minutes	*25 Questions
VII	types shown above.	30 Minutes	*25 Questions

Total Time 210 Minutes = 3½ hours   Approximately 170 Questions

*Number of questions may vary slightly.

NOTE: **One of the sections on the exam will be experimental and will not count toward your score. However you will not know which section is the experimental. The order of all sections will vary.**

GENERAL DESCRIPTION

The GMAT lasts approximately 3½ hours and consists entirely of multiple-choice questions. All questions in a section have equal value. The test is scored from 200 to 800, with an average score of about 480. Two subscores are also generated: Verbal Ability, scored 0–60 (average score 27), and Mathematical Ability, scored 0–60 (average score 28).

The most common sections of the test are:

READING COMPREHENSION—You will answer questions about reading passages from a variety of subject areas.

DATA SUFFICIENCY—For each item you will decide how much of the mathematical data you are given is sufficient for answering a question.

SENTENCE CORRECTION—You will demonstrate your knowledge of correct and effective English expression.

PROBLEM SOLVING—You will solve general math and word-type problems.

CRITICAL REASONING—You will derive logical conclusions and relationships from a variety of situations and passages.

Less common areas are:

DATA INTERPRETATION—You will demonstrate your understanding of charts, tables, and graphs.

ANALYSIS OF SITUATIONS—You will evaluate the components of a business decision as expressed in a reading passage.

General college background is measured by these sections, not specific knowledge from any specialized course or courses. No formal background in business or management is required.

QUESTIONS COMMONLY ASKED
ABOUT THE GMAT

Q: WHO ADMINISTERS THE GMAT?
A: The GMAT is written and administered by Educational Testing Service (ETS). The Graduate Management Admissions Council, made up of representatives from fifty graduate schools of management, works with ETS in an advisory capacity.

Q: CAN I TAKE THE GMAT MORE THAN ONCE?
A: Yes. But be aware that if you take the test twice, *both* scores will appear on your score report. The score report will list the results from the immediate and the two most recent you have taken since (and including) October 1983.

Q: WHAT MATERIALS MAY I BRING TO THE GMAT?
A: Bring your registration form, positive identification, a watch, three or four sharpened Number 2 pencils, and a good eraser. You may *not* bring scratch paper, calculators, or books. You may do your figuring in the space provided in the test booklet.

Q: IF NECESSARY, MAY I CANCEL MY SCORE?
A: Yes. You may cancel your score on the day of the test by informing the test center supervisor, or you may contact ETS in writing *no later than seven days* after the test date. Your score report will record your cancellation as well as completed test scores.

Q: SHOULD I GUESS ON THE GMAT?
A: If you can eliminate one or more of the multiple-choice answers to a question, it is to your advantage to guess. Eliminating one or more answers increases your chance of choosing the right answer. To discourage wild guessing, a fraction of a point is subtracted for every wrong answer, but no points are subtracted if you leave the answer blank.

Q: HOW SHOULD I PREPARE FOR THE GMAT?
A: Understanding and practicing test-taking strategies will help a great deal, especially on the verbal sections. Subject-matter review is particularly useful for the math sections. Both subject matter and strategies are fully covered in this book.

Q: WHEN IS THE GMAT ADMINISTERED?
A: The test is administered nationwide four times a year, in January, March, June, and October. These administrations are on Saturday mornings. Precise administration dates and test locations are published in the GMAT

Bulletin, which is generally available at the Testing Office, Counseling Center, or Graduate Studies Office at your undergraduate institutions.

Q: HOW AND WHEN SHOULD I REGISTER?
A: Registration forms are included in the GMAT Bulletin. In order to avoid a late registration fee, you should register at least one month prior to the test date.

Q: IS WALK-IN REGISTRATION PROVIDED?
A: Yes, on a limited basis. If you are unable to meet regular registration deadlines, you may attempt to register on the day of the test (an additional fee is required). You will be seated only if space remains after preregistered students have been seated.

Q: HOW IS MY GMAT SCORE USED?
A: The GMAT is used as part of an assessment of your probable success in graduate business school. Other factors, such as undergraduate grades, interviews, and letters of recommendation, also figure into this assessment. The importance of GMAT scores varies from institution to institution, so you are wise to contact the graduate schools to which you are applying for further information.

Q: CAN I GET MORE INFORMATION?
A: Yes. If you require information which is not available in this book, write to: Graduate Management Admission Test, Educational Testing Service, Box 966-R, Princeton, New Jersey 08541. Or telephone: (609) 771-7330.

TAKING THE GMAT: A SUCCESSFUL OVERALL APPROACH

Many who take the GMAT don't get the score that they are entitled to because they spend too much time dwelling on hard questions, leaving insufficient time to answer the easy questions they can get right. Don't let this happen to you. Use the following system to mark your answer sheet:

1. Answer easy questions immediately.
2. Place a "+" next to any problem that seems solvable but is too time-consuming.
3. Place a "−" next to any problem that seems impossible. Act quickly. Don't waste time deciding whether a problem is a "+" or a "−."

After working all the problems you can do immediately, go back and work your "+" problems. If you finish them, try your "−" problems (sometimes when you come back to a problem that seemed impossible you will suddenly realize how to solve it).

Your answer sheet should look something like this after you finish working your easy questions:

$$
\begin{array}{ll}
1. & Ⓐ \ ● \ Ⓒ \ Ⓓ \ Ⓔ \\
+2. & Ⓐ \ Ⓑ \ Ⓒ \ Ⓓ \ Ⓔ \\
3. & Ⓐ \ Ⓑ \ ● \ Ⓓ \ Ⓔ \\
-4. & Ⓐ \ Ⓑ \ Ⓒ \ Ⓓ \ Ⓔ \\
+5. & Ⓐ \ Ⓑ \ Ⓒ \ Ⓓ \ Ⓔ
\end{array}
$$

Make sure to erase your "+" and "−" marks before your time is up. The scoring machine may count extraneous marks as wrong answers.

By using this overall approach, you are bound to achieve your best possible score.

II. The Elimination Strategy

Take advantage of being allowed to mark in your testing booklet. As you eliminate an answer choice from consideration, *make sure to mark it out in your question booklet* as follows:

(A̶)̶
?(B)
(C̶)̶
(D̶)̶
?(E)

7

Notice that some choices are marked with question marks, signifying that they may be possible answers. This technique will help you avoid reconsidering those choices you have already eliminated and will help you narrow down your possible answers.

These marks in your testing booklet do not need to be erased.

Part II: Analysis of Exam Areas

This section is designed to introduce you to each GMAT area by carefully reviewing the

1. Ability Tested
2. Basic Skills Necessary
3. Directions
4. Analysis of Directions
5. Suggested Approach with Sample Questions

This section features the PATTERNED PLAN OF ATTACK for each subject area and emphasizes important test-taking techniques and strategies and how to apply them to a variety of problem types. It also includes some valuable math and verbal review.

INTRODUCTION TO READING COMPREHENSION

Reading Comprehension is usually the first section of the GMAT and often appears again later in the test. It typically consists of three or four passages and contains a total of approximately 25 questions.

Ability Tested

This section tests your ability to understand, interpret, and analyze reading passages on a variety of topics.

Basic Skills Necessary

Students who have read widely and know how to read and mark a passage actively and efficiently tend to do well on this section.

Directions

Each passage in this group is followed by questions based on its content. After reading a passage, choose the best answer to each question and blacken the corresponding space on the answer sheet. Answer all questions following a passage on the basis of what is *stated* or *implied* in that passage. You may refer back to the passage.

Analysis

1. Answer all the questions for one passage before moving on to the next one. If you don't know the answer, take an educated guess or skip it.
2. Use only the information given or implied in a passage. Do not consider outside information, even if it seems more accurate than the given information.

SUGGESTED APPROACH WITH SHORT SAMPLE PASSAGE

1. Skim the questions first, marking words which give you a clue about what to look for when you read the passage.
2. Skim the passage, reading only the first sentence of each paragraph. (optional)
3. Read the passage, marking main points, important conclusions, names, definitions, places, and numbers. Make only a few marks per paragraph.

Short Sample Passage

St. Augustine was a contemporary of Jerome. After an early life of pleasure, he became interested in a philosophical religion called Manichaeism, a derivative of a Persian religion, in which the <u>forces of good</u> constantly struggle with those of <u>evil</u>. Augustine was eventually converted to Christianity by St. Ambrose of Milan. His *Confessions* was an autobiography that <u>served as an inspiration</u> to countless thousands who believed that virtue would ultimately win.

Sample Questions with Explanations

1. St. Augustine's conversion to Christianity was probably influenced by
   - (A) his confessional leanings
   - (B) his contemporaries
   - (C) the inadequacy of a Persian religion to address Western moral problems
   - (D) his earlier interest in the dilemma of retaining virtue
   - (E) the ravages of a life of pleasure

Having skimmed this question, you should have marked the portion of the passage which mentions Augustine's conversion and paid attention to the events (influences) leading to it. (A) requires speculating beyond the facts in the paragraph; there is also no evidence in the passage to support (C) or (E). (B) is too vague and general to be the best answer. (D) points toward Augustine's earlier interest in Manichaeism, and the last sentence suggests that Augustine's interest in retaining virtue continued through his Christian doctrine. Well supported as it is, (D) is the best answer.

2. From the information in the passage, we must conclude that Augustine was a
   - (A) fair-weather optimist
   - (B) cockeyed optimist
   - (C) hardworking optimist
   - (D) failed optimist
   - (E) glib optimist

Skimming *this* question is not very helpful; it does not point specifically to any information in the passage. Questions of this sort usually assess your overall understanding of the meaning, style, tone, or point of view of the passage. In this case, you should recognize that Augustine is a serious person; therefore, more lighthearted terms like "fair-weather" (A), "cockeyed" (B), and "glib" (E) are probably inappropriate. (D) contradicts Augustine's success as an "inspiration to countless thousands." (C) corresponds with his ongoing, hopeful struggle to retain virtue in the world; it is the best answer.

3. Judging from the reaction of thousands to Augustine's *Confessions,* we
   may conclude that much of his world at that time was in a state of
   (A) opulence   (D) reformation
   (B) misery   (E) sanctification
   (C) heresy

Having skimmed this question, you should have marked the last sentence
of the passage as the place to look for the answer. That Augustine's readers
were inspired implies that they *required inspiration,* that they were in some
sort of uninspiring, or *negative* situation. (A) and (E) must therefore be
eliminated because they are positive terms. (D) is not necessarily a negative
term, and so is probably not the best answer. (C), although a negative term,
does not describe a state of being which thirsts for inspiration. (B) does, and
(B) therefore is the best choice.

A PATTERNED PLAN OF ATTACK

Reading Comprehension

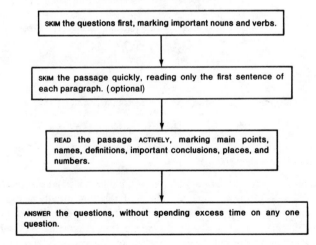

SKIM the questions first, marking important nouns and verbs.

SKIM the passage quickly, reading only the first sentence of each paragraph. (optional)

READ the passage ACTIVELY, marking main points, names, definitions, important conclusions, places, and numbers.

ANSWER the questions, without spending excess time on any one question.

INTRODUCTION TO PROBLEM SOLVING

The Problem Solving section contains 20 questions, most of which are word problems. Occasionally, questions refer to a graph or chart.

Ability Tested

The Problem Solving section tests your ability to solve mathematical problems involving arithmetic, algebra, geometry, and word problems by using problem-solving insight, logic, and application of basic skills.

Basic Skills Necessary

The basic skills necessary to do well on this section include high school algebra and intuitive geometry—no formal trigonometry or calculus is necessary. Skills in arithmetic and basic algebra, along with some logical insight into problem-solving situations, are also necessary.

Directions

Solve each problem in this section by using the information given and your own mathematical calculations. Then select the *one* correct answer of the five choices given. Use the available space on the page for scratchwork.

Note: Some problems may be accompanied by figures or diagrams. These figures are drawn as accurately as possible *except* when it is stated in a specific problem that the figure is not drawn to scale. The figure is meant to provide information useful in solving the problem or problems.

Unless otherwise stated or indicated, all figures lie in a plane.

All numbers used are real numbers.

Analysis

All scratchwork is to be done in the test booklet; get used to doing this because no scratch paper is allowed into the testing area.

You are looking for the *one* correct answer; therefore, although other answers may be close, there is never more than one right answer.

Suggested Approach with Samples

1. Take advantage of being allowed to mark on the test booklet by always underlining or circling what you are looking for. This will ensure that you are answering the right question. *Sample:*

If $x + 6 = 9$, then $3x + 1 =$

(A) 3   (B) 9   (C) 10   (D) 34   (E) 46

You should first circle or underline $3x + 1$, because this is what you are solving for. Solving for x leaves $x = 3$ and then substituting into $3x + 1$ gives $3(3) + 1$, or 10. The most common mistake is to solve for x, which is 3, and *mistakenly choose* (A) as your answer. But remember, you are solving for $3x + 1$, not just x. You should also notice that most of the other choices would all be possible answers if you made common or simple mistakes. The correct answer is (C). *Make sure that you are answering the right question.*

2. Substituting numbers for variables can often be an aid to understanding a problem. Remember to substitute simple numbers, since *you* have to do the work. *Sample:*

If $x > 1$, which of the following decreases as x decreases?

$$\text{I. } x + x^2$$
$$\text{II. } 2x^2 - x$$
$$\text{III. } \frac{1}{x + 1}$$

(A) I   (B) II   (C) III   (D) I and II   (E) II and III

This problem is most easily solved by taking each situation and substituting simple numbers. However, in the first situation, I, $x + x^2$, you should recognize that this expression will decrease as x decreases. Trying $x = 2$, gives $2 + (2)^2$, which equals 6. Now trying $x = 3$, gives $3 + (3)^2 = 12$. Notice that choices (B), (C), and (E) are already eliminated because they do not contain I. You should also realize that now you only need to try the values in II; since III is not paired with I as a possible choice, III cannot be one of the answers. Trying $x = 2$ in the expression $2x^2 - x$, gives $2(2)^2 - 2$, or $2(4) - 2$, which leaves 6. Now trying $x = 3$ gives $2(3)^2 - 3$, or $2(9) - 3 = 18 - 3 = 15$. This expression also decreases as x decreases. Therefore the correct answer is choice (D). Once again notice that III was not even attempted, because it was not one of the possible choices.

3. Sometimes you will immediately recognize the proper formula or method to solve a problem. If this is not the situation, try a reasonable approach and then work from the answers. *Sample:*

Barney can mow the lawn in 5 hours, and Fred can mow the lawn in 4 hours. How long will it take them to mow the lawn together?

(A) 5 hours   (C) 4 hours   (E) 1 hour
(B) 4½ hours   (D) 2⅖ hours

Suppose that you are unfamiliar with the type of equation for this problem. Try the "reasonable" method. Since Fred can mow the lawn in 4 hours by nimself, he will take less than 4 hours if Barney helps him. Therefore, choices (A), (B), and (C) are ridiculous. Taking this method a little further, suppose that Barney could also mow the lawn in 4 hours. Then together it would take Barney and Fred 2 hours. But since Barney is a little slower than this, the total time should be more than 2 hours. The correct answer is (D), $2\frac{2}{9}$ hours.

Using the equation for this problem would give the following calculations:

$$\frac{1}{5} + \frac{1}{4} = \frac{1}{x}$$

In 1 hour, Barney could do 1/5 of the job, and in 1 hour, Fred could do 1/4 of the job; unknown 1/x is that part of the job they could do together in one hour. Now, solving, you calculate as follows:

$$\frac{4}{20} + \frac{5}{20} = \frac{1}{x}$$

$$\frac{9}{20} = \frac{1}{x}$$

Cross multiplying gives 9x = 20
Therefore, $x = \frac{20}{9}$, or $2\frac{2}{9}$.

4. "Pulling" information out of the word problem structure can often give you a better look at what you are working with, and therefore, you gain additional insight into the problem. *Sample:*

If a mixture is 3/7 alcohol by volume and 4/7 water by volume, what is the ratio of the volume of alcohol to the volume of water in this mixture?

(A) $\frac{3}{7}$ (B) $\frac{4}{7}$ (C) $\frac{3}{4}$ (D) $\frac{4}{3}$ (E) $\frac{7}{4}$

The first bit of information that should be pulled out should be what you are looking for: "ratio of the volume of alcohol to the volume of water." Rewrite it as A:W and then into its working form: A/W. Next, you should pull out the volumes of each; A = 3/7 and W = 4/7. Now the answer can be easily figured by inspection or substitution: using (3/7)/(4/7), invert the bottom fraction and multiply to get $3/7 \times 7/4 = 3/4$. The ratio of the volume of alcohol to the volume of water is 3 to 4. The correct answer is (C). When pulling out information, actually write out the numbers and/or letters to the side of the problem, putting them into some helpful form and eliminating some of the wording.

5. Sketching diagrams or simple pictures can also be very helpful in problem solving, because the diagram may tip off either a simple solution or a method for solving the problem. *Sample:*

What is the maximum number of pieces of birthday cake of size 4″ by 4″ that can be cut from a cake 20″ by 20″?

(A) 5   (B) 10   (C) 16   (D) 20   (E) 25

Sketching the cake and marking in as follows makes this a fairly simple problem.

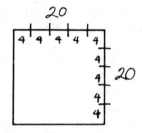

Notice that five pieces of cake will fit along each side, therefore 5 × 5 = 25. The correct answer is (E). Finding the total area of the cake and dividing it by the area of one of the 4 × 4 pieces would have also given you the correct answer, but beware of this method because it may not work if the pieces do not fit evenly into the original area.

6. Marking in diagrams as you read them can save you valuable time. Marking can also give you insight into how to solve a problem because you will have the complete picture clearly in front of you. *Sample:*

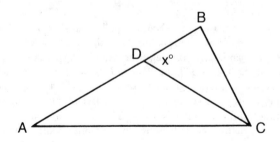

In the triangle, CD is an angle bisector, angle ACD is 30° and angle ABC is a right angle. Find the measurement of angle x in degrees.

(A) 80°   (B) 75°   (C) 60°   (D) 45°   (E) 30°

You should have read the problem and marked as follows:

In the triangle above, CD is an angle bisector (STOP AND MARK IN THE DRAWING), angle ACD is 30° (STOP AND MARK IN THE DRAWING), and angle ABC is a right angle (STOP AND MARK IN THE DRAWING). Find the measurement of angle x in degrees (STOP AND MARK IN OR CIRCLE WHAT YOU ARE LOOKING FOR IN THE DRAWING).

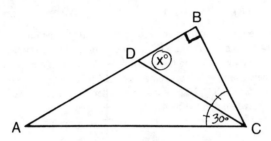

Now with the drawing marked in, it is evident that, since angle ACD is 30°, then angle BCD is also 30° because they are formed by an angle bisector (divides an angle into two equal parts). Since angle ABC is 90° (right angle) and BCD is 30°, then angle x is 60°, because there are 180° in a triangle; 180 − (90 + 30) = 60. The correct answer is (C). ALWAYS MARK IN DIAGRAMS AS YOU READ THEIR DESCRIPTIONS AND INFORMATION ABOUT THEM. THIS INCLUDES WHAT YOU ARE LOOKING FOR.

7. If it appears that extensive calculations are going to be necessary to solve a problem, check to see how far apart the choices are, and then approximate. The reason for checking the answers first is to give you a guide for how freely you can approximate. *Sample:*

The value for (.889 × 55)/9.97 to the nearest tenth is

(A) .5   (B) 4.63   (C) 4.9   (D) 7.7   (E) 49.1

Before starting any computations, take a glance at the answers to see how far apart they are. Notice that the only close answers are choices (B) and (C), except (B) is not possible, since it is to the nearest hundredth, not tenth. Now, making some quick approximations, .889 = 1 and 9.97 = 10, leaves the problem in this form

$$\frac{1 \times 55}{10} = \frac{55}{10} = 5.5$$

The closest answer is (C); therefore, it is the correct answer. Notice that choices (A) and (E) were not reasonable.

8. In some instances, it will be easier to work from the answers. Do not disregard this method, because it will at least eliminate some of the choices and could give you the correct answer. *Sample:*

Find the counting number that is less than 15 and when divided by 3 has a remainder of 1 and divided by 4 has a remainder of 2.

(A) 13   (B) 12   (C) 10   (D) 8   (E) 5

By working from the answers, you eliminate wasting time on other numbers from 1 to 14. Choices (B) and (D) can be immediately eliminated because they are divisible by 4, leaving no remainder. Choices (A) and (E) can also be eliminated because they leave a remainder of 1 when divided by 4. Therefore the correct answer is (C); 10 leaves a remainder of 1 when divided by 3 and a remainder of 2 when divided by 4.

A PATTERNED PLAN OF ATTACK

Problem Solving

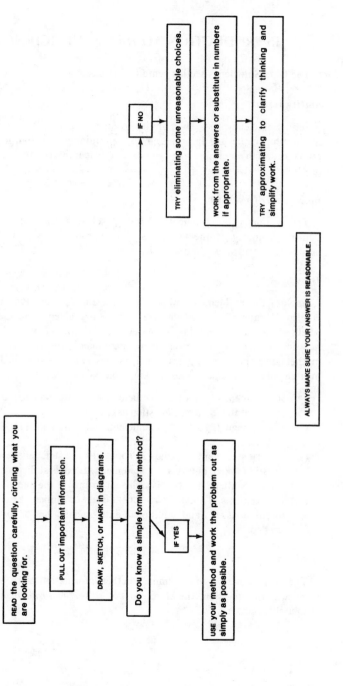

READ the question carefully, circling what you are looking for.

↓

PULL OUT important information.

↓

DRAW, SKETCH, or MARK in diagrams.

↓

Do you know a simple formula or method?

IF YES → USE your method and work the problem out as simply as possible.

IF NO → TRY eliminating some unreasonable choices.

↓

WORK from the answers or substitute in numbers if appropriate.

↓

TRY approximating to clarify thinking and simplify work.

ALWAYS MAKE SURE YOUR ANSWER IS REASONABLE.

INTRODUCTION TO DATA SUFFICIENCY

The Data Sufficiency section contains 25 questions.

Ability Tested

Data Sufficiency tests your ability to analyze a problem, to recognize relevant or irrelevant information in determining the solution of that problem, and to determine when you have sufficient information to solve that problem.

Basic Skills Necessary

This section requires competence in high school arithmetic, algebra, and intuitive geometry. Mathematical insight and problem-solving skills are also necessary. No advanced mathematics is required.

Directions

Each of the problems below consists of a question and two statements, labeled (1) and (2), in which certain data are given. You must decide whether the data given in the statements are *sufficient* to answer the question. Using the data given in the statements *plus* your knowledge of mathematics and everyday facts (such as the number of days in July or the meaning of *counterclockwise*), you are to blacken space

- (A) if statement (1) ALONE is sufficient, but statement (2) alone is not sufficient to answer the question asked;
- (B) if statement (2) ALONE is sufficient, but statement (1) alone is not sufficient to answer the question asked;
- (C) if BOTH statements (1) and (2) TOGETHER are sufficient to answer the question asked, but NEITHER statement ALONE is sufficient;
- (D) if EACH statement ALONE is sufficient to answer the question asked;
- (E) if statements (1) and (2) TOGETHER are NOT sufficient to answer the question asked, and additional data specific to the problem are needed.

Analysis

The purpose here is to determine whether information given is *sufficient* to answer the question; therefore, *do not solve the problem* unless it is absolutely necessary.

The memory aid 12TEN will simplify the directions, making them easier to memorize and/or refer to. 12TEN stands for:

1   *First* statement ALONE is sufficient, not the second. CHOOSE (A).
2   *Second* statement ALONE is sufficient, not the first. CHOOSE (B).
T   *Together* is the only way they are sufficient. CHOOSE (C).
E   *Either* statement ALONE is sufficient. CHOOSE (D).
N   *Neither* statement, TOGETHER or ALONE, is sufficient. CHOOSE (E).

REMEMBER: ONE, TWO, TOGETHER, EITHER, NEITHER, or 12TEN. (Note: *Either* means choose answer (D) *not* (E).)

Because of the structure of this type of question, you should always be able to eliminate some of the choices. If statement (1) ALONE is sufficient to answer the question, then the answer *must* be (A) or (D). If statement (1) ALONE is *not* sufficient to answer the question, then the answer *must* be (B), (C), or (E). If statements (1) and (2) ALONE are *not* sufficient, then the answer *must* be (C) or (E).

If statements (1) or (2) ALONE *are* sufficient, then you *never* try them TOGETHER.

Sometimes geometric figures are included; they should be used only for positional value, and are not to be measured as they are not necessarily drawn to scale.

Suggested Approach with Samples

1. Quickly decide what is the necessary basic information to answer the question. Then see if the data supplies that information. *Sample:*

What is the area of circle O?
(1) The circumference is 12π.
(2) The diameter is 12.

To find the area of a circle, it is necessary to have the radius. (1) gives enough information to find the radius by substituting into the circumference formula, $C = 2\pi r$, and getting $12\pi = 2\pi r$. Then simply solve for r, which is 6. Thus this area is 36π. None of this solving was necessary, only knowing that you needed the radius and could find it from the information given. (2) also gives enough information to find the radius; therefore the answer is (D), either will be sufficient.

2. Don't solve unless it is absolutely necessary. *Sample:*

What is the value of x?
(1) $3x + 12 = 36$
(2) $5x + 3y = 16$

This problem is most easily solved by inspecting the first bit of data and quickly noticing that (1) is enough to answer the question (one variable, one equation, solvable). (2) does not answer the question. This can also be determined by inspection (two variables, one equation, not solvable for a single value). The correct answer is (A), yet no actual solving had to be done.

3. Use a simple marking system to assist you in making your decision. *Sample:*

What is the average height of Tom, Bob, and Luke?
(1) Bob is 4 inches shorter than Luke, and Tom is 4 inches taller than Luke.
(2) Luke is 5 feet 6 inches tall.

(1) is not sufficient, since no actual height is given; therefore mark a slash through (1). Note that the answer is immediately narrowed to (B), (C), or (E). (2) by itself is also not sufficient, as the other two, Tom and Bob, aren't mentioned; therefore, a slash should be made through (2). Notice that the answer is now narrowed to (C) or (E). Your markings should look as follows:

What is the average height of Tom, Bob, and Luke?
(*1*) Bob is 4 inches shorter than Luke, and Tom is 4 inches taller than Luke.
(*2*) Luke is 5 feet 6 inches tall.

Now trying them together, they are sufficient. The answer is (C). In marking the data, if you are in doubt whether it is sufficient or not, put a question mark by the data and try the next bit of data. Don't waste time trying one bit of data for over about 30 seconds.

4. Don't read in specialized knowledge; use only the information given and general or common knowledge. *Sample:*

What is the runner's average speed in running around the track?
(1) One lap took 49 seconds.
(2) He ran 5 seconds faster than his previous best time.

Someone familiar with track and field would quickly assume that one lap is the standard 440 yards and would then *incorrectly answer* (A). This sort of assumption cannot be made as it is from specialized knowledge in the area and therefore is not general knowledge. The correct answer is (E) as the distance around the track is not given in either bit of data.

5. If a geometric figure is involved in the question, mark the figure with the information given and circle what you are looking for. *Sample:*

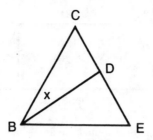

In the equilateral triangle above, what is the measure of angle x?
(1) BD is a median.
(2) Angle BDE is 90°.

Notice the markings from the information given:

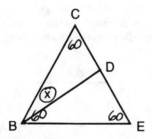

Mark in information given in data (1) as you read it, *but remember to erase that information before you try data* (2). (1) If BD is a median in an equilateral triangle, then it is also an angle bisector, making angle x equal to 30°. (Once again, the answer is not necessary, just the knowledge that it could be found.) (2) also gives enough information because if angle BDE is 90°, then angle BDC is 90°, and angle x is 30°, as there are 180° in a triangle. Marking the diagram makes the problem easier to solve.

6. If a geometric diagram is discussed, but no figure given, draw a simple diagram. *Sample:*

If the legs of a trapezoid are equal, what is the area?
(1) The smaller base is 8 inches and the legs are 6 inches.
(2) The height is 5 inches.

Drawing the diagram helps give important insight into what is needed to answer the question.

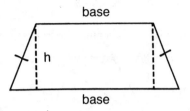

Now consider what is needed to find the area—height and length of each base since the area formula is $\frac{1}{2} h(b_1 + b_2)$ or $h(b_1 + b_2)/2$.

(1) does not give sufficient information to find the larger base or the height. (2), by itself, does not give enough information to find the bases. (1) and (2) together give enough information to find the bases and the height. The answer is (C). The Pythagorean theorem would be necessary to find the length of the difference between the smaller and larger bases. Adding this difference to the length of the shorter base would give the longer base. You now have the necessary information. Notice the markings on the diagram below, to assist you in deciding what you have to work with.

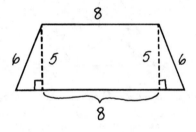

A PATTERNED PLAN OF ATTACK

Data Sufficiency

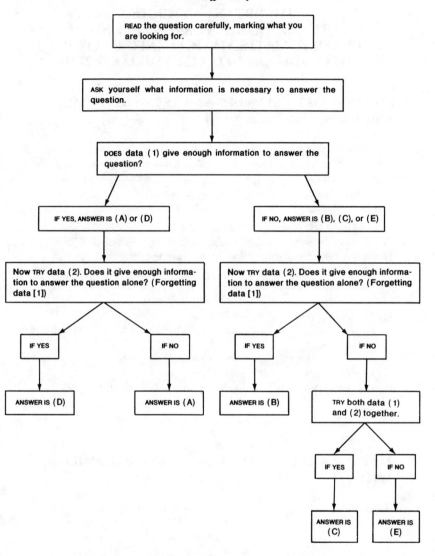

KEEP THE FOLLOWING TIPS IN MIND.
1. Don't solve unless it is absolutely necessary.
2. Use a simple marking system (slashes, question marks, etc.).
3. Don't read in specialized knowledge. Use only common information.
4. Mark in or draw geometric figures when appropriate.

IMPORTANT SYMBOLS, TERMINOLOGY, FORMULAS, AND GENERAL MATHEMATICAL INFORMATION THAT YOU SHOULD BE FAMILIAR WITH

COMMON MATH SYMBOLS AND TERMS THAT YOU SHOULD BE FAMILIAR WITH

Symbol References:

$=$ is equal to	$\geq$ is greater than or equal to
$\neq$ is not equal to	$\leq$ is less than or equal to
$>$ is greater than	$\parallel$ is parallel to
$<$ is less than	$\perp$ is perpendicular to

Natural numbers—the counting numbers: 1, 2, 3, . . .

Whole numbers—the counting numbers beginning with zero: 0, 1, 2, 3, . . .

Integers—positive and negative whole numbers and zero: . . . $-3, -2, -1, 0,$ 1, 2, . . .

Odd numbers—numbers not divisible by 2: 1, 3, 5, 7, . . .

Even numbers—numbers divisible by 2: 0, 2, 4, 6, . . .

Prime number—number divisible by only 1 and itself: 2, 3, 5, 7, 11, 13, . . .

Composite number—number divisible by more than just 1 and itself: 4, 6, 8, 9, 10, 12, 14, 15, . . .

Squares—the result when numbers are multiplied by themselves, $(2 \cdot 2 = 4)$ $(3 \cdot 3 = 9)$: 1, 4, 9, 16, 25, 36, . . .

Cubes—the result when numbers are multiplied by themselves twice, $(2 \cdot 2 \cdot 2 = 8)$, $(3 \cdot 3 \cdot 3 = 27)$: 1, 8, 27, . . .

MATH FORMULAS THAT YOU SHOULD BE FAMILIAR WITH

Triangle	Perimeter $= s_1 + s_2 + s_3$
	Area $= \frac{1}{2}bh$
Square	Perimeter $= 4s$
	Area $= s \cdot s$, or s^2
Rectangle	Perimeter $= 2(b + h)$, or $2b + 2h$
	Area $= bh$, or lw

Parallelogram

Perimeter $= 2(l + w)$, or $2l + 2w$
Area $= bh$

Trapezoid

Perimeter $= b_1 + b_2 + s_1 + s_2$

Area $= \frac{1}{2}h(b_1 + b_2)$, or $h\left(\dfrac{b_1 + b_2}{2}\right)$

Circle

Circumference $= 2\pi r$, or πd
Area $= \pi r^2$

Pythagorean theorem (for right triangles) $a^2 + b^2 = c^2$

The sum of the squares of the legs of a right triangle equals the square of the hypotenuse.

Cube

Volume $= s \cdot s \cdot s = s^3$
Surface area $= s \cdot s \cdot 6$

Rectangular Prism

Volume $= l \cdot w \cdot h$
Surface area $= 2(lw) + 2(lh) + 2(wh)$

IMPORTANT EQUIVALENTS THAT CAN SAVE YOU TIME

Memorizing the following can eliminate unnecessary computations:

$\frac{1}{100} = .01 = 1\%$

$\frac{1}{10} = .1 = 10\%$

$\frac{1}{5} = \frac{2}{10} = .2 = .20 = 20\%$

$\frac{3}{10} = .3 = .30 = 30\%$

$\frac{2}{5} = \frac{4}{10} = .4 = .40 = 40\%$

$\frac{1}{2} = \frac{5}{10} = .5 = .50 = 50\%$

$\frac{3}{5} = \frac{6}{10} = .6 = .60 = 60\%$

$\frac{7}{10} = .7 = .70 = 70\%$

$\frac{4}{5} = \frac{8}{10} = .8 = .80 = 80\%$

$\frac{9}{10} = .9 = .90 = 90\%$

$\frac{1}{4} = \frac{25}{100} = .25 = 25\%$

$\frac{3}{4} = \frac{75}{100} = .75 = 75\%$

$\frac{1}{3} = .33\frac{1}{3} = 33\frac{1}{3}\%$

$\frac{2}{3} = .66\frac{2}{3} = 66\frac{2}{3}\%$

$\frac{1}{8} = .125 = .12\frac{1}{2} = 12\frac{1}{2}\%$

$\frac{3}{8} = .375 = .37\frac{1}{2} = 37\frac{1}{2}\%$

$\frac{5}{8} = .625 = .62\frac{1}{2} = 62\frac{1}{2}\%$

$\frac{7}{8} = .875 = .87\frac{1}{2} = 87\frac{1}{2}\%$

$\frac{1}{6} = .16\frac{2}{3} = 16\frac{2}{3}\%$

$\frac{5}{6} = .83\frac{1}{3} = 83\frac{1}{3}\%$

$1 = 1.00 = 100\%$

$2 = 2.00 = 200\%$

$3\frac{1}{2} = 3.5 = 3.50 = 350\%$

MEASURES

Customary System, or English System

Length
12 inches (in) = 1 foot (ft)
3 feet = 1 yard (yd)
36 inches = 1 yard

1760 yards = 1 mile (mi)
5280 feet = 1 mile

Area
144 square inches (sq in) = 1 square foot (sq ft)
9 square feet = 1 square yard (sq yd)

Weight
16 ounces (oz) = 1 pound (lb)
2000 pounds = 1 ton (T)

Capacity
2 cups = 1 pint (pt)
2 pints = 1 quart (qt)
4 quarts = 1 gallon (gal)
4 pecks = 1 bushel

Time
365 days = 1 year
52 weeks = 1 year
10 years = 1 decade
100 years = 1 century

Metric System, or The International System of Units
(SI, *Le Système International d'Unités*)

Length—meter
Kilometer (km) = 1000 meters (m)
Hectometer (hm) = 100 meters
Dekameter (dam) = 10 meters

Meter
10 decimeters (dm) = 1 meter
100 centimeters (cm) = 1 meter
1000 millimeters (mm) = 1 meter

Volume—liter
Common measures
1000 milliliters (ml, or mL) = 1 liter (l, or L)
1000 liters = 1 kiloliter (kl, or kL)

Mass—gram
Common measures
1000 milligrams (mg) = 1 gram (g)
1000 grams = 1 kilogram (kg)
1000 kilograms = 1 metric ton (t)

WORDS AND PHRASES THAT CAN BE HELPFUL IN SOLVING PROBLEMS

Words that signal an operation:

ADDITION

- Sum
- Total
- Plus
- Increase
- More than
- Greater than

SUBTRACTION

- Difference
- Less
- Decreased
- Reduced
- Fewer
- Have left

MULTIPLICATION

- Of
- Product
- Times
- At (sometimes)
- Total (sometimes)

DIVISION

- Quotient
- Divisor
- Dividend
- Ratio
- Parts

GEOMETRY TERMS AND BASIC INFORMATION

Angles

Vertical angles—Formed by two intersecting lines, across from each other, always equal
Adjacent angles—Next to each other, share a common side and vertex
Right angle—Measures 90 degrees
Obtuse angle—Greater than 90 degrees
Acute angle—Less than 90 degrees
Straight angle, or line—Measures 180 degrees
Angle bisector—Divides an angle into two equal angles
Supplementary angles—Two angles whose total is 180 degrees
Complementary angles—Two angles whose total is 90 degrees

Lines

Two points determine a line
Parallel lines—Never meet
Perpendicular lines—Meet at right angles

Polygons

Polygon—A many-sided (more than two sides) closed figure
Regular polygon—A polygon with all sides and all angles equal
Triangle—Three-sided polygon; the interior angles total 180 degrees
    Equilateral triangle—All sides equal
    Isosceles triangle—Two sides equal
    Scalene triangle—All sides of different lengths
    Right triangle—A triangle containing a right angle
In a triangle—Angles opposite equal sides are equal
In a triangle—The longest side is across from the largest angle, and the shortest side is across from the smallest angle
In a triangle—The sum of any two sides of a triangle is larger than the third side
In a triangle—An exterior angle is equal to the sum of the remote two angles
Median of a triangle—A line segment that connects the vertex and the midpoint of the opposite side
Quadrilateral—Four-sided polygon; the interior angles total 360 degrees.
    Parallelogram—A quadrilateral with opposite sides parallel
        Rectangle—A parallelogram with all right angles
        Rhombus—A parallelogram with equal sides
        Square—A parallelogram with equal sides and all right angles
    Trapezoid—A quadrilateral with two parallel sides
Pentagon—A five-sided polygon
Hexagon—A six-sided polygon
Octagon—An eight-sided polygon

Circles

Radius of a circle—A line segment from the center of the circle to the circle itself
Diameter of a circle—A line segment that starts and ends on the circle and goes through the center
Chord—A line segment that starts and ends on the circle
Arc—A part of the circle
Circle—Composed of 360°

INTRODUCTION TO SENTENCE CORRECTION

The Sentence Correction section typically contains 25 questions.

Ability Tested

This section tests your knowledge of correct and effective English expression.

Basic Skills Necessary

Knowledge of basic rules of grammar and usage will help in this section.

Directions

Some part of each sentence below is underlined; sometimes the whole sentence is underlined. Five choices for rephrasing the underlined part follow each sentence; the first choice (A) repeats the original, and the other four are different. If choice (A) seems better than the alternatives, choose answer (A); if not, choose one of the others.

For each sentence, consider the requirements of standard written English. Your choice should be a correct and effective expression, not awkward or ambiguous. Focus on grammar, word choice, sentence construction, and punctuation. If a choice changes the meaning of the original sentence, do not select it.

Analysis

1. Several alternatives to an underlined portion may be correct; you are to pick the *best* (most clear and exact) one.

2. *Any* alternative which changes the meaning of the sentence should not be chosen, no matter how clear or correct it is.

Suggested Approach with Samples

1. Look for pronoun errors first. Focus upon words like *he, him, she, her, we, us, they, them, who, whom, whoever, whomever, you, it, which,* or *that.*

The Rotary Club applauded Tom and I for our work helping the handicapped in town find secure jobs.
(A) The Rotary Club applauded Tom and I
(B) The Rotary club applauded Tom and I
(C) The Rotary Club applauded us both
(D) The Rotary Club applauded Tom and me
(E) The Rotary Club applauded both of us

Focus on *I,* because it's a pronoun. To test whether *I* is correct, remove "Tom and." The result is, "The Rotary Club applauded . . . I." *Me* would sound better, and in fact (D) is the correct choice. (C) and (E) change the meaning of the sentence.

2. If the sentence contains no pronouns or if the pronouns are correct, focus on the *verb.*

   The trunk containing <u>costumes, makeup, and props were left</u> at the stage entrance of the theater.
   (A) costumes, makeup, and props were left
   (B) costumes, makeup, and props were all left
   (C) costumes, makeup, and props was left
   (D) costumes, makeup, and props to be left
   (E) costumes, makeup, and props left

The verb is *were left.* Since the subject is singular (*trunk*) the verb must be singular—*was* instead of *were.* Don't assume that the subject immediately precedes the verb; in this case, the subject and verb are some distance apart.

3. Another common error is faulty parallelism. Look for a series of items separated by commas and make sure each item has the same *form.*

   <u>To strive, to seek, to find, and not yielding</u> are the heroic goals of Ulysses in Tennyson's famous poem.
   (A) To strive, to seek, to find, and not yielding
   (B) To strive, to seek, to find, and to yield
   (C) To strive, to seek, to find, and not to yield
   (D) To strive, to seek, to find, and yet to yield
   (E) Striving, seeking, finding and yielding

Not yielding is incorrect; it should have the "to _____" form of the other items. (C) is the best choice; (B), (D), and (E) are correct, but they change the meaning of the sentence.

4. Another verb error happens when the verb tense (past, present, future) is inconsistent. If there are two verbs in the sentence, make sure the verb tense of each is appropriate.

   <u>If he would have worked</u> harder, he could have gone to the movies.
   (A) If he would have worked   (D) If he had worked
   (B) If he worked   (E) After working
   (C) Working

In general, if a sentence contains two "would haves," two "should haves," two "could haves," or any combination of these terms (in this case *would have* and *should have*), one of the verbs should be changed to *had*, to indicate that one of the actions (working) occurred earlier than the other (going to the movies). (D) is correct.

5. Sometimes a sentence contains an error in idiom; that is, it employs a word or phrase which is incorrect simply because it has not been established as standard usage. Such errors just don't "sound right."

   <u>After waiting on the arrival of a washer repairman for hours,</u> the customer resigned himself to using the laundromat.
   (A) After waiting on the arrival of a washer repairman for hours
   (B) With no arrival of a washer repairman for hours
   (C) After hours of waiting for the arrival of a washer repairman
   (D) Waiting after hours for the arrival of a washer repairman
   (E) In the face of hours of waiting for a washer repairman

   Waiting on is not idiomatic; the correct expression is *waiting for*. Choices (C), (D), and (E) employ this construction, but (D) and (E) significantly obscure and change the intended meaning of the original sentence.

6. Adjective or adverb misuse constitutes another type of error.

   <u>The tired mechanic, happily to be finished with a hard day's work,</u> closed the hood over the newly tuned engine.
   (A) The tired mechanic, happily to be finished with a hard day's work
   (B) Happily, the tired mechanic being finished with a hard day's work
   (C) Tired but happy with a hard day's work being done, the mechanic
   (D) The tired mechanic, happy to be finished with a hard day's work
   (E) With the pleasant fatigue of a job well done, the mechanic

   Happily is used here to describe a person, the mechanic. The correct part of speech for describing a person or thing is an adjective, *happy*. (D) is the correct choice—grammatically correct, logical, economical, and clear without unnecessarily changing the intended meaning of the original sentence.

7. A type of error that affects a whole phrase rather than just one word is a dangling element, or misplaced modifier, error.

   <u>Looking through the lens of a camera,</u> Mount Rushmore seemed much smaller and farther away than it had only seconds before.
   (A) Looking through the lens of a camera
   (B) With camera in hand
   (C) Through the effects of the lens of a camera she looked through
   (D) When she looked through the camera lens
   (E) Against the camera

The sentence seems to say that Mount Rushmore is looking through the camera lens. Choice (D) makes it clear that a person is looking through the lens and does so without the excessive wordiness of choice (C).

8. A sentence may contain a comparison error.

She wished that her career could be <u>as glamorous as the other women</u> but was not willing to work as hard as they had.
(A) as glamorous as the other women
(B) as glamorous as the other women's careers
(C) with the glamour of other women
(D) more glamorous than the careers of the other women
(E) glamorous

Here two very different *in*comparable things are being compared: her career is compared to the other women. Choice (B), the most clear, complete, and sensible construction, compares her career to the careers of other women.

Summary

Generally, watch out for pronouns, verbs, and awkward larger structures (illustrated by errors like faulty parallelism). Other possible errors which have not been explained above are fully explained in the answer sections following the practice tests.

A PATTERNED PLAN OF ATTACK

Sentence Correction

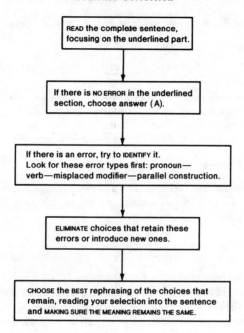

READ the complete sentence, focusing on the underlined part.

If there is NO ERROR in the underlined section, choose answer (A).

If there is an error, try to IDENTIFY it. Look for these error types first: pronoun—verb—misplaced modifier—parallel construction.

ELIMINATE choices that retain these errors or introduce new ones.

CHOOSE the BEST rephrasing of the choices that remain, reading your selection into the sentence and MAKING SURE THE MEANING REMAINS THE SAME.

INTRODUCTION TO CRITICAL REASONING

The Critical Reasoning section lasts 30 minutes and typically contains 25 questions.

Ability Tested

This section tests your ability to analyze and evaluate short passages or statements drawn from a variety of sources and presented in a variety of modes.

Basic Skills Necessary

Students who can read critically and understand major issues and points of view tend to do well in this section. Ability to eliminate irrelevant and unimportant issues is also important.

Directions

You will be presented with brief passages or statements and will be required to evaluate their reasoning. In each case, select the best answer choice, even though more than one choice may present a possible answer. Choices which are unreasonable or incompatible with common-sense standards should be eliminated.

Analysis

1. Use only information given or implied in a passage. Do not consider outside information, even if it seems more accurate than the given information.
2. Note the stress on choosing the BEST answer; the testmakers strongly imply that there may be more than one good answer.
3. No special expertise in logic is necessary; do not arrive at your answer choice through the use of formal logical principles; rely on common sense.

Suggested Approach with Samples

1. In most cases, the question will have the following structure: reading passage—question—multiple choices. Always read the question first so that you have an idea of what to look for when you read the passage.

Reading Passage: Whatever else might be said about American elections, they are already quite unlike Soviet elections in that Americans make choices. And one choice they can make in this free country is to stay home.

Question: What is the author's point in the above passage?

Multiple Choices:
(A) Americans who do decide to vote make more choices than those who do not.
(B) American elections embody many negative aspects, most of which are not embodied by Soviet elections.
(C) Choosing not to vote is the prerogative of a free citizen.
(D) All citizens vote in every Soviet election.
(E) Most American voters are not well informed enough to vote wisely.

Prereading the question allows you to read the passage with a *focus*. In this case, you are looking for the author's point; recognizing the concluding sentence as the author's point is valuable here.

2. Keep the question in mind when reading a passage, and also note the major issue and supporting evidence in the passage. Ask yourself, what is this passage, in general, about? The answer relative to the passage above is "free choice." Evidence supporting the issue of free choice is (1) the fact that Americans make choices when they vote and (2) the fact that Americans may make the choice not to vote.

3. When considering the multiple choices, immediately eliminate those items which are (1) irrelevant to the question and/or the major issue of the passage and (2) not at all addressed by the passage. Consider the passage above. The author's point is necessarily connected with the major issue of the passage—in this case, free choice. The author stresses the free choice *not to vote*, by way of making the point. You may eliminate all choices which do not address the free choice not to vote: (A) is irrelevant because it addresses the number of choices rather than the freedom of choice; (B) raises issues scarcely addressed in the passage—that is, the negative aspects of elections. (D) doesn't address the issue of choosing not to vote; though it notes that all Soviet citizens must vote, it neglects the main point—that Americans don't have to; (E) is irrelevant to the issue of free choice, stressing instead voter information. The best choice is (C), which addresses the major issue, free choice, and also the author's specific point, the free choice not to vote.

4. A question may require you to evaluate tone:

> *Interviewer:* How do you like the clean, fresh taste of new MaxoShine Toothbrightener?
>
> *Interviewee:* My dentist tells me that no toothpaste will affect the natural color of my teeth.

In the above exchange, the interviewer's question implies which of the following attitudes toward MaxoShine?
(A) sincere curiosity
(B) unqualified enthusiasm
(C) unabashed ignorance
(D) scientific objectivity
(E) disguised dislike

The question asks about the interviewer's attitude, and questions like this which ask you to define the author's *stance* in one way or another are often answerable through noting the tone. In order to detect tone, do this: (1) When you read the passage in question, do so *actively,* trying to suit the "personality" of the words to the purpose or structure of the passage. In the passage above, the purpose of the interviewer is to advocate the product, and the structure of the passage is a dialogue. (2) When you read, imagine the way in which such an interviewer might deliver the question and try to mentally approximate the tone of a conversational exchange.

Note that the tone of the interviewer is extremely positive, and that certain modifiers within the interviewer's question stress that positive attitude (modifiers such as *clean, fresh, new*). Noting this tone leads you to eliminate choices which indicate a neutral or negative attitude and to realize that the only answer choice coincident with the interviewer's positive tone is (B).

A question about the interviewee might lead you to consider the negative attitude expressed there and also to note that the interviewee does not really answer the question asked

5. Recognizing the "type" of question asked will help to lead you to a correct answer. Questions will commonly ask you to (1) identify the author's main point, (2) identify the author's underlying assumptions, (3) identify information which strengthens the author's conclusion, (4) identify flaws in the argument or conclusion, or characteristics which weaken it.

Identifying the Author's Main Point

Identifying the main issue, as described above, will help you to answer this type of question.

Identifying the Author's Underlying Assumptions

The assumption of the author is that which motivates his or her argument. For instance, an argument in favor of increased government spending *assumes* that present government spending is too low. An example:

United States dependence on foreign oil has tended to overshadow the beneficial effects of gasoline-powered machines on our society. More than ever before, the American automobile allows us to enjoy the many pleasures this country offers.

The argument above is based upon which of the following assumptions?

I.   Many American pleasures cannot be walked to.
II. The automobile is a significant gasoline-powered machine.
III. U.S. dependence on foreign oil is beneficial.

(A) I only   (D) I and II
(B) II only   (E) I and III
(C) III only

Answer and Explanation: (D) I and II. I is true (eliminate B and C because neither contains I). II is true (eliminate A and E). Choose (D) because it's the only choice left. Notice that by working from the roman numerals in this way, you did not need to spend time considering III.

Identifying Information Which Strengthens the Author's Argument or Conclusion

Focus on the *conclusion,* note the supporting evidence given, and look for an answer choice which supplies additional support specifically appropriate to the conclusion.

Identifying Information Which Weakens the Author's Argument or Conclusion

Look for answer choices which contradict or call into question the supporting evidence. An example:

United States dependence on foreign oil has tended to overshadow the beneficial effects of gasoline-powered machines on our society. More than ever before, the American automobile allows us to enjoy the many pleasures this country offers.

This argument would be weakened by pointing out that

   I. smog generated by automobiles is not a pleasure
  II. at the turn of the century, Americans rarely ventured far from home
 III. inflation helped by rising oil prices has made many automobiles virtually unaffordable

(A) I and III   (D) I and II
(B) II and III   (E) I, II, and III
(C) II only

Answer and Explanation: (A) I and III. This problem also combines roman numeral choices and letter choices; it's a kind of *multiple-multiple choice.* Work from the numeral choices, asking yourself whether each is *true* or *false.* Statement I is true—it would weaken the argument for pleasure. Eliminate (B) and (C) because they do not contain I. II is false—it would *not* weaken the argument for driving as a modern pleasure. Eliminate (D) and (E) because both contain II. III is true—it would weaken the argument for automobiles as a source of pleasure. Choose (A), the only remaining possibility.

The strategies reviewed in this introduction are further explained and illustrated in the answers and explanations which follow each practice test. To summarize:

1. Preread questions when appropriate.
2. Focus on the major issue and supporting evidence.
3. Eliminate answer choices which are irrelevant.
4. Note the tone of the passage.
5. Note the "type" of question asked.

A PATTERNED PLAN OF ATTACK

Critical Reasoning

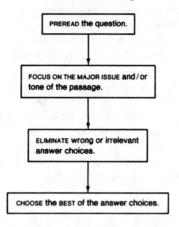

PREREAD the question.

FOCUS ON THE MAJOR ISSUE and/or tone of the passage.

ELIMINATE wrong or irrelevant answer choices.

CHOOSE the BEST of the answer choices.

Critical Reasoning Practice Problems

Questions 1 and 2 refer to the following passage

The new vehicle inspection program is needed to protect the quality of the state's air, for us and for our children. Auto exhausts are a leading contributor to coughing, wheezing, choking, and pollution. The state's long-term interests in the health of its citizens and in this area as a place to live, work, and conduct business depend on clean air.

1. Which of the following, if true, would most seriously weaken the argument above?
    (A) Since smog devices were made mandatory automotive equipment by the existing inspection program three years ago, pollution has decreased dramatically and continues to decrease.
    (B) Pollution problems are increasing in other states as well as in this one.
    (C) Sometimes coughing, wheezing, and choking are caused by phenomena other than pollution.
    (D) Vehicle inspectors are not always careful.
    (E) The state should not impose its interests upon the citizenry but should instead allow public health to be regulated by private enterprise.

2. Which of the following is an unstated assumption made by the author?
   (A) Working and conducting business may be different activities.
   (B) The state has been interested in the health of its citizens even before this inspection program was proposed.
   (C) Exhaust emissions contribute to pollution.
   (D) The new inspection program will be effective.
   (E) Our ancestors did not suffer from air pollution.

We doubt that the latest government report will scare Americans away from ham, bacon, sausages, hot dogs, bologna, and salami or that it will empty out the bars or cause a run on natural food supplies. If a diet were to be mandated from Washington, Americans probably would order the exact *opposite* course. Therefore the diet that does make sense is to eat a balanced and varied diet composed of foods from *all* food groups and containing a reasonable caloric intake.

3. Which of the following is (are) specifically implied by the passage?
   I. Vitamins are necessary to combat disease.
   II. A recent report warned of the risks of meat and alcoholic beverages.
   III. Unorthodox suggestions for a more nutritional diet were recently made by the government.
   (A) I only   (D) I and II
   (B) II only   (E) II and III
   (C) III only

In his first message to Congress, Harry Truman said, "The responsibility of the United States is to serve and not dominate the world."

4. Which of the following is one basic assumption underlying Truman's statement?
   (A) The United States is capable of dominating the world.
   (B) The United States chooses to serve rather than dominate the world.
   (C) World domination is a virtue.
   (D) One must be decisive when facing a legislative body for the first time.
   (E) The United States, preceding Truman's administration, had been irresponsible.

Without sign ordinances, everyone with the price of a can of spray paint can suddenly decide to publicly create their own personal Picassos, and soon the entire town would start to look like something out of *Alice in Wonderland*. Therefore we need sign ordinances.

5. The author makes which of the following basic assumptions?

  I. Spray paint is used for many signs.
  II. The entire town looking like *Alice in Wonderland* is undesirable.
  III. Sign ordinances are effective.

  (A) I only (B) II only (C) III only (D) I and III (E) I, II, and III

Speaker: One need not look very far to find abundant examples of incivility and brutality in the most genteel corners of American society.

Questioner: Then why don't we step up law enforcement in the slums of our cities?

6. The question reveals which of the following misunderstandings?
  (A) the misunderstanding that incivility and brutality have become more abundant
  (B) the misunderstanding that law enforcement is related to the problems of incivility and brutality
  (C) misunderstanding of the speaker's position relative to incivility and brutality
  (D) misunderstanding of the meaning of the word *genteel*
  (E) misunderstanding of the meaning of the words *incivility* and *brutality*

Experience shows that for every burglar shot by a homeowner there are many more fatal accidents involving small children, family slayings that could have been avoided but for the handy presence of a gun, and thefts of handguns by the criminals they are intended to protect against.

7. Which of the following facts, if true, would most seriously weaken the above contention?
  (A) Criminals tend to sell the handguns they steal during the commission of a burglary.
  (B) Burglars are also capable of causing fatal accidents.
  (C) Every burglar shot by a homeowner is stopped from committing scores of further burglaries and injuring scores of other citizens.
  (D) The number of burglars shot by homeowners is larger than the number of burglars shot by renters.
  (E) Not all fatal accidents involve guns.

Questions 8 and 9 refer to the following passage

Voters on June 8 approved a $495 million bond issue for a state prison construction that is an obvious priority. Now the legislature has voted to put five more general obligation bond issues on the November ballot, adding another $1.5 billion to the state's long-term debt. Those on the November menu include $500 million for building and remodeling public schools, $450 million to extend the veterans home loan program, $200 million to subsidize low-interest mortgages for first-time home buyers, $85 million to acquire land for environmental protection, and $280 million to help counties expand or remodel their jails.

8. Which of the following statements is a point to which the author is most probably leading?
   (A) Two of these bond issues are certainly more important than the others.
   (B) We must face the obvious conclusion that prison construction is much less important than the improvement of public education and social programs for lawful citizens.
   (C) The cost of these bond issues is, on the face of it, negligible.
   (D) The voters cannot be expected to help make financial decisions for the state because most voters are suffering from their own severe financial problems.
   (E) These five bond proposals are quite enough, and between now and November voters will have to study them carefully to make sure that five are not too many.

9. Which of the following facts would most strongly weaken an argument for approval of the five new bond issues?
   (A) Environmental protection is not an overriding concern of the constituency.
   (B) The state's long-term debt cannot lawfully exceed $1.5 billion.
   (C) Improvements in education, the environment, criminal prosecution, and the real estate market are favored by the voters.
   (D) Similar bond proposals in other states have not been successful.
   (E) Two bills related to the housing of criminals are quite enough.

Famous painter James Whistler said, "Industry in art is a necessity—not a virtue—and any evidence of the same, in the production, is a blemish, not a quality."

10. Whistler is arguing that
    (A) of necessity, art becomes industrialized
    (B) the qualities of art are its virtues
    (C) blemished paintings are the work of overindustrious artists
    (D) the product reflects the means of production
    (E) the artist must work hard, but the art should look easy

Deliberations of our governing bodies are held in public in order to allow public scrutiny of each body's actions and take to task those actions which citizens feel are not, for whatever reason, in their best interests.

11. With which of the following statements would the author of the above passage probably agree?
    (A) Deliberations of our governing bodies should be held in public.
    (B) Public scrutiny usually results in the criticism of our governing bodies.
    (C) The best interests of the public usually do not coincide with the motives of our governing bodies.
    (D) No government decisions ought to be kept from the public.
    (E) Citizens in other countries are not cared for by the government.

Questions 12 and 13 refer to the following passage

Recent studies indicate that more violent crimes are committed during hot weather than during cold weather. Thus, if we could control the weather, the violent crime rate would drop.

12. The argument above makes which of the following assumptions?

    I. The relationship between weather conditions and crime rate is merely coincidental.
    II. The relationship between weather conditions and crime rate is causal.
    III. The relationship between weather conditions and crime rate is controllable.

    (A) I and II
    (B) II and III
    (C) I, II, and III
    (D) I only
    (E) II only

13. The argument would be strengthened if it pointed out that
    (A) the annual crime statistics for New York are higher than those for Los Angeles
    (B) in laboratory tests, increased heat alone accounted for increased aggressive behavior between members of the test group
    (C) poor socioeconomic conditions, more uncomfortable in hot weather than in cold, are the direct causes of increased crime
    (D) weather control will be possible in the near future
    (E) more people leave their doors and windows open during hot weather

The state's empty $4 million governor's mansion on the banks of the Capitol River may be sort of a suburban Taj Mahal, as the governor once said. But why shouldn't the state unload it?

14. Which of the following is one of the author's basic assumptions?
    (A) The governor's mansion is out of place in the suburbs.
    (B) The reader is aware of the state's intention to "unload" the governor's mansion.
    (C) No one has yet lived in the governor's mansion.
    (D) The state is trying to sell the governor's mansion.
    (E) The governor was correct.

Answers for Critical Reasoning Practice Problems

1. (A) The argument for further supervision of vehicle use is most weakened by the statement that present safeguards are already doing the job. (C) and (D) slightly weaken the argument but do not address the overall position of the author.

2. (D) In order to argue for a new inspection program, the author must assume that that particular program, if enacted, will be effective. (C), the only other choice related to the points of the argument, expresses stated information rather than an unstated assumption.

3. (B) Since the author doubts that Americans will stop eating meats or visiting bars, one must conclude that the author is referring to the latest government report warning of the risks of meat and alcoholic beverages. Statement I concerning vitamins may be true, but is not *specifically* implied other than in a very general sense (nutrition). Statement III is not true: there is nothing to suggest that the government report made "unorthodox" suggestions.

4. (A) Truman's statement is not warranted unless one assumes the U.S. capability to dominate the world; that assumed capability makes the choice between serving and dominating possible and is thus a basic assumption.

5. (E) All of the statements are assumptions of the author essential to the argument. The author assumes spray paint to be the medium that graffiti painters use and implicitly abhors the possibility of a town looking like *Alice in Wonderland*. In addition, his or her desire for sign ordinances assumes that they work and are effective in deterring spray painting.

6. (D) The questioner understands the speaker to be referring to a problem restricted to the slums and so does not understand that *genteel* refers to upper-class situations.

7. (C) This choice most directly addresses the argument of the passage. The passage argues that for every burglar shot, there are scores of slayings of the innocent; (C) argues that for every burglar shot, there are scores of prevented slayings.

8. (E) By listing high costs, the author is probably leading to the conclusion that the state's debt is being strained, a conclusion expressed in (E). (C) contradicts the author's emphasis on high costs. (A), (B), and (D) are neither expressed nor implied by the passage; their choice would rely on extraneous assumptions.

9. (B) This fact indicates that the passage of all the bond measures, which would take the debt over $2.5 billion, is illegal.

10. (E) Whistler is saying that constant effort (industry) is necessary but that the artwork (production) should not evidence that effort.

11. (A) By describing in very positive terms the effects of public deliberations, the author suggests the opinion that such deliberations *should* be public.

12. (E) The only correct choice is II; it is argued that hot weather *causes* crime. This is not mere coincidence, and the statement does not state that we *can* control the weather.

13. (B) The argument posits an exclusive relationship between hot weather and crime. (A), (C), and (E) contradict such an exclusive relationship. (D) is irrelevant to the relationship, and (B) provides evidence supporting and strengthening the heat-crime relationship.

14. (B) The author's final question necessarily rests on the assumption that the reader is aware of the state's intention; the author omits information expressing or explaining this intention.

INTRODUCTION TO DATA INTERPRETATION

A LESS COMMON QUESTION TYPE

Data Interpretation questions (charts and graphs) used to appear as a separate section on the GMAT. Now there are occasional charts and graphs problems in the Problem Solving and Data Sufficiency sections of the exam.

Ability Tested

You will need to understand and to derive information from charts, tables, and graphs. Many of the problems require brief calculations based on the data, so your mathematical ability is also tested.

Basic Skills Necessary

The mathematics associated with Data Interpretation does not go beyond high-school level. Your familiarity with a wide range of chart and graph types will help you feel comfortable with these problems and read the data accurately.

Directions

You are given data represented in chart or graph form. Following each set of data are questions based on that data. Select the *best* answer to each question by referring to the appropriate chart or graph and mark your choice on the answer sheet. Use only the given or implied information to determine your answer.

Analysis

1. Remember that you are looking for the *best* answer, not necessarily the perfect answer. Often, graph questions ask you for an *approximate* answer; if this happens, don't forget to round off numbers to make your work easier.
2. Use only the information given; never "read into" the information on a graph.

SUGGESTED APPROACH WITH SAMPLE QUESTIONS

Here are some helpful strategies for extracting accurate information followed by some sample graph questions.

1. Skim the questions and quickly examine the whole graph before starting to work problems; this sort of prereading will tell you what to look for.

2. Use your answer sheet as a straightedge in order to align points on the graph with their corresponding number values.

3. Sometimes the answer to a question is available in supplementary information given with a graph (headings, scale factors, legends, etc.); be sure to read this information.

4. Look for the obvious: dramatic trends, high points, low points, etc.— obvious information often leads directly to an answer.

Data Interpretation Questions

Questions 1–3 refer to the graph.

1. The 1970–72 gross receipts for Monster Burger exceeded those of Pizza In A Pot by approximately how much?
   (A) 0.2 million   (C) 8.2 million   (E) 17 million
   (B) 2 million   (D) 8.4 million

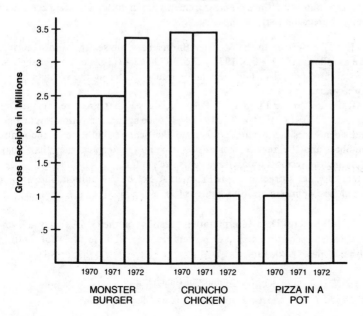

**Gross Receipts of Several Fast-Food Restaurants
1970-1972**

2. From 1971 to 1972, the percent increase in receipts for Pizza In A Pot
   exceeded the percent increase of Monster Burger by approximately how
   much?
   (A) 0%   (B) 2%   (C) 10%   (D) 15%   (E) 43%

3. The 1972 decline in Cruncho Chicken's receipts may be attributed to
   (A) an increase in the popularity of burgers
   (B) an increase in the popularity of pizza
   (C) a decrease in the demand for chicken
   (D) a predictable slump attributable to the deceleration of the Vietnam-
       ese War
   (E) it cannot be determined from the information given

Answers and Explanations

This is a bar graph. Typically, this type of graph has a number scale along
one edge and individual categories along another edge. Here we have
multiple bars representing each fast-food category; each single bar stands for
the receipts from a single year.

You may be tempted to write out the numbers as you do your arithmetic
(3.5 million = 3,500,000). This is unnecessary, as it often is on graphs which
use large numbers. Since *all* measurements are in millions, adding zeros does
not add precision to the numbers.

1. (B) Referring to the Monster Burger bars, we see that gross receipts
are as follows: 1970 = 2.5, 1971 = 2.5, 1972 = 3.4 (use your answer sheet as
a straightedge to determine this last number). Totaling the receipts for all
three years, we get 8.4.

Referring to the Pizza In A Pot bars, we see that gross receipts are as
follows: 1970 = 1, 1971 = 2.1, 1972 = 3 (once again, use your straightedge,
but do not designate numbers beyond the nearest tenth, since the graph
numbers and the answer choices prescribe no greater accuracy than this).
Totaling the receipts for all three years, we get 6.1.

So Monster Burger exceeds Pizza In A Pot by 2.3 million. The answer
which best approximates this figure is (B).

2. (C) Several Data Interpretation questions on the GMAT may ask you
to calculate percent increase or percent decrease. The formula for figuring
either of these is the same:

$$\frac{\text{amount of the change}}{\text{``starting'' amount (follows the word } from)}$$

In this case, we may first calculate the percent increase for Monster Burger.

Gross receipts in 1971 = 2.5
Gross receipts in 1972 = 3.4
Amount of the change = .9

The 1971 amount is the "starting" or "from" amount.

$$\frac{\text{amount of the change}}{\text{"starting" amount}} = \frac{.9}{2.5} = .36 = 36\%$$

Percent increase for Pizza In A Pot:

Gross receipts in 1971 = 2.1
Gross receipts in 1972 = 3
Amount of the change = .9

$$\frac{\text{amount of the change}}{\text{"starting" amount}} = \frac{.9}{2.1} = .428 = 43\%$$

So, Pizza In A Pot exceeds Monster Burger by 7% (43% − 36%). The answer which best approximates this figure is (C).

3. (E) Never use information that you know is not given. In this case, the multiple factors which could cause a decline in receipts are not represented by the graph. All choices except (E) require you to speculate beyond the information given.

Questions 4–6 refer to the graph.

4. The gross receipts for 1971 are approximately what percentage of the gross receipts for all three years?
    (A) 30%
    (B) 46.3%
    (C) 46.7%
    (D) 50%
    (E) it cannot be determined from the information given

5. Over all three years, the average percentage of gross receipts for Cruncho Chicken exceeds the average percentage of gross receipts for Pizza In A Pot by approximately how much?
    (A) 53%   (B) 30%   (C) 23%   (D) 8%   (E) 4%

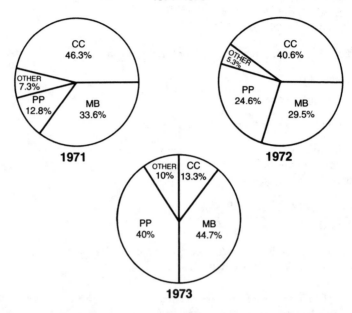

**Gross Receipts of All Major
Fast-Food Restaurants
1971–1973**

Gross Receipts for 1971: $7,500,000   MB—Monster Burger
Gross Receipts for 1972: $8,550,000   CC—Cruncho Chicken
Gross Receipts for 1973: $8,100,000   PP—Pizza In A Pot

6. The gross receipts earned by other restaurants in 1973 amount to *precisely* how much?
   (A) $1,810,650
   (B) $810,000
   (D) $547,500
   (D) $453,150
   (E) a precise amount cannot be determined

Answers and Explanations

This is a circle graph, or pie chart. 100 percent is represented by the whole circle, and the various "slices" represent portions of that 100 percent. The larger the slice, the higher the percentage.

4. (A) You can solve this problem without referring to the graphs; the necessary information is available in the list of gross receipts below the graphs. Don't write out all the zeros when calculating with these large figures; brief figures are easier to work with.

Gross receipts for 1971 = 7.5 million.
Gross receipts for all three years = 7.5 + 8.6 + 8.1 = 24.2 million.

$$\frac{7.5}{24.2} = 31\%$$

The answer which best approximates 31% is 30%. (A). Notice that even without doing the calculations, you may approximate 30% by realizing that the gross receipts for any one year are about one-third of the total.

5. (D) To calculate the average percentage for Cruncho Chicken, add the percentages for each year and divide by 3.

$$46.3 + 40.6 + 13.3 = 100.2 \div 3 = 33.4\%$$

Do the same for Pizza In A Pot.

$$12.8 + 24.6 + 40 = 77.4 \div 3 = 25.8\%$$

Cruncho Chicken exceeds Pizza In A Pot by 33.4 − 25.8 = 7.6%. (D), 8%, best approximates this figure.

6. (B) In 1973, other restaurants earned precisely 10%. 10% of $8,100,000 = $810,000, (B).

A PATTERNED PLAN OF ATTACK

Data Interpretation

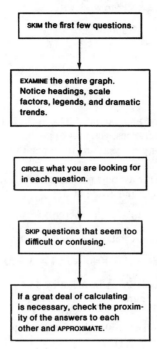

SKIM the first few questions.

EXAMINE the entire graph. Notice headings, scale factors, legends, and dramatic trends.

CIRCLE what you are looking for in each question.

SKIP questions that seem too difficult or confusing.

If a great deal of calculating is necessary, check the proximity of the answers to each other and APPROXIMATE.

Part III: Practice-Review-Analyze-Practice

Three Full-Length Practice Tests

This section contains three full-length practice simulation GMATs. The practice tests are followed by complete answers, explanations, and analysis techniques. The format, levels of difficulty, question structure, and number of questions are similar to those on the actual GMAT. The actual GMAT is copyrighted and may not be duplicated and these questions are not taken directly from the actual tests.

When taking these exams, try to simulate the test conditions by following the time allotments carefully.

PRACTICE TEST 1

Section I: Reading Comprehension—30 Minutes; 25 Questions
Section II: Problem Solving—30 Minutes; 20 Questions
Section III: Sentence Correction—30 Minutes; 25 Questions
Section IV: Data Sufficiency—30 Minutes; 25 Questions
Section V: Critical Reasoning—30 Minutes; 25 Questions
Section VI: Problem Solving—30 Minutes; 20 Questions
Section VII: Data Sufficiency—30 Minutes; 25 Questions

ANSWER SHEET FOR PRACTICE TEST 1
(Remove This Sheet and Use It to Mark Your Answers)

SECTION I   SECTION II   SECTION III

SECTION I

1 Ⓐ Ⓑ Ⓒ Ⓓ Ⓔ
2 Ⓐ Ⓑ Ⓒ Ⓓ Ⓔ
3 Ⓐ Ⓑ Ⓒ Ⓓ Ⓔ
4 Ⓐ Ⓑ Ⓒ Ⓓ Ⓔ
5 Ⓐ Ⓑ Ⓒ Ⓓ Ⓔ
6 Ⓐ Ⓑ Ⓒ Ⓓ Ⓔ
7 Ⓐ Ⓑ Ⓒ Ⓓ Ⓔ
8 Ⓐ Ⓑ Ⓒ Ⓓ Ⓔ
9 Ⓐ Ⓑ Ⓒ Ⓓ Ⓔ
10 Ⓐ Ⓑ Ⓒ Ⓓ Ⓔ
11 Ⓐ Ⓑ Ⓒ Ⓓ Ⓔ
12 Ⓐ Ⓑ Ⓒ Ⓓ Ⓔ
13 Ⓐ Ⓑ Ⓒ Ⓓ Ⓔ
14 Ⓐ Ⓑ Ⓒ Ⓓ Ⓔ
15 Ⓐ Ⓑ Ⓒ Ⓓ Ⓔ
16 Ⓐ Ⓑ Ⓒ Ⓓ Ⓔ
17 Ⓐ Ⓑ Ⓒ Ⓓ Ⓔ
18 Ⓐ Ⓑ Ⓒ Ⓓ Ⓔ
19 Ⓐ Ⓑ Ⓒ Ⓓ Ⓔ
20 Ⓐ Ⓑ Ⓒ Ⓓ Ⓔ
21 Ⓐ Ⓑ Ⓒ Ⓓ Ⓔ
22 Ⓐ Ⓑ Ⓒ Ⓓ Ⓔ
23 Ⓐ Ⓑ Ⓒ Ⓓ Ⓔ
24 Ⓐ Ⓑ Ⓒ Ⓓ Ⓔ
25 Ⓐ Ⓑ Ⓒ Ⓓ Ⓔ

SECTION II

1 Ⓐ Ⓑ Ⓒ Ⓓ Ⓔ
2 Ⓐ Ⓑ Ⓒ Ⓓ Ⓔ
3 Ⓐ Ⓑ Ⓒ Ⓓ Ⓔ
4 Ⓐ Ⓑ Ⓒ Ⓓ Ⓔ
5 Ⓐ Ⓑ Ⓒ Ⓓ Ⓔ
6 Ⓐ Ⓑ Ⓒ Ⓓ Ⓔ
7 Ⓐ Ⓑ Ⓒ Ⓓ Ⓔ
8 Ⓐ Ⓑ Ⓒ Ⓓ Ⓔ
9 Ⓐ Ⓑ Ⓒ Ⓓ Ⓔ
10 Ⓐ Ⓑ Ⓒ Ⓓ Ⓔ
11 Ⓐ Ⓑ Ⓒ Ⓓ Ⓔ
12 Ⓐ Ⓑ Ⓒ Ⓓ Ⓔ
13 Ⓐ Ⓑ Ⓒ Ⓓ Ⓔ
14 Ⓐ Ⓑ Ⓒ Ⓓ Ⓔ
15 Ⓐ Ⓑ Ⓒ Ⓓ Ⓔ
16 Ⓐ Ⓑ Ⓒ Ⓓ Ⓔ
17 Ⓐ Ⓑ Ⓒ Ⓓ Ⓔ
18 Ⓐ Ⓑ Ⓒ Ⓓ Ⓔ
19 Ⓐ Ⓑ Ⓒ Ⓓ Ⓔ
20 Ⓐ Ⓑ Ⓒ Ⓓ Ⓔ

SECTION III

1 Ⓐ Ⓑ Ⓒ Ⓓ Ⓔ
2 Ⓐ Ⓑ Ⓒ Ⓓ Ⓔ
3 Ⓐ Ⓑ Ⓒ Ⓓ Ⓔ
4 Ⓐ Ⓑ Ⓒ Ⓓ Ⓔ
5 Ⓐ Ⓑ Ⓒ Ⓓ Ⓔ
6 Ⓐ Ⓑ Ⓒ Ⓓ Ⓔ
7 Ⓐ Ⓑ Ⓒ Ⓓ Ⓔ
8 Ⓐ Ⓑ Ⓒ Ⓓ Ⓔ
9 Ⓐ Ⓑ Ⓒ Ⓓ Ⓔ
10 Ⓐ Ⓑ Ⓒ Ⓓ Ⓔ
11 Ⓐ Ⓑ Ⓒ Ⓓ Ⓔ
12 Ⓐ Ⓑ Ⓒ Ⓓ Ⓔ
13 Ⓐ Ⓑ Ⓒ Ⓓ Ⓔ
14 Ⓐ Ⓑ Ⓒ Ⓓ Ⓔ
15 Ⓐ Ⓑ Ⓒ Ⓓ Ⓔ
16 Ⓐ Ⓑ Ⓒ Ⓓ Ⓔ
17 Ⓐ Ⓑ Ⓒ Ⓓ Ⓔ
18 Ⓐ Ⓑ Ⓒ Ⓓ Ⓔ
19 Ⓐ Ⓑ Ⓒ Ⓓ Ⓔ
20 Ⓐ Ⓑ Ⓒ Ⓓ Ⓔ
21 Ⓐ Ⓑ Ⓒ Ⓓ Ⓔ
22 Ⓐ Ⓑ Ⓒ Ⓓ Ⓔ
23 Ⓐ Ⓑ Ⓒ Ⓓ Ⓔ
24 Ⓐ Ⓑ Ⓒ Ⓓ Ⓔ
25 Ⓐ Ⓑ Ⓒ Ⓓ Ⓔ

ANSWER SHEET FOR PRACTICE TEST 1
(Remove This Sheet and Use It to Mark Your Answers)

SECTION IV	SECTION V	SECTION VI	SECTION VII
1 Ⓐ Ⓑ Ⓒ Ⓓ Ⓔ	1 Ⓐ Ⓑ Ⓒ Ⓓ Ⓔ	1 Ⓐ Ⓑ Ⓒ Ⓓ Ⓔ	1 Ⓐ Ⓑ Ⓒ Ⓓ Ⓔ
2 Ⓐ Ⓑ Ⓒ Ⓓ Ⓔ	2 Ⓐ Ⓑ Ⓒ Ⓓ Ⓔ	2 Ⓐ Ⓑ Ⓒ Ⓓ Ⓔ	2 Ⓐ Ⓑ Ⓒ Ⓓ Ⓔ
3 Ⓐ Ⓑ Ⓒ Ⓓ Ⓔ	3 Ⓐ Ⓑ Ⓒ Ⓓ Ⓔ	3 Ⓐ Ⓑ Ⓒ Ⓓ Ⓔ	3 Ⓐ Ⓑ Ⓒ Ⓓ Ⓔ
4 Ⓐ Ⓑ Ⓒ Ⓓ Ⓔ	4 Ⓐ Ⓑ Ⓒ Ⓓ Ⓔ	4 Ⓐ Ⓑ Ⓒ Ⓓ Ⓔ	4 Ⓐ Ⓑ Ⓒ Ⓓ Ⓔ
5 Ⓐ Ⓑ Ⓒ Ⓓ Ⓔ	5 Ⓐ Ⓑ Ⓒ Ⓓ Ⓔ	5 Ⓐ Ⓑ Ⓒ Ⓓ Ⓔ	5 Ⓐ Ⓑ Ⓒ Ⓓ Ⓔ
6 Ⓐ Ⓑ Ⓒ Ⓓ Ⓔ	6 Ⓐ Ⓑ Ⓒ Ⓓ Ⓔ	6 Ⓐ Ⓑ Ⓒ Ⓓ Ⓔ	6 Ⓐ Ⓑ Ⓒ Ⓓ Ⓔ
7 Ⓐ Ⓑ Ⓒ Ⓓ Ⓔ	7 Ⓐ Ⓑ Ⓒ Ⓓ Ⓔ	7 Ⓐ Ⓑ Ⓒ Ⓓ Ⓔ	7 Ⓐ Ⓑ Ⓒ Ⓓ Ⓔ
8 Ⓐ Ⓑ Ⓒ Ⓓ Ⓔ	8 Ⓐ Ⓑ Ⓒ Ⓓ Ⓔ	8 Ⓐ Ⓑ Ⓒ Ⓓ Ⓔ	8 Ⓐ Ⓑ Ⓒ Ⓓ Ⓔ
9 Ⓐ Ⓑ Ⓒ Ⓓ Ⓔ	9 Ⓐ Ⓑ Ⓒ Ⓓ Ⓔ	9 Ⓐ Ⓑ Ⓒ Ⓓ Ⓔ	9 Ⓐ Ⓑ Ⓒ Ⓓ Ⓔ
10 Ⓐ Ⓑ Ⓒ Ⓓ Ⓔ	10 Ⓐ Ⓑ Ⓒ Ⓓ Ⓔ	10 Ⓐ Ⓑ Ⓒ Ⓓ Ⓔ	10 Ⓐ Ⓑ Ⓒ Ⓓ Ⓔ
11 Ⓐ Ⓑ Ⓒ Ⓓ Ⓔ	11 Ⓐ Ⓑ Ⓒ Ⓓ Ⓔ	11 Ⓐ Ⓑ Ⓒ Ⓓ Ⓔ	11 Ⓐ Ⓑ Ⓒ Ⓓ Ⓔ
12 Ⓐ Ⓑ Ⓒ Ⓓ Ⓔ	12 Ⓐ Ⓑ Ⓒ Ⓓ Ⓔ	12 Ⓐ Ⓑ Ⓒ Ⓓ Ⓔ	12 Ⓐ Ⓑ Ⓒ Ⓓ Ⓔ
13 Ⓐ Ⓑ Ⓒ Ⓓ Ⓔ	13 Ⓐ Ⓑ Ⓒ Ⓓ Ⓔ	13 Ⓐ Ⓑ Ⓒ Ⓓ Ⓔ	13 Ⓐ Ⓑ Ⓒ Ⓓ Ⓔ
14 Ⓐ Ⓑ Ⓒ Ⓓ Ⓔ	14 Ⓐ Ⓑ Ⓒ Ⓓ Ⓔ	14 Ⓐ Ⓑ Ⓒ Ⓓ Ⓔ	14 Ⓐ Ⓑ Ⓒ Ⓓ Ⓔ
15 Ⓐ Ⓑ Ⓒ Ⓓ Ⓔ	15 Ⓐ Ⓑ Ⓒ Ⓓ Ⓔ	15 Ⓐ Ⓑ Ⓒ Ⓓ Ⓔ	15 Ⓐ Ⓑ Ⓒ Ⓓ Ⓔ
16 Ⓐ Ⓑ Ⓒ Ⓓ Ⓔ	16 Ⓐ Ⓑ Ⓒ Ⓓ Ⓔ	16 Ⓐ Ⓑ Ⓒ Ⓓ Ⓔ	16 Ⓐ Ⓑ Ⓒ Ⓓ Ⓔ
17 Ⓐ Ⓑ Ⓒ Ⓓ Ⓔ	17 Ⓐ Ⓑ Ⓒ Ⓓ Ⓔ	17 Ⓐ Ⓑ Ⓒ Ⓓ Ⓔ	17 Ⓐ Ⓑ Ⓒ Ⓓ Ⓔ
18 Ⓐ Ⓑ Ⓒ Ⓓ Ⓔ	18 Ⓐ Ⓑ Ⓒ Ⓓ Ⓔ	18 Ⓐ Ⓑ Ⓒ Ⓓ Ⓔ	18 Ⓐ Ⓑ Ⓒ Ⓓ Ⓔ
19 Ⓐ Ⓑ Ⓒ Ⓓ Ⓔ	19 Ⓐ Ⓑ Ⓒ Ⓓ Ⓔ	19 Ⓐ Ⓑ Ⓒ Ⓓ Ⓔ	19 Ⓐ Ⓑ Ⓒ Ⓓ Ⓔ
20 Ⓐ Ⓑ Ⓒ Ⓓ Ⓔ	20 Ⓐ Ⓑ Ⓒ Ⓓ Ⓔ	20 Ⓐ Ⓑ Ⓒ Ⓓ Ⓔ	20 Ⓐ Ⓑ Ⓒ Ⓓ Ⓔ
21 Ⓐ Ⓑ Ⓒ Ⓓ Ⓔ	21 Ⓐ Ⓑ Ⓒ Ⓓ Ⓔ		21 Ⓐ Ⓑ Ⓒ Ⓓ Ⓔ
22 Ⓐ Ⓑ Ⓒ Ⓓ Ⓔ	22 Ⓐ Ⓑ Ⓒ Ⓓ Ⓔ		22 Ⓐ Ⓑ Ⓒ Ⓓ Ⓔ
23 Ⓐ Ⓑ Ⓒ Ⓓ Ⓔ	23 Ⓐ Ⓑ Ⓒ Ⓓ Ⓔ		23 Ⓐ Ⓑ Ⓒ Ⓓ Ⓔ
24 Ⓐ Ⓑ Ⓒ Ⓓ Ⓔ	24 Ⓐ Ⓑ Ⓒ Ⓓ Ⓔ		24 Ⓐ Ⓑ Ⓒ Ⓓ Ⓔ
25 Ⓐ Ⓑ Ⓒ Ⓓ Ⓔ	25 Ⓐ Ⓑ Ⓒ Ⓓ Ⓔ		25 Ⓐ Ⓑ Ⓒ Ⓓ Ⓔ

Time: 30 Minutes
25 Questions

DIRECTIONS

Each passage in this group is followed by questions based on its content. After reading a passage, choose the best answer to each question and blacken the corresponding space on the answer sheet. Answer all questions following a passage on the basis of what is *stated* or *implied* in that passage. You may refer back to the passage.

Each method of counting bacteria has advantages and disadvantages; none is 100 percent accurate. Cell counts may be made with a counting chamber, a slide marked with a grid to facilitate counting of cells and to determine the volume of liquid in the area counted. Counts are made under a microscope and calculations made to determine the number of cells per ml of the original culture. Electronic cell counters can be used to count cells suspended in a liquid medium which passes through a hole small enough to allow the passage of only one bacterial cell at a time. The counter actually measures the rise in electric resistance of the liquid each time a cell passes through the hole. Smear counts are similar to cell counts: a known volume of culture is spread over a known area (1 cm^2) of a slide and then stained. Counts are made from several microscope fields, and calculations are made. In membrane filter counts a known volume of a culture is passed through a filter, which is then examined microscopically for cells. The advantage of cell counts, smear counts, and membrane filter counts is that they are quickly accomplished with little complicated equipment; however, both living and dead cells are counted.

The serial-dilution method involves the making of a series of dilutions, usually by a factor of 10, into a nutrient medium. The highest dilution producing growth gives a rough indication of the population of the original culture; for example, if the highest dilution to produce growth is the 1:100 dilution, the original culture had between 100 and 1,000 cells per ml.

Plate counts are made by making serial dilutions (usually in sterile tap water or an isotonic solution) of the original culture. Samples of known volume of the dilutions are transferred to petri dishes and mixed with nutrient agar. After a suitable incubation period the colonies on the plates with between 30 and 300 colonies are counted. Because each colony is assumed to have arisen from a single cell, calculations can be made to determine the original population size. Plate counts have the advantage of not including dead cells, and they can be used when the population is so low as to make other methods impractical, but they require more time than direct counts, and they detect only those organisms that can grow under the conditions of incubation; the development of one colony from more than one cell is also a source of error. In connection with this technique a modification of the membrane filter count can be used. After filtration, the filter is placed on a pad soaked in nutrient media and allowed to incubate; resulting colonies are counted and appropriate calculations made.

A colorimeter or spectrophotometer is used in turbidimetric methods; the instrument measures the amount of light transmitted by test tubes with and without cultures; the difference represents the light absorbed or scattered by the bacterial cells and gives an indication of their concentration.

The total cell volume in a sample can be determined by centrifuging the sample in a calibrated centrifuge tube. From the known volume of a single cell and the volume of the sample cells, the original population size can be calculated.

The dry weight of washed, dehydrated cells gives a reliable indication of population size. Chemical assays for the concentration of nitrogen or other cell constituents present in cells in fairly constant amounts are used to calculate population size. Because living cells produce chemical changes in their environments, these changes may reflect the number of cells present; changes in pH or in the concentration of a substrate or product may be measured.

In a typical growth curve there is no increase in number of viable cells in the lag phase, but the cells increase in size, imbibe water, and synthesize enzymes as they become adjusted to the new medium. This phase is long if the inoculum consists of dormant cells and/or cells that were previously cultivated on a different medium. Dormant cells have fewer ribosomes than actively growing ones, and some time is required for the formation of ribosomes on which enzymes are then synthesized.

In the logarithmic phase the growth rate is most rapid, and the length of the generation time is at its minimum. The growth rate is constant. This portion of the curve plots as a straight line on semilogarithmic paper. Cells are physiologically active; their characteristic biochemical abilities are most obvious at this time. Almost all cells in the culture are alive, and the population is more nearly uniform than in any other phase of the growth curve. As logarithmic growth proceeds, the food supply diminishes and waste products accumulate.

At the stationary phase the food supply has fallen to a limiting concentration and the waste products have reached an inhibiting concentration. There is no change in the number of viable cells; the production of new cells is balanced by the deaths of other cells. The growth rate is zero, but the population size is at its highest level, called the maximum crop.

During the death phase the number of viable cells decreases as the number of deaths surpasses the number of new cells produced—slowly at first, then more rapidly. The number of viable cells decreases at a logarithmic rate. The length of the death phase varies with the species. It may be only a few days in the case of some gram-negative cocci, but for most species it lasts a few weeks or even months.

Cells can be maintained indefinitely in a logarithmic phase by continuously adding nutrients and removing toxic metabolic products and excess cells in a siphon overflow. The growth rate is controlled by the rate of introduction of fresh medium. Because the overflow contains cells as well as waste products, the population size remains constant.

1. One method of counting bacteria which does not suffer from a major disadvantage of a "cell count" is a
   (A) plate count
   (B) smear count
   (C) membrane filter count
   (D) serial-dilution count
   (E) down for the count

2. The lag phase is the time during which
   (A) some cells multiply faster than others which "lag" behind
   (B) cells nourish themselves, grow, and eventually reproduce
   (C) cell population is stable
   (D) actively growing cells contribute ribosomes to dormant ones
   (E) adjustment to the new environment is negligible

3. According to the passage, the typical result of incubation is
   (A) impractical
   (B) the precise population of the original culture
   (C) mutation of the nutrient agar
   (D) growth
   (E) 30 to 300 colonies

4. One of the characteristics of the logarithmic phase might be described as
   (A) physiological stasis
   (B) ennervation
   (C) mitosis
   (D) conspicuous consumption
   (E) the recycling of waste products

5. The passage allows us to conclude that a biologist in a hurry to do a bacterial count might choose to
    (A) seek out a spectrophotometer   (D) incubate
    (B) estimate the total cell volume   (E) use a petri dish
    (C) perform a smear count

6. During which phase is the population size described with a term commonly applied to agricultural production?
    (A) stationary phase   (D) death phase
    (B) lag phase   (E) harvest phase
    (C) logarithmic phase

Let us take the terms "subjective" and "objective" and see if we can make up our minds what we mean by them in some such statement as this: "Philosophers and artists are subjective; scientists, objective." First of all we must point out that the two terms make up a semantic pair. The one has no meaning without the other. We may define each by antonym with the other. We may define them by synonym by translating the last syllable and say that "subjective" pertains to a subject, and "objective" pertains to an object. By operation analysis we may say that subjects perceive or conceive objects in the process of knowing. The word "knowing" reminds us that we are talking about the central nervous system and should waste no time in examining our terms for their sensory, affective, and logical components. It is easy to see from the following discussion that no particular sensory mechanism is necessarily involved and that although the sentence might be uttered with some considerable emotional content, it is used here entirely without feelings of praise or blame. The terms are primarily logical. What, then, is the basic logical relation that establishes whatever meaning they have? What goes on in the world when a poet is being subjective, and how does it differ from what goes on when a scientist is being objective?

When the poet sings "Drink to me only with thine eyes," he is responding immediately or in retrospect to an object, his beloved, outside himself; but he is fundamentally concerned with the sensations and emotions which that object stimulates in him; and whether the object justifies his praise in the opinion of others, or indeed whether there actually is such an object, is quite irrelevant to his purpose, which is the weaving of a beautiful pattern of sound and imagery into a richly affective concept of feminine loveliness. This it is to be subjective.

Now the scientist is primarily concerned with the identity and continuity of the external object that stimulates his response. Scientists

characteristically have been rather unphilosophic about these objects
that they observe so objectively, and philosophers have been characteristically unscientific about them. I must point out that here the word
"philosopher" has shifted its sense from the one set up for it in Chapter
1; here it means that special sort of theoretical scientist who tries to
make up his mind what he means by meaning—philosophers call him an
epistemologist. Epistemologists Ogden and Richards in the youthful,
rebellious days of *The Meaning of Meaning* seem not to have thought
through this problem of the object. At least the following footnote gives
that impression.

> In particular, by using the same term "meaning" both for the
> "goings on" inside their heads (the images, associations, etc.,
> which enabled them to interpret signs) and for the referents (the
> things to which the signs refer) philosophers have been forced to
> locate Grantchester, Influenza, Queen Anne, and indeed the whole
> Universe equally inside their heads—or, if alarmed by the prospect
> of cerebral congestion, at least "in their minds" in such wise that
> all these objects become conveniently "mental." Great care, there-
> fore, is required in the use of the term "meaning," since its
> associations are dangerous.

It need not seem absurd to locate the Eiffel Tower, or Everest, or the
Grand Canyon for that matter, "in the mind" because it is so perfectly
obvious that they can exist as the Eiffel Tower, Everest, or the Grand
Canyon nowhere else. Perhaps we can take a step toward clarification of
this puzzling state of affairs and move a little closer to our definition of
"objective" by suggesting a distinction between an object and a thing.
Let us define object as the external cause of a thing. Whether objects
"exist" is obviously not discussable, for the word "object" as used here
must necessarily stand not for a thing but for a hypothesis. There is, for
example, no way of telling whether objects are singular or plural,
whether one should say the stimulus of the Eiffel Tower experience or
the stimuli of the Eiffel Tower experience. If, then, it is impossible even
for the scientist to escape the essential subjectivity of his sensations,
generalizations, and deductions, what do we mean by calling him
objective?

7. Faced with this statement, "What you say you see is just in your head,"
   the author might do which of the following?
   (A) become incensed
   (B) agree that the statement is quite true

    (C) argue against the appropriateness of the word "just"
    (D) assume that the person making the statement is not a scientist
    (E) laugh

8. Which of the following is *not* a semantic pair?

(A) chaos/order	(D) light/darkness	
(B) fact/fiction	(E) virtue/vice	
(C) sitting/standing		

9. The sentence examined by the author in the first paragraph would have an affective component if
    (A) "artists" were changed to "painters"
    (B) "philosophers" were changed to "logical positivists"
    (C) the physical characteristics of philosophers, artists, and scientists were vividly described
    (D) "subjective" and "objective" were changed, respectively, to "irrational" and "rational"
    (E) "subjective" and "objective" were changed, respectively, to "lunatic" and "trustworthy"

10. According to the passage, "objectivity" depends on the assumption that
    (A) discrete objects exist external to the mind
    (B) one's vocation in life should be logical
    (C) subjectivity is a cognitive weakness
    (D) science is a viable discipline
    (E) the Eiffel Tower is a singular stimulus rather than a diffuse experience

11. The author's attitude toward Ogden and Richards is

(A) conciliatory	(D) perplexed	
(B) metaphorical	(E) evasive	
(C) critical		

12. Drawing from the passage, we may question whether
    (A) love makes the world go 'round
    (B) science has a right to elevate its methodology
    (C) the writer is subjective or objective
    (D) you are really there reading this page right now
    (E) people should be accorded the same relative status as things

    In economics, demand implies something slightly different from the common meaning of the term. The layman, for example, often uses the term to mean the amount that is demanded of an item. Thus, if the price were to decrease and individuals wanted more of the item, it is commonly said that demand increases. To an economist, demand is a relationship between a series of prices and a series of corresponding quantities that are demanded at these prices. If one reads the previous sentences carefully, it should become apparent that there is a distinction between the quantity demanded and demand. This distinction is often a point of confusion and we all should be aware of and understand the difference between these two terms. We repeat, therefore, that demand is a relationship between price and quantities demanded, and therefore suggests the effect of one (e.g., price) on the other (e.g., quantity demanded). Therefore, knowledge of the demand for a product enables one to predict how much more of a good will be purchased if price decreases. But the increase in quantity demanded does not mean demand has increased, since the relationship between price and quantity demanded (i.e., the demand for the product) has not changed. Demand shifts when there is a change in income, expectations, taste, etc., such that a different quantity of the good is demanded at the same price.

In almost all cases, a consumer wants more of an item if the price decreases. This relationship between price and quantity demanded is so strong that it is referred to as the "law of demand." This "law" can be explained by the income and substitution effects. The income effect occurs because price increases reduce the purchasing power of the individual and, thus, the quantity demanded of goods must decrease. The substitution effect reflects the consumer's desire to get the "best buy." Accordingly, if the price of good A increases, the individual will tend to substitute another good and purchase less of good A. The negative correlation between price and quantity demanded is also explained by the law of diminishing marginal utility. According to this law, the additional utility the consumer gains from consuming a good decreases as successively more units of the good are consumed. Because the additional units yield less utility or satisfaction, the consumer is willing to purchase more only if the price of the good decreases.

Economists distinguish between individual and market demand. As the term implies, individual demand concerns the individual consumer and illustrates the quantities that individuals demand at different prices. Market demand includes the demand of all individuals for a particular good and is found by summing the quantities demanded by all individuals at the various prices.

The other side of the price system is supply. As in the case of demand, supply is a relationship between a series of prices and the associated quantities supplied. It is assumed that as price increases the individual or firm will supply greater quantities of a good. There is a positive correlation between quantity supplied and product price.

Economists also distinguish between a change in supply and quantity supplied. The distinction is similar to the one made with respect to demand. Also, as in the case of demand, economists distinguish between individual firm supply and market supply, which is the summation of individual supply.

Taken together, supply and demand yield equilibrium price and quantity. Equilibrium is a state of stability, with balanced forces in which prices and quantity will remain constant. Moreover, there are forces in the market that will act to establish equilibrium if changes in demand or supply create disequilibrium. For example, if prices are above equilibrium, the quantity supplied exceeds quantity demanded and surpluses occur that have a downward pressure on prices. These pressures will persist until equilibrium is established. If prices are below equilibrium, the good will become scarce and there will be an upward pressure on price.

In reality, equilibrium is seldom attained, for the factors affecting the market are constantly changing. In a dynamic market of this kind, there is a continual process of adjustment as the market searches or gropes for equilibrium. The rapidity of adjustment will depend to a large extent on the quality of information that is available to firms and consumers.

Through the market interaction of demand and supply, a "market price" is established. This price serves two very important roles of rationing and allocating goods. Since wants far exceed resources, there must be a device by which to determine who gets the goods. In the market system, price plays this rationing role by supplying goods to all who pay the price of the product. As an allocator of goods, price insures that resources are utilized in their most valuable uses. In short, in a market system, price serves both a demand-inhibiting and a supply-eliciting function. Naturally, the market system does not work perfectly.

In most economies, the government plays a role in the market system. Governments enforce the "rules of the game," impose taxes, and may control prices through price ceilings or price supports. These actions necessarily may create shortages or surpluses. In most developed and interdependent economies, the necessity of the government playing some role in the economy seldom is disputed.

13. Assume that firms develop an orange-flavored breakfast drink high in vitamin C that is a good substitute for orange juice but sells for less. Based upon assertions in the passage, which of the following would occur with respect to the demand for orange juice?

(A) health food stores would resurrect the law of diminishing marginal utility

(B) assuming that the price of fresh orange juice remained constant, more orange juice would be consumed

(C) the law of demand would prevail

(D) assuming that the price of fresh orange juice remained constant, the demand would not change

(E) there is not enough information in the passage to answer this question

14. According to the passage, a group of individuals will
    (A) derive less satisfaction from a product
    (B) exert individual demand under appropriate conditions
    (C) shift the demand line to the right
    (D) constitute a market
    (E) emphasize supply over demand

15. According to the passage, a change in demand would occur in which of the following situations?
    (A) the gasoline price increases, resulting in the increased sale of Datsuns (whose price remains stable)
    (B) the gasoline price increases, resulting in the increased sale of Datsuns (which go on sale in response to increased gas prices)
    (C) the gasoline price decreases on the same day that a new 43-mpg car enters the market
    (D) a federal order imposes a price ceiling on gasoline
    (E) a federal order lifts price regulations for gasoline

16. According to the passage, quantity supplied and product price are not
    (A) correlative   (D) symbiotic
    (B) disjunctive   (E) consequential
    (C) related

17. Assume that the demand for houses increases. Drawing from the passage, decide which of the following would most likely cause such a shift.
    (A) interest rates on mortgages increase
    (B) the government predicts a large increase in the extent of unemployment
    (C) in a poverty area, a new government program provides jobs for all who need them
    (D) announcement of a low-priced type of mobile home which is a good substitute for houses
    (E) the increased cost of lumber

18. The final sentence in the passage hints that
    (A) interdependence goes hand in hand with development
    (B) there are underdeveloped countries whose attitude toward government control may be hostile
    (C) disputes over government control usually come from an illiterate populace
    (D) socialism is a sophisticated achievement
    (E) capitalism is a sophisticated achievement

19. According to the final paragraph, the government's intervention in the economy may cause
    (A) higher prices
    (B) disequilibrium
    (C) lower prices
    (D) the market to tend toward socialism
    (E) the market to tend toward capitalism

20. According to the passage, when most people use the term "demand," they are usually referring to
    (A) an aggressive personality
    (B) a run on the banks
    (C) a collective public action
    (D) a desire to acquire more for less
    (E) the relationship between "quantity demanded" and "demand"

21. The distinction between "demand" and "quantity demanded" is similar to
    (A) the distinction between "supply" and "quantity supplied"
    (B) the distinction between "utility" and "marginal utility"
    (C) the distinction between "individuals" and "markets"
    (D) the distinction between "equilibrium" and "disequilibrium"
    (E) the distinction between "upward pressure" and "downward pressure"

22. Applying information from the passage, decide which of the following market situations is implied by an overfull new-car lot.
    (A) the market is indicating a need for smaller cars
    (B) the size of the lot had been miscalculated initially
    (C) prices are above equilibrium
    (D) prices are below equilibrium
    (E) a state of stability exists

23. When he says, "Naturally, the market system does not work perfectly," the author's tone is
    (A) in sharp contrast to that of his earlier statements

(B) matter-of-fact
(C) snide
(D) vociferous
(E) conciliatory

24. The passage implies that equilibrium is a state more theoretical than practical because
    (A) it was conceived long before it was practiced
    (B) imbalance is to be desired
    (C) influences upon demand and supply are never stable
    (D) disequilibrium reifies competition
    (E) the market is in flux

25. According to the passage, in a market system, price serves
    (A) one complete function
    (B) two functions
    (C) three functions
    (D) many possible functions
    (E) many necessary functions

STOP. IF YOU FINISH BEFORE TIME IS CALLED, CHECK YOUR WORK ON THIS SECTION ONLY. DO NOT WORK ON ANY OTHER SECTION IN THE TEST.

SECTION II: PROBLEM SOLVING

Time: 30 Minutes
20 Questions

DIRECTIONS

In this section solve each problem, using any available space on the page for scratchwork. Then indicate the *best* answer in the appropriate space on the answer sheet.

1. Approximately how many revolutions will be made by a car tire with a 14-inch diameter if the car travels ½ mile?
   (A) 120   (B) 180   (C) 360   (D) 720   (E) 1440

2. If a man travels f miles an hour for t hours and r miles an hour for s hours, what is his average rate in miles per hour for the entire distance traveled?
   (A) ft + rs

   (B) (ft + rs)/2

   (C) $\dfrac{f}{t} + \dfrac{r}{s}$

   (D) $\dfrac{ft + rs}{t + s}$

   (E) $\dfrac{ft + rs}{t - s}$

3. The closest approximation of 69.28 × .004/.03 is
   (A) .092   (B) .92   (C) 9.2   (D) 92   (E) 920

Products	1960	1962	1964	1966	1968	1970
A	$4.20	$4.60	$5.00	$5.40	$5.80	$6.20
B	$6.30	$6.45	$6.60	$6.75	$6.90	$7.05

4. The chart above shows the prices of products A and B from 1960 to 1970. Using the chart, in what year will product A cost 40¢ more than product B?
   (A) 1974   (B) 1976   (C) 1977   (D) 1978   (E) 1980

5. Sid can do a job in 6 hours. If Jan works with him, the job will be completed in 2 hours. How many minutes would it take Jan to do the job alone?
   (A) 60   (B) 90   (C) 180   (D) 210   (E) 360

74

6. The large square above consists of squares and isosceles right triangles. If the large square has side 4 cm, then the area of the shaded portion in square cm is
   (A) 2   (B) 4   (C) 6   (D) 8   (E) 12

7. The purchase price of an article is $48. In order to include 15% of cost for overhead and to provide $12 of net profit, the markup should be
   (A) 15%   (B) 25%   (C) 35%   (D) 40%   (E) 45%

8. Manny rides a bicycle 6 miles east, 5 miles north, 10 miles west, and 8 miles south, at a rate of 10 miles per hour. If Irv leaves at the same time and from the same place and walks directly to Manny's final destination at a rate of 5 miles per hour, he will
   (A) arrive at the same time as Manny
   (B) arrive before Manny
   (C) arrive after Manny
   (D) none of the above
   (E) cannot be determined from the information given

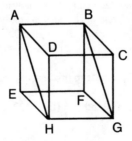

9. In the cube above, AH and BG are diagonals and the surface area of side ABFE is 16. What is the area of rectangle ABGH?
   (A) $4\sqrt{2}$ (B) $16\sqrt{2}$ (C) $16 + \sqrt{2}$ (D) 16   (E) $15\sqrt{3}$

10. If $x = y + y^2$, and y is a negative integer which decreases in value, then x
    (A) increases in value   (D) remains the same
    (B) fluctuates   (E) none of the above
    (C) decreases in value

11. A sporting goods store sold 64 Frisbees in one week, some for $3.00 and the rest for $4.00 each. If receipts from Frisbee sales for the week totaled $204, what is the fewest number of $4.00 Frisbees that could have been sold?
    (A) 24   (B) 12   (C) 8   (D) 4   (E) 2

12. Three businessmen wish to invest in a new company. Each man is willing to pay one-third of the total investment. After careful calculations, they realize that each of them would pay $7,200 less if they could find two more equal investors. How much is the total investment in the new business?
    (A) $64,000   (B) $54,000   (C) $21,600   (D) $5,400
    (E) cannot be determined

13. An astronaut weighing 207 pounds on Earth would weigh 182 pounds on Venus. The weight of the astronaut on Venus would be approximately what percent of his weight on Earth?
    (A) 50%   (B) 60%   (C) 70%   (D) 80%   (E) 90%

14. A man invested $1,000, part at 5% and the rest at 6%. His total income was $53. How much did he invest at 5%?
    (A) $500   (B) $600   (C) $700   (D) $900   (E) $950

15. A furniture store owner decided to drop the price of his recliners by 20% to spur business. By the end of the week he had sold 50% more recliners. What is the percentage increase of the gross?
    (A) 10%   (B) 15%   (C) 20%   (D) 25%   (E) 50%

16. If it takes a machine $\frac{2}{3}$ minute to produce one item, how many items will it produce in 2 hours?
    (A) $\frac{1}{3}$ (B) $\frac{4}{3}$ (C) 80   (D) 120   (E) 180

17. If two numbers have only the number 1 as a common divisor, then they are called "relatively prime." Which of the following are *not* relatively prime?

I. 3   II. 4   III. 7   IV. 12

   (A) I and II, I and III
   (B) I and IV, II and IV
   (C) II and III, II and IV
   (D) II and IV, III and IV
   (E) I and II, I and IV

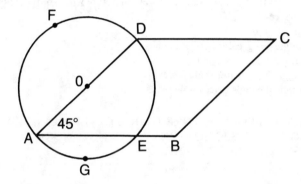

18. In the rhombus, BC = 6, AE ≃ 4, and angle DAE = 45°. AD is the diameter of the circle. If a man started at C and followed around the outer edge of this figure to D, F, A, G, E, B, and back to C, approximately how far did he travel?

   (A) $14 + (^{27}/_4)\pi$ (C) $12 + 6\pi$ (E) $12 + (^9/_2)\pi$
   (B) $14 + 6\pi$ (D) $14 + (^9/_2)\pi$

19. A bus leaves Burbank at 9:00 A.M., traveling east at 50 miles per hour. At 1:00 P.M. a plane leaves Burbank traveling east at 300 miles per hour. At what time will the plane overtake the bus?

   (A) 12:45 P.M.   (C) 1:40 P.M.   (E) 1:55 P.M.
   (B) 1:10 P.M.   (D) 1:48 P.M.

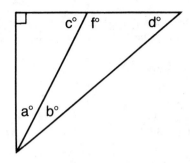

20. In the right triangle, c = 2a and d > 2b; therefore which of the following must be true?

    (A) c > b + d
    (B) angle a is greater than angle b
    (C) angle a equals angle b
    (D) angle b is greater than angle a
    (E) angle d equals twice angle a

STOP. IF YOU FINISH BEFORE TIME IS CALLED, CHECK YOUR WORK ON THIS SECTION ONLY. DO NOT WORK ON ANY OTHER SECTION IN THE TEST.

SECTION III: SENTENCE CORRECTION

Time: 30 Minutes
25 Questions

DIRECTIONS

Some part of each sentence below is underlined; sometimes the whole sentence is underlined. Five choices for rephrasing the underlined part follow each sentence; the first choice (A) repeats the original, and the other four are different. If choice (A) seems better than the alternatives, choose answer (A); if not, choose one of the others.

For each sentence, consider the requirements of standard written English. Your choice should be a correct and effective expression, not awkward or ambiguous. Focus on grammar, word choice, sentence construction, and punctuation. If a choice changes the meaning of the original sentence, do not select it.

1. Because she worked the night shift, arriving at 10 P.M. and leaving at 6 A.M.
   - (A) arriving at 10 P.M. and leaving at 6 A.M.
   - (B) having arrived at 10 P.M. and leaving at 6 A.M.
   - (C) she arrived at 10 P.M. and left at 6 A.M.
   - (D) with an arrival at 6 and a departure at 10
   - (E) from 10 P.M. to 6 A.M.

2. Although voters were expected to be apathetic, the issues proved so controversial that 90% of those registered showed up at the polls.
   - (A) of those registered showed up at the polls
   - (B) of the registered showed up at the polls
   - (C) of the registered voted
   - (D) were registered to vote
   - (E) who were not showed up at the polls

3. If the majority of your opponents have control, you may become defeated.
   - (A) If the majority of your opponents have control, you may become defeated.
   - (B) If the majority of your opponents take control, you may lose.
   - (C) If the majority of your opponents assumes control, you may see defeat.
   - (D) If the majority of your opponents has control, you may lose.
   - (E) Most of your opponents will have control, and you may lose.

79

4. Laying low in the tall jungle grass was a lion and his mate, both waiting for the opportunity to catch some food.
   (A) Laying low in the tall grass was
   (B) The tall jungle grass concealing their low-lying bodies,
   (C) In the tall jungle grass, laying low, were
   (D) Lying low in the tall jungle grass,
   (E) Lying low in the tall jungle grass were

5. Planning a career in business is often easier than to pursue it.
   (A) Planning a career in business is often easier than to pursue it.
   (B) To plan a career in business is often easier than pursuing it.
   (C) Planning a business career is often easier than pursuing it.
   (D) The planning of a business career is often easier than its pursuit.
   (E) A business career plan is often easier than a business career.

6. Focusing across several generations, Alex Haley wrote Roots, a novel explaining both his family history and the history of American bigotry.
   (A) Focusing across several generations
   (B) Centering around several generations
   (C) Living through several generations
   (D) With an eye on several generations
   (E) Telling of several generations

7. The huge crowd at the football game cheered the players making the touchdown from the stands.
   (A) The huge crowd at the football game cheered the players making the touchdown from the stands.
   (B) The huge crowd from the stands at the football game cheered the players making the touchdown.
   (C) Making the touchdown, the huge football game crowd cheered the players from the stands.
   (D) The huge crowd at the football game cheered from the stands as the players made the touchdown.
   (E) Cheers arose from the stands as the football game players made the touchdown.

8. The new union contract forbade working overtime past regular hours, and those who did not comply to this were severely censured.
   (A) working overtime past regular hours, and those who did not comply to this
   (B) working overtime, and those who did so
   (C) working after hours, and those not compliant
   (D) overtime, and those who did not comply with this
   (E) noncompliance with the antiovertime clause

9. A fight broke out when the foreign ambassador <u>took a joke serious and punched the jokester hardly</u>.
   - (A) took a joke serious and punched the jokester hardly
   - (B) took a joke seriously and hardly punched the jokester
   - (C) hardly took a joke and seriously punched the jokester
   - (D) took a joke seriously and punched the jokester hard
   - (E) gave a hard punch to a serious jokester

10. <u>She likes everyone as much as him</u>, and so he does not feel special.
   - (A) She likes everyone as much as him
   - (B) She likes everyone as much as she
   - (C) She has a liking for everyone equal to him
   - (D) She has a liking for everyone equal to he
   - (E) Everyone she likes is equal to him

11. The public soon became outraged at <u>the Cabinet member whom betrayed the public trust</u>, and they demanded his ouster.
   - (A) the Cabinet member whom betrayed the public trust
   - (B) the untrustworthy Cabinet member
   - (C) the Cabinet member with whom they betrayed the public trust
   - (D) the Cabinet member who, after betraying the public trust
   - (E) the Cabinet member who betrayed the public trust

12. Opinions about the ballot issue, of course, <u>varies according with the ethnic and economic status</u> of each voter.
   - (A) varies according with the ethnic and economic status
   - (B) varies according to ethnic and economic status
   - (C) changes with ethnicity and the economy
   - (D) vary according to the ethnic and economic status
   - (E) vary according to ethnic and economical status

13. While declaring his support for a nuclear weapons freeze, <u>a small bomb exploded some distance from the Cabinet minister, who was startled but unharmed</u>.
   - (A) a small bomb exploded some distance from the Cabinet minister, who was startled but unharmed
   - (B) a small bomb startled the Cabinet minister, but did not harm him
   - (C) a small bomb startled the Cabinet minister from a distance, but did not harm him
   - (D) the Cabinet minister was startled by a bomb that exploded some distance from him, but unharmed
   - (E) the Cabinet minister was startled but unharmed by a small bomb that exploded some distance from him

14. Several disgruntled visitors had left the board meeting <u>before it had considered the new municipal tax cut.</u>
    - (A) before it had considered the new municipal tax cut
    - (B) before it considered the new municipal tax cut
    - (C) before the members considered the new municipal tax cut
    - (D) with the consideration of the new municipal tax cut yet to come
    - (E) previous to the new municipal tax cut

15. Some Detroit car manufacturers promise to give rebates to new customers between June 1 and June 30, <u>granting the returned money during June but not thereafter.</u>
    - (A) granting the returned money during June but not thereafter
    - (B) during June but not thereafter
    - (C) but not thereafter
    - (D) no money after that
    - (E) denying those who purchase before or after June

16. <u>The chairperson adapted the committee's recommendations to meet his own needs, without considering the negative affects of his changes.</u>
    - (A) The chairperson adapted the committee's recommendations to meet his own needs, without considering the negative affects of his changes.
    - (B) Without considering the negative affects of his changes, the chairperson adapted the committee's recommendations to meet his own needs.
    - (C) The chairperson adapted the committee's recommendations to meet his own needs, without considering the negative effects of his changes.
    - (D) Necessarily, the chairperson adapted committee recommendations, despite negative effects.
    - (E) Negative effects notwithstanding, the chairman adapted the recommendations of the committee.

17. <u>After having read through the stack of bills laying on my desk,</u> I began wondering whether to file for bankruptcy.
    - (A) After having read through the stack of bills laying on my desk
    - (B) Having read through the stack of bills lying on my desk
    - (C) Reading through the stack of bills littering my desk
    - (D) The stack of bills lying on the desk, after I had read them
    - (E) After having read through the stack of bills lying on my desk

18. Revisionist historians have argued that the entry of the United States
    into World War II was favored by the Chief Executive and his closest
    advisors.
    (A) have argued that the entry of the United States into
    (B) arguing about the United States entry into
    (C) entering an argument about the United States and
    (D) had been having an argument that the entry of the United States
        into
    (E) claim that the entry of the United States into

19. Gerrymandering is when a voting area is unfairly divided so that one
    political party gains advantage.
    (A) is when a voting area is unfairly divided
    (B) divides a voting area unfairly
    (C) makes fair voting unfair
    (D) occurs when a voting area is unfairly divided
    (E) is when a voting area is divided unfairly

20. Frank Buck, "the great white hunter," was always portrayed on film as
    fearless and having great skill in hunting dangerous animals.
    (A) fearless and having great skill in hunting dangerous animals
    (B) fearless and very skillful in hunting dangerous animals
    (C) having no fear and having great skill in hunting dangerous animals
    (D) fearless and with skill in hunting dangerous animals
    (E) hunting dangerous animals without fear and with skill

21. If a police officer were to mistake the citizen's friendly intentions, and
    supposes her to be dangerous, he might draw his revolver.
    (A) and supposes her to be dangerous
    (B) and supposed her to be dangerous
    (C) and supposes danger from her
    (D) and suspect her to be dangerous
    (E) and suspected her to be dangerous

22. After having finished the marathon, both the winner and the losers felt
    proud of their achievement.
    (A) After having finished the marathon
    (B) Having finished the marathon
    (C) Having been finished after the marathon
    (D) Finishing the marathon
    (E) The marathon finished

23. The actor, along with his butler, bodyguard, chauffeur, two maids, and four dogs, are on board the train bound for Cannes.
    (A) The actor, along with his butler, bodyguard, chauffeur, two maids, and four dogs, are on board
    (B) The actor and his butler and also his chauffeur, together with two maids and including four dogs, are on board
    (C) The actor, along with his butler, bodyguard, chauffeur, two maids, and four dogs, is on board
    (D) The actor, along with his butler, bodyguard, chauffeur, two maids, and four dogs, are climbing onto
    (E) The actor's butler, bodyguard, chauffeur, two maids, and four dogs are on board

24. Unaffected by both rising inflation and high interest rates were that type of enterprising American able to create a product adaptable to shifting public tastes.
    (A) were that type of enterprising American able to create a product
    (B) was that type of enterprising American able to create a products
    (C) were the productions of American enterprise
    (D) were enterprising Americans who were able to create products
    (E) enterprising Americans creating products

25. Neither the director nor the investors in *Rocky III* predicts that it will earn less money than the other two "Rocky" films.
    (A) Neither the director nor the investors in *Rocky III* predicts
    (B) Neither the investors in *Rocky III* nor its director predicts
    (C) The director of *Rocky III,* along with its investors, predict
    (D) Neither the investors nor the directors of *Rocky III* predicts
    (E) About *Rocky III,* neither the director nor the investors predict

STOP. IF YOU FINISH BEFORE TIME IS CALLED, CHECK YOUR WORK ON THIS SECTION ONLY. DO NOT WORK ON ANY OTHER SECTION IN THE TEST.

SECTION IV: DATA SUFFICIENCY

Time: 30 Minutes
25 Questions

DIRECTIONS

Each of the problems below consists of a question and two statements, labeled (1) and (2), in which certain data are given. You must decide whether the data given in the statements are *sufficient* to answer the question. Using the data given in the statements *plus* your knowledge of mathematics and everyday facts (such as the number of days in July or the meaning of *counterclockwise*), you are to blacken space

- (A) if statement (1) ALONE is sufficient, but statement (2) alone is not sufficient to answer the question asked;
- (B) if statement (2) ALONE is sufficient, but statement (1) alone is not sufficient to answer the question asked;
- (C) if BOTH statements (1) and (2) TOGETHER are sufficient to answer the question asked, but NEITHER statement ALONE is sufficient;
- (D) if EACH statement ALONE is sufficient to answer the question asked;
- (E) if statements (1) and (2) TOGETHER are NOT sufficient to answer the question asked, and additional data specific to the problem are needed.

1. What is Mary's age?
    (1) In two years, Mary will be twice as old as Beth is now.
    (2) Susan's age is the average of Mary's and Beth's ages.

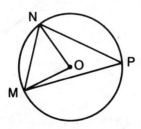

2. Within the circle with center O, how many degrees is angle MNO?
    (1) Angle ONP = 31°
    (2) Angle NPM = 48°

85

3. Does A = C?
   (1) A ≠ B
   (2) B ≠ C

4. How much precipitation does Springfield need this month to attain its long-term average of 35 inches per year?
   (1) Over the last 11 months, the city has averaged 3 inches of precipitation per month.
   (2) Springfield has accumulated 94.3% of its mean annual precipitation during the last 11 months.

5. What is the area of a circular garden?
   (1) The circumference is 314 feet.
   (2) The radius is 50 feet.

6. Five persons sat next to each other around a circular table to play cards. Did Grace sit next to Bill?
   (1) Dora sat next to Ethyl and Carl.
   (2) Grace sat next to Carl.

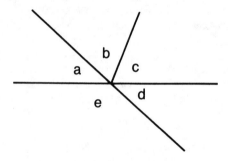

7. How many degrees is angle e?
   (1) a + d = 82°
   (2) b + d = 111°

8. Which is the smallest of 3 numbers that average 7?
   (1) One of the numbers is 4.
   (2) One of the numbers is 6.

9. In the equation 3a − 7b + 14 = 0, what is the value of b?
   (1) a = b
   (2) a = 3

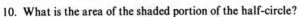

10. What is the area of the shaded portion of the half-circle?
    (1) B is the midpoint of $\overgroup{AC}$.
    (2) Angle ABC is a right angle.

11. What is the value of $\dfrac{14m^4}{s^6}$?
    (1) $m^2 = 3s^3$
    (2) $s^6 = 64$

12. Is m, which does not equal zero, a positive number?
    (1) $m = m^2$
    (2) $m^2 = m^3$

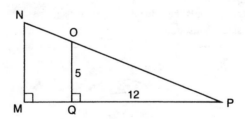

13. How long is MN?
    (1) $ON = 6\frac{1}{2}$
    (2) $MQ = 6$

14. A man's suit was discounted to $140. What was its list price?
    (1) There would be a $10 fee for alterations.
    (2) The sale was at "30% off."

15. In the expression $3x - 2y < z$, is y positive?
    (1) $x = 3$
    (2) $z = 17$

16. What is the value of p?
    (1) $2p + 3r = 11$
    (2) $p - r = 5$

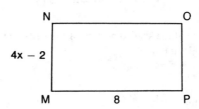

17. What is the width MN of rectangle MNOP?
    (1) $OP = x + 4$
    (2) The area is 48.

18. What is the range of a sportscar on one tank of gasoline?
    (1) The tank holds 50 liters.
    (2) It consumes 8 liters of gasoline each 100 kilometers.

19. Is the diagonal of square Q a rational number?
    (1) The area equals the side multiplied by itself.
    (2) The side equals $\sqrt{8}$.

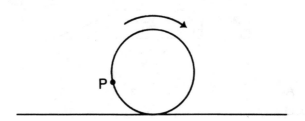

20. What is the diameter of the wheel above?
    (1) The wheel has rolled 36 feet.
    (2) Point P has touched the ground 5 times.

21. What is the value of j if h is k% of j?
    (1) h is 25% of 40.
    (2) $k = 20$

22. How long would it take Sue to paint the room?
    (1) Working with Bob, the project would last 2 hours.
    (2) Bob could accomplish the painting alone in 3¼ hours.

23. Is x < 2?
    (1) $x > x^2$
    (2) $(1/x) > 3$

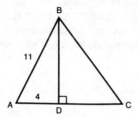

24. Given BD perpendicular to AC, what is the area of triangle BCD?
    (1) Angle BAD = 69°
    (2) BD = CD

25. How many rectangular tiles are required for the kitchen floor?
    (1) Each tile is 48 square inches.
    (2) The kitchen measures 10 feet by 7 feet.

STOP. IF YOU FINISH BEFORE TIME IS CALLED, CHECK YOUR WORK ON THIS SECTION ONLY. DO NOT WORK ON ANY OTHER SECTION IN THE TEST.

SECTION V: CRITICAL REASONING

Time: 30 Minutes
25 Questions

DIRECTIONS

You will be presented with brief passages or statements and will be required to evaluate their reasoning. In each case, select the best answer choice, even though more than one choice may present a possible answer. Choices which are unreasonable or incompatible with common-sense standards should be eliminated.

1. Which of the following most logically completes the passage at the blank below?

   The English language, lacking the rigidity of most European tongues, has been bent and shaped in at least as many ways as there are countries or regions where it is spoken. Though purists often argue that "standard" English is spoken only in certain high-minded enclaves of the American northeast, the fact is that it is the most widely used language in the world and is not likely to yield that distinction for a very long time, if ever. Nevertheless, _____.

   (A) it remains one of the most widely spoken languages throughout the world
   (B) it can be understood in just about every corner of the globe
   (C) even making allowances for regional peculiarities, English as it is spoken has been much abused in recent times
   (D) though we may be proud of these facts, English remains one of the most difficult languages to master
   (E) English, as it is spoken, lacks the rigidity of the classical and more historic European languages

90

2. Life imitates art.

Which of the following, if true, most strongly supports the above statement?

   (A) When Warren Beatty filmed *Reds,* he tried to suggest not only the chaos of the Russian Revolution but also its relationship to the present.
   (B) The number of professional ballet companies has increased over the last five years, but the number of dance majors has decreased.
   (C) On Tuesday, the business section of the newspaper had predicted the drop in interest rates that occurred on Friday.
   (D) Truman Capote wrote *In Cold Blood* as a result of a series of brutal slayings by two crazed killers.
   (E) Soon after the advent of color television, white shirts became less popular as dressy attire for men, and pastel-colored shirts began to sell well.

When President Lyndon Johnson signed the Voting Rights Act in 1965, he used fifty pens, handing them out as souvenirs to a joyous gathering in the President's Room of the Capitol, where Abraham Lincoln had signed the Emancipation Proclamation on January 1, 1863. When President Reagan signed an extension of the Voting Rights Act in 1982, he spoke affectionately of "the right to vote," signed with a single pen, then concluded the four-minute ceremony by rising from his desk, announcing, "It's done."

3. If the passage above is true, which of the following is most probably true?
   (A) The Voting Rights Act did not require an extension.
   (B) The Voting Rights Act is not significantly related to the Emancipation Proclamation.
   (C) President Reagan saw himself as more like Lincoln than did Johnson.
   (D) President Reagan did not regard the extension of the act as an occasion for fanfare.
   (E) President Reagan objected strenuously to an extension of the Voting Rights Act.

4. *Congressman:*   Serving a few months as a Capitol page can be an exciting and enriching experience for high school students from around the country.

      Student: If the circumstances are right.

The student's response suggests which of the following?
(A) belligerence
(B) acquiescence
(C) skepticism
(D) disbelief
(E) ignorance

Questions 5 and 6 refer to the passage below

On average, federal workers receive salaries 35.5 percent higher than private-sector salaries. For instance, federal workers in California average $19,206 a year, 25 percent higher than the average pay in the private sector, which is $15,365.

5. This information would best support which of the following opinions?

(A) Private-sector salaries in California are above average.
(B) The private sector is being paid fairly.
(C) Federal jobs are more secure than private-sector jobs.
(D) Public-sector work is more difficult than private-sector work.
(E) Federal pay is out of line.

6. Which of the following statements is consistent with the information in the passage?
(A) Salaries of California federal workers more nearly approximate the salaries in the private sector than do the salaries of federal workers nationwide.
(B) There are more generous vacation leave privileges for private workers than for federal workers.
(C) Social programs have been curtailed in the face of large state deficits.
(D) State workers in California receive salaries comparable to those of private workers.
(E) Recently, federal workers have begun demanding higher compensation benefits.

Money talks as never before in state and local elections, and the main cause is TV advertising. Thirty seconds can go as high as $2000. Political fundraising is one of the few growth industries left in America. The way to stop the waste might be for television to be paid by state and local government, at a standard rate, to provide air time to all candidates to debate the issues. This might be boring at first. But eventually candidates might actually brush up their debating skills and electrify the TV audience with content, not style.

7. Which of the following presuppositions is (are) necessary to the argument above?

    I. Candidates spend too much money on television advertising.
   II. Television can be used to educate and inform the public.
  III. The freedom of speech doesn't abridge the freedom to spend.

(A) I only
(B) II only
(C) III only
(D) I and II
(E) I, II, and III

Questions 8 and 9 refer to the following passage

According to a recent study by the National Academy of Public Administration, postal patrons are regularly affronted by out-of-order stamp vending machines, branch post office lobbies locked at night, and twenty-two-cent letters that take as long to get there as eight-cent letters did a decade ago.

8. Which of the following, if true, would weaken the implication of one of the writer's observations?
(A) Most out-of-order vending machines are located in run-down neighborhoods.
(B) Late-night vandalism has plagued post offices nationwide.
(C) Postage rates rose 88 percent from 1971 to 1987, but the cost of first class mail is still cheaper in the U.S. than anywhere else.
(D) As a public corporation, the Postal Service has increased its capital assets by $3 billion.
(E) Ten years ago, most letters reached their destination within twenty-four hours.

9. Which of the following transitions probably begins a sentence critical of the argument above?
   (A) However
   (B) In addition
   (C) Despite
   (D) In reality
   (E) Therefore

Of all the petty little pieces of bureaucratic arrogance, it's hard to imagine one smaller than that of the city schools in not admitting a British subject whose father is working—as a legal alien—for a nearby petrochemical company. Someone apparently decided that if the boy had been an illegal alien, a recent U.S. Supreme Court decision in a Texas case would have required the district to admit him, but since he is legal, there is no such requirement. That is nonsense.

10. Which of the following best expresses the point of the author's argument?
   (A) The city schools outside Texas should not base decisions on a precedent set in Texas.
   (B) The stability of a parent's job should have no bearing on the educational opportunity offered his or her child.
   (C) Bureaucratic arrogance has resulted in unsound legal interpretation.
   (D) Legal sense and nonsense are sometimes indistinguishable.
   (E) Both legal and illegal aliens should receive equal treatment.

By appropriating bailout money for the depressed housing industry, Congress is opening the door to a flood of special relief programs for other recession-affected businesses.

11. The author's attitude toward Congress's action is probably
   (A) neutral
   (B) disapproving
   (C) confused
   (D) happy
   (E) irate

A researcher has concluded that women are just as capable as men in math but that their skills are not developed because society expects them to develop other and more diverse abilities.

12. Which of the following is a basic assumption of the researcher?
    (A) Ability in math is more important than ability in more diverse subjects.
    (B) Ability in math is less important than ability in more diverse subjects.
    (C) Women and men should be equally capable in math.
    (D) Women might be more capable than men in math.
    (E) Women tend to conform to social expectations.

Questions 13 and 14 refer to the following passage

Beginning this fall, Latino and Asian students will not be allowed to transfer out of bilingual classes (that is, a program in which courses are given in a student's native language) until they pass strict competency tests in math, reading, and writing—as well as spoken English. The board and its supporters say this will protect children from being pushed out of bilingual programs before they are ready. They have hailed this as a victory for bilingual education.

13. Which of the following, if true, is the strongest criticism of the position of the board?
    (A) A foreign student may be quite competent in math without being competent in English.
    (B) Some native students already in English-speaking classes are unable to pass the competency tests.
    (C) Most foreign students require many months of practice and instruction before mastering English skills.
    (D) Many students prefer to transfer out of bilingual classes before they have achieved competency in English.
    (E) Holding back students will double the number of students in bilingual classes—twice as many Latino and Asian children isolated from the English-speaking mainstream.

14. The argument above would be most strengthened if the author were to explain
    (A) how efficient the bilingual program is
    (B) how well staffed the bilingual program is
    (C) whether the community supports the bilingual program
    (D) whether any board members do not support the bilingual program
    (E) how the students feel about the bilingual program

The $464 million "reserve" in the 1987–88 budget adopted by the legislature in June turns out to have been based mainly on wishful thinking. Because of tax cuts approved by voters on the June ballot, along with the continuing recession and other events affecting income and expenses, the actual reserve in prospect may be as low as $7 million.

15. The author is probably leading to which of the following conclusions?
    (A) These facts warrant an investigation into who squandered $457 million.
    (B) A reserve in the budget is not so necessary as we might wish it to be.
    (C) The legislature would be wise not to add any new spending to the budget adopted in June.
    (D) The recession will probably not last much longer, but while it does the legislature must adjust the budget accordingly.
    (E) Legislative budgets are typically careless and unheeding of variable factors which may affect their accuracy.

Questions 16 and 17 refer to the following passage

"The sum of behavior is to retain a man's dignity without intruding upon the liberty of others," stated Sir Francis Bacon. If this is the case, then not intruding upon another's liberty is impossible.

16. The conclusion strongly implied by the author's arguments is that

    (A) retaining one's dignity is impossible without intruding upon another's liberty
    (B) retaining dignity never involves robbing others of liberty
    (C) dignity and liberty are mutually exclusive
    (D) there is always the possibility of a "dignified intrusion"
    (E) B. F. Skinner's *Beyond Freedom and Dignity* takes its cue from Bacon

17. The author's argument would be weakened if it were pointed out that

    I. Bacon's argument has been misinterpreted out of context
    II. neither liberty nor dignity can be discussed in absolute terms
    III. retaining dignity always involves a reduction of liberty

    (A) I, II, and III   (D) II and III only
    (B) III only   (E) I and II only
    (C) I only

Jonathan Swift said, "laws are like cobwebs which may catch small flies but let wasps and hornets break through."

18. Jonathan Swift would most probably believe that
    (A) prosecutors should be tough on criminals
    (B) pesticides should be used to deter large insects
    (C) small crimes should not be prosecuted
    (D) the powerful can often avoid serious criminal sentences
    (E) laws do not stop people from committing crimes

19. Which of the following most logically completes the passage at the blank below?

    In a civilized society, members of the community will often defer to others, even against their own better judgment. This situation may occur in public, in gatherings with strangers, or in the household with one's family or friends. It is a sign of a more sophisticated culture that one's immediate interests are thought to be secondary to those of another. On first examination this may seem to be selflessness, but _____.

    (A) actually it is not; it is just ignorance
    (B) rather it may take many names
    (C) actually it is
    (D) to some extent it does serve the ends of the individual concerned
    (E) sometimes it can harbor animosities and hostility

Questions 20 through 23 refer to the following passage

The older we get, the less sleep we should desire. This is because our advanced knowledge and capabilities are most enjoyable when used; therefore, "mindless" sleep becomes a waste of time.

20. Which of the following distinctions is *not* expressed or implied by the author?
    (A) between sleep and wakefulness
    (B) between youth and maturity
    (C) between productivity and waste
    (D) between a desire and a requirement
    (E) between more sleep and less sleep

21. The author of this statement assumes that
    (A) less sleep is not desirable
    (B) sleep advances knowledge and capabilities
    (C) mindlessness coincides with wakefulness
    (D) knowledge and capabilities naturally improve with age
    (E) sleep is only for the young

22. This author's statement might be strengthened if he or she pointed out that
    (A) advanced knowledge is often manifested in creative dreams
    (B) the mind is quite active during sleep
    (C) few empirical studies have concluded that sleep is an intellectual stimulant
    (D) advanced capabilities are not necessarily mind-associated
    (E) dreams teach us how to use waking experiences more intelligently

23. The author's statement might be weakened by pointing out that
    (A) eight hours of sleep is a cultural, not a physical, requirement
    (B) the most capable people rarely sleep
    (C) rest is a positive contribution to knowledge and capability
    (D) young children enjoy themselves less than knowledgeable adults
    (E) people rarely waste time during their waking hours

   Don't spend the night tossing and turning! Take Eezy-Z's for a sound, restful sleep . . . you'll wake up refreshed, energized, with no drugged-up hangover. Remember . . . Eezy-Z's when you need that sleep!

24. Which of the following is *not* a claim of Eezy-Z's?
    (A) a good night's sleep
    (B) added energy
    (C) no aftereffects
    (D) quickly falling asleep
    (E) a restful slumber

   On a swimming team—
      All freestyle swimmers are Olympic winners.
      No blue-eyed swimmer is an Olympic winner.
      All Olympic winners go on to lucrative professional careers.

25. If it is determined that all of the above are true, then which of the following must also be true about the swimming team?
    (A) All those who go on to professional careers are freestyle swimmers.
    (B) Only freestyle swimmers go on to professional careers.
    (C) Some blue-eyed swimmers go on to lucrative professional careers.
    (D) No blue-eyed swimmer is a freestyle swimmer.
    (E) Only blue-eyed swimmers don't go on to lucrative careers.

STOP. IF YOU FINISH BEFORE TIME IS CALLED CHECK YOUR WORK ON THIS SECTION ONLY. DO NOT WORK ON ANY OTHER SECTION IN THE TEST.

SECTION VI: PROBLEM SOLVING

Time: 30 Minutes
20 Questions

DIRECTIONS

In this section solve each problem, using any available space on the page for scratchwork. Then indicate the *best* answer in the appropriate space on the answer sheet.

1. What is the largest integer if the sum of three consecutive even integers is 318?
   (A) 100   (B) 104   (C) 106   (D) 108   (E) 111

2. If $2/x = 4$ and if $2/y = 8$, then $x - y =$
   (A) ⅛   (B) ¼   (C) ¾   (D) 4   (E) 24

3. On a map, 1 centimeter represents 35 kilometers. Two cities 245 kilometers apart would be separated on the map by how many centimeters?
   (A) 5   (B) 7   (C) 9   (D) 210   (E) 280

4. If the ratio of the side of Cube A to the side of Cube B is 2:1, then which of the following could be the ratio of the surface areas?
   (A) 1:2   (B) 2:1   (C) 3:1   (D) 4:1   (E) 8:1

5. The denominator of a fraction is 5 greater than the numerator. If the numerator and the denominator are increased by 2, the resulting fraction is equal to $7/12$. What is the value of the original fraction?
   (A) $5/12$ (B) ½   (C) $9/14$ (D) ⅔   (E) $12/17$

6. How much tea worth 93¢ per pound must be mixed with tea worth 75¢ per pound to produce 10 pounds worth 85¢ per pound?
   (A) 2⅔   (B) 3½   (C) 4⁴⁄₉   (D) 5⁵⁄₉   (E) 9½

7. If 15 students in a class average 80% on an English exam and 10 students average 90% on the same exam, what is the average in percent for all 25 students?
   (A) 83%   (B) 83½%   (C) 84%   (D) 85%   (E) 86⅔%

100

8. Mr. Smitherly leaves Beverly Hills at 8 A.M. and drives north on the highway at an average speed of 50 miles per hour. Mr. Dinkle leaves Beverly Hills at 8:30 A.M. and drives north on the same highway at an average speed of 60 miles per hour. Mr. Dinkle will
   (A) overtake Mr. Smitherly at 9:30 A.M.
   (B) overtake Mr. Smitherly at 10:30 A.M.
   (C) overtake Mr. Smitherly at 11:00 A.M.
   (D) be 30 miles behind at 8:35 A.M.
   (E) never overtake Mr. Smitherly

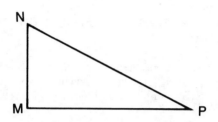

9. On △ MNP, MN ⊥ MP, MP = 24, and NP = 26. Find the area of △ MNP in square units.
   (A) 312   (B) 240   (C) 120   (D) 60
   (E) cannot be determined

10. How many feet will an automobile travel in one second if it is moving at the rate of 30 miles per hour?
    (A) 44   (B) 66   (C) 88   (D) 176   (E) 2640

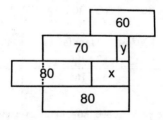

11. The horizontal length of each rectangle is marked within. What is the total horizontal length of x + y ?
    (A) 40 (B) 50 (C) 80 (D) 90 (E) cannot be determined

12. Tom has enough money to buy 45 bricks. If the bricks each cost 10 cents less, Tom could buy 5 more bricks. How much money does Tom have to spend on bricks?

(A) $100   (B) $50   (C) $45   (D) $40   (E) $30

13. How many combinations are possible if a person has 4 sport jackets, 5 shirts, and 3 pairs of slacks?

(A) 4   (B) 5   (C) 12   (D) 60   (E) 120

14. John received a 10% raise each month for three consecutive months. What was his salary after the three raises if his starting salary was $1000 per month?

(A) $1248   (B) $1300   (C) $1331   (D) $1410
(E) none of these

15. Find the total surface area in square meters of a rectangular solid whose length is 7 meters, width is 6 meters, and depth is 3 meters.

(A) $32m^2$ (B) $81m^2$ (C) $126m^2$ (D) $162m^2$ (E) $252m^2$

16. The average of 9 numbers is 7 and the average of 7 other numbers is 9. What is the average of all 16 numbers?

(A) 9   (B) 8   (C) $7\frac{7}{8}$ (D) $7\frac{1}{2}$ (E) $7\frac{1}{4}$

17. Which of the following cannot be weighed using a balance scale and these unit weights: 1, 4, 7, and 10?

(A) 13   (B) 15   (C) 17   (D) 19   (E) 21

18. In a class of 200 students, 120 study Spanish and 100 study French. If a student must study at least one of these two languages, what percent of the students study French but not Spanish?

A) 80%   (B) 40%   (C) 30%   (D) 20%   (E) 10%

Toys	Cost to Manufacture	Profit per Toy
A	$2.5796	$2.4431
B	$2.5768	$2.4312

19. According to the chart above, how many of each toy would have to be manufactured so that the total price of toy A exceeds the total price of toy B by $147.00?

(A) 100   (B) 1000   (C) 10,000   (D) 100,000
(E) 1,000,000

20. If the diameter of circle R is 30% of the diameter of circle S, the area of circle R is what percent of the area of circle S?

(A) 9% (B) 15% (C) 30% (D) 60% (E) 90%

STOP. IF YOU FINISH BEFORE TIME IS CALLED, CHECK YOUR WORK ON THIS SECTION ONLY. DO NOT WORK ON ANY OTHER SECTION IN THE TEST.

SECTION VII: DATA SUFFICIENCY

Time: 30 Minutes
25 Questions

DIRECTIONS

Each of the problems below consists of a question and two statements, labeled
(1) and (2), in which certain data are given. You must decide whether the
data given in the statements are *sufficient* to answer the question. Using the
data given in the statements *plus* your knowledge of mathematics and
everyday facts (such as the number of days in July or the meaning of
counterclockwise), you are to blacken space

- (A) if statement (1) ALONE is sufficient, but statement (2) is not sufficient
  to answer the question asked;
- (B) if statement (2) ALONE is sufficient, but statement (1) alone is not
  sufficient to answer the question asked;
- (C) if BOTH statements (1) and (2) TOGETHER are sufficient to answer the
  question, but NEITHER statement ALONE is sufficient;
- (D) if EACH statement ALONE is sufficient to answer the question asked;
- (E) if statements (1) and (2) TOGETHER are NOT sufficient to answer the
  question asked, and additional data specific to the problem are
  needed.

1. What are the individual prices of three cameras?
   (1) The three cameras have an average price of $172.
   (2) Two are identical and sell for $332 together.

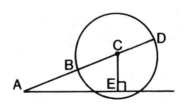

2. In the figure above, what is the area of right triangle ACE?
   (1) $\overline{AE}$ equals 16 inches.
   (2) $\overline{BD}$ equals 12 inches.

104

3. What is the numerical value of the ratio n/m?
   (1) mn = 14
   (2) m = 6n

4. How many black shoes were sold by Shepard's Shoe Emporium?
   (1) Three-quarters of the shoes sold were brown.
   (2) The Emporium sold 1284 left shoes.

5. A farmer wants to fence in a rectangular lot of 3000 square feet in which to raise pigs. Should he employ configuration X or configuration Y in order to minimize the cost of fencing?
   (1) Lot X would be 75 feet long and lot Y would be 50 feet wide.
   (2) Lot X would be 87½ percent longer than wide and lot Y would be 20 percent longer than wide.

6. How many brothers does David have?
   (1) His parents have seven surviving children.
   (2) He has twice as many sisters as brothers.

7. Given three different integers, does the exponential quantity $(a - b)^c$ exceed zero?
   (1) b < a
   (2) c = 2a

8. Otto and his wife Anna leave home at 1 P.M. and bicycle in different directions. How far apart are they at 4 P.M.?
   (1) Otto rides at 12 mph westward for two hours and then stops.
   (2) Anna rides at 10 mph southward for one hour and then rides westward at the same speed for three hours.

9. How long would it take Joan to count the books in a small library?
   (1) She counts twice as fast as Emily.
   (2) Working together, Joan and Emily count the books in 26 hours.

10. How many Mondays are in December of a particular year?
    (1) There are four Tuesdays that December.
    (2) There are four Saturdays that December.

11. What is the value of x + y + z?
    (1) y + z = 2x
    (2) $\frac{1}{x} + \frac{1}{y} + \frac{1}{z} = \frac{4}{9}$

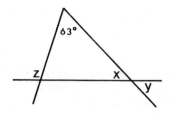

12. How many degrees is angle x?
    (1) y = 47°
    (2) z = 110°

13. How long is the diagonal through the center of a particular cube?
    (1) A diagonal across one face is 4.24 centimeters.
    (2) The surface area of the cube is 54 square centimeters.

14. At what temperature do degrees Hotter (°H) and degrees Warmer (°W)
    have the same numerical value?
    (1) 80°H is equivalent to 36°W.
    (2) °W = 0.6 (°H − 20)

15. One number is five more than half a second number, which is evenly
    divisible by a third number. What is the second number?
    (1) The first number is one less than the second.
    (2) The third number is two less than half the second.

16. Each of 200 electrical switches controls a separate light bulb. How many
    of the switches are in the OFF position?
    (1) 40 percent of the bulbs are glowing.
    (2) 5 percent of the bulbs are burnt out.

17. Beverage cans are manufactured of steel or aluminum. From the
    following graphs, what was the percentage change in number of bever-
    age cans manufactured from 1975 to 1980?

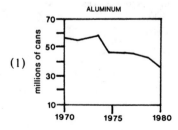

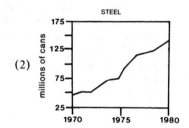

18. Is the product cd positive?
    (1) $3c = -8d^3$
    (2) $d > c + 4$

19. How much wallpaper is needed to cover the two largest walls of a narrow room which is 9 feet high?
    (1) The room is 10 feet wide.
    (2) The room is 24 feet long.

20. A savings account earned 1% simple interest each month, credited on the last day of the month. On December 8 there was $1115.67 in the account. During which month did the account first exceed $1100?
    (1) $1000 was deposited on the previous December 31.
    (2) There were no deposits or withdrawals this year.

21. If $x < y$, is $(x - y) < yz$?
    (1) $y < 0$
    (2) $z < 0$

22. How many people are employed at a certain manufacturing plant with an annual payroll of $2,342,000?
    (1) Three-fourths of the employees are clerical, at an average salary of $16,020.
    (2) With 8 percent more employees, the payroll would equal $2,548,000.

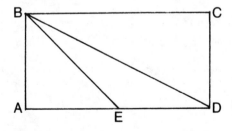

23. In the figure above, ABCD is a rectangle and E is the midpoint of one side. What is the area of triangle BCD?
    (1) $\overline{BE}$ = 5 inches
    (2) $\overline{CD}$ = 3 inches

24. Given that m = n + 2, what is the value of $m^2 - 4m + 4$?
    (1) n = 3
    (2) $n^2 = 400$

25. An ice-cream stand sells two sizes of cones, Generous and Colossal. How many Colossal cones were sold one day?
    (1) The total sales were $209.15.
    (2) Generous cones sold for 75¢ and Colossal cones sold for $1.25.

STOP. IF YOU FINISH BEFORE TIME IS CALLED, CHECK YOUR WORK ON THIS SECTION ONLY. DO NOT WORK ON ANY OTHER SECTION IN THE TEST.

ANSWER KEY FOR PRACTICE TEST 1

Section I Reading Comprehension	Section II Problem Solving	Section III Sentence Correction	Section IV Data Sufficiency
1. A	1. D	1. C	1. E
2. C	2. D	2. A	2. B
3. D	3. C	3. D	3. E
4. D	4. E	4. E	4. D
5. C	5. C	5. C	5. D
6. A	6. D	6. E	6. A
7. C	7. D	7. D	7. A
8. C	8. B	8. B	8. C
9. E	9. B	9. D	9. D
10. A	10. A	10. A	10. A
11. C	11. B	11. E	11. A
12. D	12. B	12. D	12. D
13. C	13. E	13. E	13. D
14. D	14. C	14. C	14. B
15. A	15. C	15. C	15. E
16. B	16. E	16. C	16. C
17. C	17. B	17. B	17. D
18. B	18. D	18. A	18. C
19. B	19. D	19. B	19. B
20. D	20. B	20. B	20. E
21. A		21. D	21. C
22. C		22. B	22. C
23. B		23. C	23. D
24. C		24. D	24. B
25. B		25. B	25. C

ANSWER KEY FOR PRACTICE TEST 1

Section V Critical Reasoning	Section VI Problem Solving	Section VII Data Sufficiency
1. C	1. D	1. C
2. E	2. B	2. E
3. D	3. B	3. B
4. C	4. D	4. E
5. E	5. B	5. D
6. A	6. D	6. C
7. D	7. C	7. D
8. E	8. C	8. C
9. A	9. C	9. C
10. C	10. A	10. C
11. B	11. E	11. E
12. E	12. C	12. D
13. E	13. D	13. D
14. A	14. C	14. B
15. C	15. D	15. A
16. A	16. C	16. E
17. E	17. D	17. C
18. D	18. B	18. A
19. D	19. C	19. B
20. D	20. A	20. B
21. D		21. C
22. C		22. E
23. C		23. C
24. D		24. D
25. D		25. E

HOW TO SCORE YOUR EXAM

1. Add the total number of correct responses for each section.
2. Add the total number of incorrect responses (only those attempted or marked in) for each section.
3. The total number of incorrect responses should be divided by 4, giving the adjustment factor.
4. Subtract this adjustment factor from the total number of correct responses to obtain a raw score.
5. This score is then scaled from 200 to 800.

Example:
A. If the total number of correct answers was 100 out of a possible 205.
B. And 60 problems were attempted but missed.
C. Dividing the 60 by 4 gives an adjustment factor of 15.
D. Subtracting this adjustment factor of 15 from the original 100 correct gives a raw score of 85.
E. This raw score is then scaled to a range of 200 to 800.

ANALYZING YOUR TEST RESULTS

The charts on the following pages should be used to carefully analyze your results and spot your strengths and weaknesses. The complete process of analyzing each subject area and each individual problem should be completed for each Practice Test. These results should then be reexamined for trends in types of errors (repeated errors) or poor results in specific subject areas. THIS REEXAMINATION AND ANALYSIS IS OF TREMENDOUS IMPORTANCE TO YOU IN ASSURING MAXIMUM TEST PREPARATION BENEFIT.

PRACTICE TEST 1: ANALYSIS SHEET

	Possible	Completed	Right	Wrong
Section I: Reading Comprehension	25			
Section II: Problem Solving	20			
Section III: Sentence Correction	25			
Section IV: Data Sufficiency	25			
Section V: Critical Reasoning	25			
Section VI: Problem Solving	20			
Section VII: Data Sufficiency	25			
OVERALL TOTALS	165			

WHY??????????????????????????????????

ANALYSIS—TALLY SHEET FOR PROBLEMS MISSED

One of the most important parts of test preparation is analyzing WHY! you missed a problem so that you can reduce the number of mistakes. Now that you have taken the practice test and corrected your answers, carefully tally your mistakes by marking them in the proper column.

REASON FOR MISTAKE

	Total Missed	Simple Mistake	Misread Problem	Lack of Knowledge
Section I: Reading Comprehension				
Section II: Problem Solving				
Section III: Sentence Correction				
Section IV: Data Sufficiency				
Section V: Critical Reasoning				
Section VI: Problem Solving				
Section VII: Data Sufficiency				
OVERALL TOTALS				

Reviewing the above data should help you determine WHY you are missing certain problems. Now that you have pinpointed the type of error, take the next practice test focusing on avoiding your most common type.

COMPLETE ANSWERS AND EXPLANATIONS FOR PRACTICE TEST 1

SECTION I: READING COMPREHENSION

1. (A) According to the first paragraph, a disadvantage of cell counts, smear counts, and membrane filter counts is that "both living and dead cells are counted." This is not true of plate counts, which "have the advantage of not including dead cells" (paragraph 3).

2. (C) During the lag phase, "there is no increase in number of viable cells." (B) is partially true; it would be correct if not for the claim that cells reproduce.

3. (D) The third paragraph shows that incubation produces colonies, which means that there is population *growth*. Choice (E) describes only the range of colonies which are counted; it is too limited to be the best choice.

4. (D) During the logarithmic phase, "the food supply diminishes" (through consumption, of course), and "waste products accumulate" (conspicuous evidence of such consumption). (A) contradicts the passage, which speaks of the rapid growth rate during this phase.

5. (C) The smear count is one of the methods which is "quickly accomplished." The other choices are related to more time-consuming procedures.

6. (A) During the stationary phase, the highest level of population size is called the "maximum crop." "Crop" is, of course, commonly used as an agricultural term.

7. (C) The author concludes by saying that "it is impossible even for the scientist to escape the essential subjectivity of his sensations, generalizations, and deductions." Since everything is subjective, since different people each see the same thing a bit differently, one is seeming to devalue this case by saying that "what you say you see is *just* in your head." "In your head" is not an unimportant place; according to the passage, it is the *only* place.

8. (C) Early in the passage we are told that, in a semantic pair, "the one [term] has no meaning without the other. We may define each by antonym with the other." In short, semantic pairs are pairs of direct opposites. Only (C) is not such a pair.

9. (E) The author makes the point that this sentence does not have affective (emotional) content because "it is used here entirely without feelings of praise or blame." Choice (E) changes the force of the sentence by substituting terms which are always associated with praise or blame. (D) is a possibility along these lines, but "irrational" and "rational" are not as emotionally charged as "lunatic" and "trustworthy" are.

10. (A) The author tells us that scientists, who he defines as "objective," are "primarily concerned with the identity and continuity of the external object that stimulates [their] response." That is, to be objective one must believe that the world is a collection of stable objects, each of which always looks the same. (E) is a single example consistent with this assumption, but is not itself broad enough to support the question of objectivity in general. (D) is also too broad to be the best answer. (C) is not an assumption allowed by the passage.

11. (C) We are told by the author that Ogden and Richards "seem not to have thought through this problem of the object." Such a statement is clearly critical. And the author is not "perplexed" or "evasive" about what he means, because he goes on to quote and analyze Ogden and Richards in a clear, straightforward manner.

12. (D) In general, the passage questions whether any object (including this book) has objective reality. At one point the author says, "whether objects 'exist' is obviously not discussable." Since the writer himself supports his ideas with evidence, we may not pick (C), because the question whether he is subjective or objective is not implied in his own approach.

13. (C) This situation establishes a relationship between price and quantity which parallels the paragraph 2 explanation of the "law of demand." This section discusses "the consumer's desire to get the 'best buy,' " and goes on to say that "if the price of good A increases, the individual will tend to substitute another good and purchase less of good A." Since the appearance of a lower-priced breakfast drink makes orange juice more "expensive," in relation, the law of demand as so described would prevail.

14. (D) The third paragraph distinguishes between "individual demand" and "market demand"; the former is exercised by a single person, whereas the latter is exerted by a *group* of individuals. With this distinction in mind, we may conclude that a group of individuals constitutes a market. (B) contradicts the paragraph. (A), (C), and (E) might be true under certain conditions, but those conditions are not specified in the question or in the passage.

15. (A) Initially, the passage emphasizes a distinction between "demand" and "quantity demanded," concluding that "demand shifts when there is a change in income, expectations, taste, etc., such that a different quantity of the good is demanded at the *same* price." This statement fits (A) precisely. All other choices include or allow for a *changing* price.

16. (B) Paragraph 4 states, "there is a positive correlation between quantity supplied and product price." Since that means that quantity and price are related, any choice (in this case all choices except B) with a relational connotation does not tell us what the two items are *not*.

17. (C) The passage says that "demand shifts when there is a change in income, expectations, taste, etc., such that a different quantity of the good is demanded at the same price." (A), (D), and (E) all involve a *changing* price, and (B) would reduce income so that demand would *decrease*.

18. (B) The last sentence says that it is "developed" or "interdependent" economies that acquiesce to the idea that government must control economy to some extent. This leaves underdeveloped countries unspoken for and raises the possibility they might *not* acquiesce to government control.

19. (B) The paragraph states that government action "may create shortages or surpluses." Shortages and surpluses are associated with disequilibrium in paragraph 6.

20. (D) The third sentence in the passage supports this answer. (C) may be true, but is too general to be the best answer.

21. (A) This is stated explicitly in paragraph 5.

22. (C) When prices are above equilibrium, "the quantity supplied exceeds quantity demanded and surpluses occur." An overfull car lot implies such a condition.

23. (B) Choices (C), (D), and (E) are tones appropriate to persuasion, but not to factual accounts such as this one. (A) is not correct because the author's earlier statements have been describing disequilibrium, a condition in which the market does not work perfectly.

24. (C) The seventh paragraph states, "In reality, equilibrium is seldom attained, for the factors affecting the market are constantly changing." The factors he speaks of are demand and supply, so (C) is a better answer than (E), which is too general.

25. (B) This answer is explicitly stated in the next to last paragraph: ". . . price serves both a demand-inhibiting and supply-eliciting function."

SECTION II: PROBLEM SOLVING

1. (D) First calculate the circumference of the circle using the equation
C = πD (or C = 2πr). C = 14 (²²⁄₇) = 44. The circumference is 44 inches;
now change ½ mile to feet (2640) to inches 2640 × 12 = 31,680.
Dividing 31,680 by 44 = 720 revolutions.

2. (D) Average rate is total distance (found by multiplying rate times time
and adding ft + rs) divided by total time (t + s); therefore the average
rate is (ft + rs)/t + s.

3. (C) This problem is most easily completed by rearranging and approximating as follows:

$$\frac{69.28 \times .004}{.03} \simeq 69 \times \frac{.004}{.03} \simeq 69 \times .1 = 6.9$$

which is the only reasonably close answer to 9.2.

4. (E) Simply continue the chart as follows, adding 40¢ for each two years
to Product A and 15¢ for each two years to Product B:

Products	1972	1974	1976	1978	1980
A	$6.60	$7.00	$7.40	$7.80	$8.20
B	$7.20	$7.35	$7.50	$7.65	$7.80

It is evident that the correct answer is 1980.

5. (C) Since Sid and Jan are working at different rates, we need to equate
them to the same time, one hour. This gives the equation ⅙ + 1/x = ½,
as in one hour, Sid does ⅙ of the job, plus in one hour Jan does 1/x of the
job; together in one hour they could do ½ of the job.

$$\text{Solving } \frac{1}{6} + 1/x = \frac{1}{2}$$
$$1/x = \frac{1}{2} - \frac{1}{6}$$
$$1/x = \frac{3}{6} - \frac{1}{6}$$
$$1/x = \frac{2}{6}$$
$$2x = 6$$
$$x = 3 \text{ hours or } 180 \text{ minutes}$$

Notice that you could have eliminated answers (A), (B), and (E) as they
are not reasonable choices.

6. **(D)** Since the large square has side 4 cm, then its area must be 16. By careful grouping of areas, you will see that there are 4 unshaded smaller squares, and 4 shaded smaller squares (match the shaded parts to four squares) therefore ½ of the area is shaded, or 8 sq cm.

7. **(D)** The net profit is 25% since $12 is 25% of $48. Now add in 15% for overhead and you have 25% + 15% = 40%.

8. **(B)** The following diagram shows Manny's path.

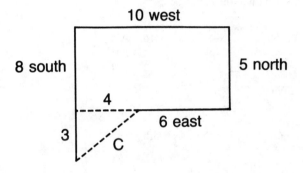

Manny traveled 29 miles at 10 miles per hour, so it took him 2.9 hours. The distance Irv travels is calculated by subtracting travel in opposite directions and using the Pythagorean theorem. 6 east and 10 west leaves 4 west, while 5 north and 8 south leaves 3 south. The right triangle has legs of 3 and 4.

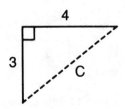

Therefore the hypotenuse must be 5 (3:4:5 ratio) or using the theorem,

$$a^2 + b^2 = c^2$$
$$3^2 + 4^2 = c^2$$
$$9 + 16 = c^2$$
$$25 = c^2$$
$$5 = c$$

Irv must travel 5 miles at 5 miles per hour, or 1 hour. Since they both start at the same time, Irv arrives much earlier than Manny.

9. **(B)** Since the surface area of side ABFE is 16, then each side is 4. Now use the Pythagorean theorem to find the length of the diagonal that is also the length of the rectangle.

$$4^2 + 4^2 = AH^2$$
$$16 + 16 = AH^2$$
$$32 = AH^2$$
$$\sqrt{32} = AH$$

Simplifying

$$\sqrt{32} = \sqrt{16 \times 2} = \sqrt{16} \times \sqrt{2} = 4\sqrt{2}$$

Now multiplying length times width gives

$$4 \times 4\sqrt{2} = 16\sqrt{2}$$

Notice you may have recognized the ratio of a 45°:45°:90° triangle as $1:1:\sqrt{2}$ and found the diagonal quickly using $4:4:4\sqrt{2}$.

10. **(A)** Substituting small negative integers is the most effective method for this problem.

Let $y = -1$
then $x = -1 + (-1)^2$
              $x = -1 + 1$
              $x = 0$
Now let $y = -2$
then $x = -2 + (-2)^2$
              $x = -2 + 4$
              $x = 2$

Therefore x increases in value.

11. **(B)** Let x be the number of \$4 Frisbees, then $64 - x$ is the number of \$3 Frisbees. This gives the equation $3(64 - x) + 4(x) = 204$. Solving gives

$$192 - 3x + 4x = 204$$
$$192 + x = 204$$
$$x = 12$$

Therefore, the fewest number of $4 Frisbees is 12. Note that you could have worked from the answers by substituting in each possibility.

12. (B) If each could save $7200, then all 3 could save $21,600. Let x stand for the amount each of the five businessmen invests, then the difference between the five and three investments would be

$$5x - 3x = 21,600$$
or $$2x = 21,600$$
$$x = 10,800$$

Hence each of the five invests $10,800, therefore the total investment is 5 × 10,800 or $54,000.

Note that answers (C), (D), and (E) were not reasonable. Another method could have used one of the original investor's savings and worked from the equation $1/3 \ x - 1/5 \ x = 7200$.

13. (E) Since this is an approximation, round off

$$\frac{\text{Venus weight of 182}}{\text{Earth weight of 207}} \text{ to } \frac{180}{200} \text{ which is 90\%}$$

14. (C) Let x be the amount invested at 5%, then $1000 - x$ is the amount invested at 6%. This gives the equation $5(x) + 6(1000 - x) = 5300$. Solving gives

$$5x + 6000 - 6x = 5300$$
$$6000 - x = 5300$$
$$-x = -700$$
$$x = 700$$

Therefore $700 was invested at 5%.
Note that answers (A), (D), and (E) were not reasonable.

15. (C) The best way to solve this problem is by using simple numbers. If the recliners originally sold at $100 each, then a 20% reduction would leave a price of $80 each. If the owner sold 50% more recliners, it would be the same as $40 more for each original sale. This would be $120, ($80 + $40), which is 20% more than $100 per recliner.

An alternate method would be to let 3/2 represent a 50% increase, then 3/2 times 80% = 120%, which is a 20% increase over the original 100%.

16. (E) First change 2 hours into 120 minutes.
(Always get a common unit of measurement.)

Then dividing 120 by $\frac{2}{3}$ gives

$$\overset{60}{\cancel{120}} \times \frac{3}{\underset{1}{\cancel{2}}} = 180$$

The correct answer is (E), 180 items. Notice choices (A) and (B) are ridiculous answers.

17. (B) Checking each possible pair of numbers for common divisions:

$$\left.\begin{array}{ll} \text{I.} & 3 \\ \text{II.} & 4 \end{array}\right\} \quad \begin{array}{l} \text{Only common divisor 1} \\ \text{These are relatively prime} \end{array}$$

$$\left.\begin{array}{ll} \text{I.} & 3 \\ \text{III.} & 7 \end{array}\right\} \quad \begin{array}{l} \text{Only common divisor 1} \\ \text{These are relatively prime} \end{array}$$

$$\left.\begin{array}{ll} \text{I.} & 3 \\ \text{IV.} & 12 \end{array}\right\} \quad \begin{array}{l} \text{Common divisors are 1 and 3} \\ \text{These are } not \text{ relatively prime} \end{array}$$

Since I and IV are *not* relatively prime, check the choices to see which include I and IV. Notice that I and II are only in choices (B) and (E), therefore those are the two possible choices. A closer look eliminates choice (E) because I and II have numbers that are relatively prime. For good measure, checking II and IV:

$$\left.\begin{array}{ll} \text{II.} & 4 \\ \text{IV.} & 12 \end{array}\right\} \quad \begin{array}{l} \text{Common divisors are 1 and 4} \\ \text{These are } not \text{ relatively prime} \end{array}$$

Therefore I and IV, and II and IV are *not* relatively prime giving the correct answer of (B).

18. (D) Since ABCD is a rhombus, all sides are equal, therefore BC = CD = 6, and BC + CD = 12. AB = 6, minus AE $\simeq$ 4 leaves 6 − 4 $\simeq$ 2, which is the approximate length of BE. Adding 12 + 2 = 14, gives the distance around the rhombus that will be traveled. Now using the formula for circumference of a circle = $2\pi r$ or πD leaves 6π as the circumference of the complete circle. Because the inscribed angle is 45°, arc DE is 90° (inscribed angle is half of the arc it intercepts). This 90° will not be traveled as it is in the interior of the figure, therefore only 270° of the 360° in the complete circle will be traveled, or ¾ of the circle. ¾ × 6π = $9\pi/2$. This added to the original 14 gives answer (D) 14 + ($9\pi/2$), or 14 + (9/2)π.

19. **(D)** Set up the equation as follows:

Let t be the length of time it will take the plane to overtake the bus, then t + 4 is the time that the bus has traveled before the plane starts. The distance that the bus has traveled by 1 P.M. is 50(t + 4), since distance equals rate times time (d = rt). The distance the plane will travel is 300t. Now setting these two equal to each other (they will have to travel the same distance for one to overtake the other) gives 50(t + 4) = 300t. Solve the equation as follows:

$$50(t + 4) = 300t$$
$$50t + 200 = 300t$$
$$200 = 250t$$

Therefore $\frac{4}{5} = t$

⅘ of an hour (⅘ × 60) is 48 minutes. Hence it will take 48 minutes for the plane to overtake the bus and since the plane is starting at 1 P.M. it will overtake the bus at 1:48 P.M.

20. **(B)** In the right triangle, if c = 2a, then angle a = 30° and c = 60°. Since angle f is supplementary to angle c, angle f must be 120°. If angle f is 120°, then there are 60° left to be divided between angles d and b (remember there are 180° in a triangle). Since d > 2b, then b must be less than 30°, therefore the correct answer is **(B)** angle a (30°) is greater than angle b (less than 30°).

Notice the way you should have marked the diagram to assist you.

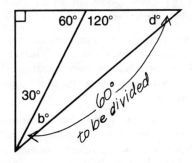

SECTION III: SENTENCE CORRECTION

1. (C) The original sentence is a fragment; so are choices (B), (D), and (E).

2. (A) The original is better than any of the alternatives.

3. (D) *Majority* is a collective noun which may take either a singular or plural verb, depending on whether the group as a whole or the individuals are emphasized. But *lose* is a clearer and more economical expression than *become defeated*. Choices (B), (C), and (E) change the meaning of the sentence.

4. (E) The verb *lying* (resting) is correct here; also, *were* is the correct verb because the subject, *a lion and his mate,* is plural. Choices (B) and (D) would make the sentence a fragment.

5. (C) The original is flawed by faulty parallelism. *Planning* is not parallel to *to pursue* (the former a gerund, the latter an infinitive). Choice (C) corrects this problem; *planning* is parallel to *pursuing*.

6. (E) *Focusing across* is idiomatically incorrect and also logically unsound (*focusing on* is better). The only choice that is both idiomatically correct and preserves the meaning of the original is (E).

7. (D) *From the stands,* in the original, is a misplaced modifier suggesting that the players made the touchdown from the stands, which is highly impossible. Choice (E) leaves *crowd* out of the sentence (a significant omission), and all other choices except (D) contain misplaced modifiers.

8. (B) The original contains two important errors. *Overtime* and *past regular hours* are repetitious and *comply to this* is both vague and nonidiomatic. Choice (B) corrects both of these weaknesses. (D) is a correct expression but retains the vague pronoun *this,* which possibly refers to either the contract or the overtime.

9. (D) Both errors in the original result from a confusion of adjectives and adverbs. *Seriously,* an adverb, correctly modifies the verb *took;* and *hard,* used as an adverb meaning *with strength,* correctly modifies *punched.* Choices (B), (C), and (E) significantly change the meaning of the original.

10. (A) The original is correct. This sentence may use either the pronoun *him* or the pronoun *he* because it may be an "abbreviation" of either "She likes everyone as much as *she likes* him" or "She likes everyone as much as he *likes everyone.*" The omitted but implied phrase determines the pronoun. All other choices are either ungrammatical or change the meaning of the sentence.

11. (E) The correct pronoun in this case is *who,* the subject of *betrayed.*

12. (D) The original contains two errors. *Varies* does not agree with the plural subject, *opinions;* and *according with* is not idiomatic. (C) is a correct phrase but changes and obscures the meaning of the sentence.

13. (E) The introductory phrase is a dangling modifier, corrected by following *freeze* with *the Cabinet minister* to make clear to whom the introductory phrase refers. Choice (D) is not best because *but unharmed* is left in an awkward position.

14. (C) The original contains two errors. *It* suggests that the meeting, not the members, does the considering, and *had considered* is a verb tense simultaneous with *had left* and does not indicate that considering the tax cut occurred after the visitors had left. Choice (D) is unnecessarily wordy and leaves unsaid who did the considering.

15. (C) *Granting the returned money during June* is repetitious, and of the choices offered, (C) is the clearest and most economical expression.

16. (C) The error in the original is a diction error. *Effects* (results) is preferable to *affects.* Choices (D) and (E) are economical but change the meaning of the original significantly.

17. (B) The original contains two errors. *After having read* is redundant (*having read* already contains the *after* meaning), and *laying* (which means *putting*) is incorrect (*lying* is correct).

18. (A) The original is better than any of the alternatives.

19. (B) *Is when* is not acceptable because *gerrymandering* is not a time; choice (E) repeats this error. (D) is not best because it leaves vague whether gerrymandering is synonymous with unfair division. (C) is very general and vague.

20. (B) The original is flawed by faulty parallelism. *Fearless* is not parallel to *having great skill.* Choice (B) corrects this problem. *Fearless* is parallel to *skillful.* (C) and (E) are both unnecessarily wordy.

21. (D) *Supposes* is not the correct verb tense; in order to be parallel with *to mistake,* the verb in the underlined portion must also connect idiomatically with *to. Suspect* is the only possible choice.

22. (B) *Having finished* expresses the past tense by itself, so *after* is repetitious (its meaning is already implied in *having finished*). None of the other choices expresses the past tense both economically and clearly.

23. (C) The verb in this sentence should be *is* (not *are*) to agree with the singular subject, *actor*. A parenthetical phrase enclosed by commas and beginning with words such as *along with, including,* and *as well as* changes the number of neither the subject nor the verb. Choice (B) correctly uses *are* because the subject in this sentence has been made plural; however, the construction is awkward and wordy. Choice (D) retains the incorrect *are* and changes the meaning of the sentence. (E) leaves out the fact that the actor is on the train.

24. (D) In the original, the verb *were* does not agree with the subject, *type*. (B) is incorrect because it uses the plural *products* with *a*. (E) is incorrect because it results in a sentence fragment. (D) is an economical and clear choice that retains the meaning of the original.

25. (B) When subjects are connected with *nor* or *or*, the verb is governed by the subject closest to it; in (A) and (D) the closer subject does not agree with the verb. (E) is awkward. In (B), the subject, *director,* agrees with the verb, *predicts.*

SECTION IV: DATA SUFFICIENCY

1. (E) The two statements may be translated into the equations

$$(1) M + 2 = 2B$$
$$(2) S = (M + B)/2$$

As two equations are insufficient to determine three variables, Mary's age is indeterminate.

2. (B) The central angle MON must be 96°, twice the inscribed angle NPM. Further, the triangle MNO has two radii as sides, so it is isosceles, and angle OMN = MNO. Therefore 2(MNO) + 96° = 180°, and one may solve for MNO = 42°.

3. (E) The relation between two quantities is uncertain given merely that each is unequal to a third quantity.

4. (D) Either statement allows us to calculate the required precipitation, P.

$$(1) P = 35 - 33$$
$$(2) P = 35(1 - 0.943)$$

5. (D) The area can be calculated from $A = \pi r^2$ if we know the radius, which is given in the second statement. The first statement gives the circumference, from which the radius may be found by $r = C/2\pi$.

6. (A) Since Ethyl, Dora, and Carl are consecutive, Grace and Bill must be in the remaining adjacent seats.

7. (A) Because vertical angles are equal, a = d. From statement (1) we can find that angle a = 41°. In the figure, angles a and e are supplementary, so angle e = 180 - 41 = 139°.

8. (C) With both statements, we know that the third number must exceed 7, so the smallest number is 4. But with the first statement alone, all we know is 4 + x + y = 3.7, and one of the unknown numbers could be less than 4.

9. (D) Either statement transforms the equation so there is only one unknown, which therefore could be found:

$$(1) 3b - 7b + 14 = 0$$
$$(2) 9 - 7b + 14 = 0$$

10. **(A)** Angle ABC, inscribed on a diameter, is necessarily 90°, so the second statement adds nothing new. But the first statement implies the triangle has an altitude equal to the circle's radius, 6. So the shaded area equals the area of the semicircle, ($\frac{1}{2} \times \pi \times 6^2$) minus the area of the triangle ($\frac{1}{2}$bh = $\frac{1}{2} \times 12 \times 6$ = 36).

11. **(A)** From the first statement, m^2/s^3 = 3, and squaring each side, m^4/s^6 = 9. Substituting into the original expression, $14(m^4/s^6)$ = 14×9 = 126.

12. **(D)** The sole solution is m = 1 = 1 × 1 = 1 × 1 × 1 and so m is positive. Note that $-1 \neq (-1)(-1) \neq (-1)(-1)(-1)$.

13. **(D)** Either statement suffices to determine MN to be $7\frac{1}{2}$. Because of similar triangles, MN:OQ = MP:QP = NP:OP. From the Pythagorean theorem, OP = 13. By addition, NP = ON + OP = $6\frac{1}{2}$ + 13 = $19\frac{1}{2}$; also MP = 18. Therefore MN:5 = 18:12 = $19\frac{1}{2}$:13 and we can solve for MN.

14. **(B)** The sale price equaled the list price L minus 30%. So $140 = 0.7L, and L = 140/0.7 = $200.

15. **(E)** Making substitutions from both statements yields the expression $9 - 2y < 17$. To solve for y, we first subtract 9 from both sides and then divide by -2; the latter operation reverses the sense of the inequality. The solution $y > -4$ records that y may be positive, zero, or negative (between 0 and -4).

16. **(C)** Since there are two unknowns, we need two equations to solve for p and r. From (2), p = r + 5. Substituting that for p in (1) yields 2r + 10 + 3r = 11, or r = $\frac{1}{5}$. Since p = r + 5, p = $\frac{1}{5}$ + 5 = $\frac{26}{5}$.

17. **(D)** From the first statement, x + 4 = 4x − 2, because opposite sides of a rectangle are equal. So x = 2 and the width x + 4 = 6. Or we can use the area of the second statement, as width = area/length = $\frac{48}{8}$ = 6.

18. **(C)** The question asks how far the car can travel, and the answer would be $\frac{50}{8} \times 100$ = 625 kilometers. It is essential to realize that liters measure volume and kilometers measure distance.

19. **(B)** Necessarily the diagonal equals the side times $\sqrt{2}$, so from the second statement, d = $\sqrt{8} \times \sqrt{2}$ = $\sqrt{16}$ = 4, a rational number.

20. (E) Since P is not now touching the ground, all we know is that the wheel has traveled more than 5 circumferences but less than $5\frac{1}{4}$. So, $5\pi d < 36 < 5\frac{1}{4}\pi d$. Hence the diameter is uncertain, somewhere in the range 2.18 to 2.29 feet.

21. (C) From statement (1) we find h = 10. From (2) k = 20. Then the question translates to: The number 10 is 20% of what number j? Therefore $10 = 0.2j$, and $j = 10/0.2 = 50$.

22. (C) Remember that rate = 1/time, so Sue's rate = 1/s where s is the time for her to paint the room. Since

    Sue's rate + Bob's rate = joint rate,
    $1/s + 1/3\frac{1}{4} = \frac{1}{2}$, and this can be solved for
    s = 5.2 hours.

23. (D) The first statement implies that x is a positive number but less than 1. The second statement yields $x < \frac{1}{3}$. Either statement answers the question that, yes, x is less than 2.

24. (B) From the Pythagorean theorem we know that $AD^2 + BD^2 = AB^2$, so $BD^2 = 16 + 121$, and $BD = \sqrt{137}$. The second statement tells us that the base and height of the triangle are equal, so $A = \frac{1}{2}bh = \frac{1}{2}\sqrt{137} \times \sqrt{137} = \frac{137}{2}$.

25. (C) The number of tiles would equal the area of the kitchen divided by the area of one tile, or $(120 \times 84)/48 = 210$ tiles.

SECTION V: CRITICAL REASONING

1. (C) The transitional word *nevertheless* establishes a juxtaposition of the phrases immediately before and after it. Therefore (A) and (B) are incorrect. Choice (D) may be a good answer, but (C) is better, as it addresses a concern initially introduced in the paragraph and brings the passage full circle.

2. (E) Only (C) and (E) describe situations in which a media event precedes a real-life event. In (C) the medium is not an artistic one; in (E) television may be regarded as an art form.

3. (D) Choices (B) and (E) are contradicted by the passage, and the passage does not support the probability of (A) or (C). Choice (D) is reasonable, plausible, and probable, given the information in the passage.

4. (C) The student's qualification shows that he or she doubts whether the Congressman's statement is absolutely true, but the response is not so pronounced as to suggest any of the other choices.

5. (E) The passage restricts its attention to salaries, and its details clearly indicate that federal pay is significantly high, thus possibly supporting the conclusion in (E).

6. (A) This statement is consistent with the comparison between federal and private workers established in the passage. Choice (D) contradicts information in the passage, (C) is irrelevant, and (B) and (E) are not mentioned in the passage.

7. (D) The argument presupposes both that candidates are spending too much on television advertising ("the waste") and that television can be used to inform the public ("provide air time to all candidates to debate the issues"). Statement III is irrelevant to the argument.

8. (E) This choice weakens the point made by the final observation. Each of the other choices either strengthen points made by the observation or are irrelevant.

9. (A) Only this choice necessarily introduces a contrasting statement, one which would probably take issue with the points of the argument. (C) and (D) might possibly begin critical, contrasting statements but may have other uses as well.

10. (C) Geographic location and employment status are irrelevant issues, so (A) and (B) should be eliminated. (D) and (E) are too general and vague.

Only (C) makes explicit the point of the author's argument, that interpretation of the Texas law is arrogant and unsound.

11. (B) By describing the special relief programs as a "flood," the author gives the programs a negative connotation and suggests disapproval.

12. (E) The researcher concluded that women could be just as capable as men in math but that they develop other abilities because of social pressures. Thus, the researcher assumes that women do conform to social expectations.

13. (E) Choices (A) and (B) are irrelevant to the argument, and (D) is an illogical criticism. (E) is a logical conclusion that poses a significant problem.

14. (A) All of the other choices are much less relevant than the issue of how efficiently and effectively the program helps students to achieve competency.

15. (C) Each of the other choices requires assumptions and conclusions not supported or implied by the argument. The stress in the argument on reduced funds leads logically to the conclusion that further spending is unwise.

16. (A) Bacon advocates retaining dignity without intruding upon liberty. The author implies that retaining dignity is impossible without intruding upon another's liberty by stating that not intruding upon liberty is impossible. (B), (C), and (D) contradict the author's argument, and (E) presents an irrelevant issue.

17. (E) I and II only. The author both relies on an interpretation of Bacon's statement and discusses liberty and dignity in absolute terms; I and II subvert such reliance. III supports, reiterates in fact, the author's argument.

18. (D) Jonathan Swift is comparing laws to a cobweb, noting that little insects get caught but big insects can break on through. He thus is indicating that the legal system is inequitable: that the "small" will get caught (sentenced) while those with more power can avoid sentencing.

19. (D) The passage sets up the thesis that sometimes individuals yield to others' interests. Choices (A) and (E) are unsubstantiated or not mentioned in the passage; (C) does not fit the structure of the sentence; (B) could possibly be the correct answer, but (D) more nearly completes the thought of the passage and is neatly juxtaposed with the first part of the incomplete sentence.

20. (D) The author does not address the distinction between how much

sleep we desire and how much our bodies require. Each of the other distinctions is addressed in the passage.

21. (D) In the passage, becoming older corresponds with "*advanced knowledge and capabilities.*" Choices (A), (B), and (C) should be eliminated because each is contradicted by the assumptions of the passage (the passage suggests that *more* sleep is undesirable, knowledge and capabilities are connected with *wakefulness,* and mindlessness is connected with *sleep*). Choice (E) is a generalization not at all concerned with amount of sleep and therefore not relevant to the passage.

22. (C) Choices (A), (B), and (E) present information that supports the value of sleep, and (D) dissociates advanced capabilities from the mind, thus damaging the author's mind/mindlessness distinction.

23. (C) Only choice (C) asserts the positive value of sleep and thus weakens the author's stance in favor of decreased sleep.

24. (D) The commercial either explicitly states or implies all but (D). It makes no reference to how long it will take to fall asleep or how quickly the drug works. It does, however, claim to provide a restful, good night's sleep, with added energy and no aftereffects the next morning.

25. (D) Since no blue-eyed swimmer is an Olympic winner, then no blue-eyed swimmer may be a freestyle swimmer, since *all* freestyle swimmers are Olympic winners. (B) and (E) are false because they exclude other possibilities which may, in fact, exist.

SECTION VI: PROBLEM SOLVING

1. **(D)** This problem is most easily answered by dividing 318 by 3 to get 106 which must be the middle number; therefore the largest is 108. You could have used the equation

$$\underset{(2x)}{\text{Smallest}} + \underset{(2x + 2)}{\text{Middle}} + \underset{(2x + 4)}{\text{Largest}} = 318$$

and worked from there.

2. **(B)** Solving the first equation for x

$$\frac{2}{x} = 4$$
$$2 = 4x$$
$$\frac{2}{4} = x$$

Therefore $\frac{1}{2} = x$
Now solving the second equation for y

$$\frac{2}{y} = 8$$
$$2 = 8y$$
$$\frac{2}{8} = y$$

Therefore $\frac{1}{4} = y$
Substituting these values for $x - y$ gives $\frac{1}{2} - \frac{1}{4} = \frac{2}{4} - \frac{1}{4} = \frac{1}{4}$
Therefore $x - y = \frac{1}{4}$, and the correct answer is **(B)**.

3. **(B)** Solve by setting up a proportion.

If 1 cm = 35 km
then x cm = 245 km

and
$$\frac{1}{x} = \frac{35}{245}$$
$$35x = 245$$
$$\frac{35x}{35} = \frac{245}{35}$$
$$x = 7$$

4. **(D)** If cube A has side 2, then the surface area is 24 square units since the area of one face is 2×2, or 4, and there are 6 equal faces to a cube. If cube B has side 1, then the surface area is 6 square units since the area of one face is 1×1, or 1, and there are 6 faces. Therefore the ratio could be 24:6, or 4:1.

5. **(B)** Set up the problem as follows

$$\frac{x + (2)}{x + 5 + (2)} = \frac{7}{12}, \text{ or } \frac{x + 2}{x + 7} = \frac{7}{12}$$

By observation $x = 5$ since $\dfrac{5 + 2}{5 + 7} = \dfrac{7}{12}$

Substituting into the original fraction $\dfrac{x}{x + 5}$ gives $\dfrac{5}{5 + 5} = \dfrac{5}{10} = \dfrac{1}{2}$

A longer method would have been to solve $\dfrac{x + 2}{x + 7} = \dfrac{7}{12}$ as follows:

Cross multiplying gives

$$12x + 24 = 7x + 49$$
$$5x = 25$$
$$x = 5$$

and then substitute in $\dfrac{x}{x + 5}$

6. **(D)** The only reasonable answer is 5⅝ since 85¢ per pound is slightly closer to 93¢ per pound than 75¢ per pound. Then slightly more than half of the 10 pounds must be 93¢ per pound.

Algebraically, let x stand for the pounds of 93¢ tea, then $10 - x$ is the 75¢ tea. This leads to the equation

$$.93x + .75 (10 - x) = .85 (10)$$

Solving gives
$$93x + 750 - 75x = 850$$
$$18x = 100$$
$$x = \frac{100}{18}$$

Therefore $x = 5\frac{5}{9}$

7. (C) In this type of problem (weighted average) you must multiply the number of students times their respective scores and divide this total by the number of students as follows:

$$
\begin{array}{r}
15 \times 80\% = 1200 \\
\underline{10} \times 90\% = \underline{\ 900} \\
25 \qquad\qquad 2100
\end{array}
$$

Now divide 25 into 2100. This gives an average of 84%, therefore the correct answer is (C).

8. (C) Let x be the length of time Mr. Dinkle travels, then $x + \frac{1}{2}$ is the time Mr. Smitherly travels. This gives the equation $50(x + \frac{1}{2}) = 60x$, to see when they will meet. Solving gives

$$
\begin{aligned}
50x + 25 &= 60x \\
25 &= 10x \\
2.5 &= x
\end{aligned}
$$

Therefore, it will take Mr. Dinkle $2\frac{1}{2}$ hours to overtake Mr. Smitherly. Since Mr. Dinkle starts at 8:30 A.M., he will overtake Mr. Smitherly at 11:00 A.M.
Note that answers (A), (D), and (E) are not reasonable.

9. (C) The area of $\triangle MNP = \frac{1}{2} bh = \frac{1}{2} (MP) (MN)$.
Since $\triangle MNP$ is a right triangle the Pythagorean theorem says

$$
\begin{aligned}
c^2 &= a^2 + b^2 \\
(NP)^2 &= (MP)^2 + (MN)^2 \\
26^2 &= 24^2 + (MN)^2 \\
676 &= 576 + (MN)^2 \\
(MN)^2 &= 100 \\
MN &= \sqrt{100} = 10
\end{aligned}
$$

Hence the area of MNP $= \frac{1}{2} (MN) (MP)$
$= \frac{1}{2} (10) (24)$
$= 120$

10. (A) 30 miles per hour $= \dfrac{30 \text{ miles}}{1 \text{ hour}}$

Since 1 mile = 5280 feet
and 1 hour = 60 minutes = 3600 seconds

$$
\frac{30 \text{ miles}}{1 \text{ hour}} = \frac{30 \times 5280 \text{ feet}}{1 \times 3600 \text{ seconds}}
$$

$$= \frac{\overset{1}{\cancel{30}} \times 528\cancel{0}}{1 \times \cancel{3600}} = \frac{528}{12}$$
$$\underset{12}{}$$

$$= 44 \text{ feet per second}$$

Hence the automobile will travel 44 feet in one second.

11. (E) The horizontal length of x cannot be determined because there is no indication of the overlapping length of the rectangle to the left of x. If x cannot be determined, then x + y cannot be determined.

12. (C) Let c = cost of each brick. Let M = total money. Thus M = 45c and M = 50 (c − 10).

Therefore 45c = 50 (c − 10)
$$\qquad\quad 45c = 50c − 500$$
$$\qquad\quad 500 = 5c$$
$$\qquad\quad 100 = c$$

Thus M = 4500 cents, or $45.00.

13. (D) Since each of the 4 sport jackets may be worn with 5 different shirts, we have 20 possible combinations. These may be worn with each of the 3 pairs of slacks for a total of 60 possible combinations. Stated simply, 5 × 4 × 3 = 60 possible combinations.
Notice answers (A) and (B) are not reasonable.

14. (C) We have

10% of 1000 is 100. (1000 + 100) = 1100
10% of 1100 is 110. (1100 + 110) = 1210
10% of 1210 is 121. (1210 + 121) = 1331

15. (D) A rectangular solid consists of six rectangular faces. This one in particular has two 7 × 6, two 6 × 3, and two 7 × 3 rectangles with areas of 42, 18, and 21, respectively. Hence the total surface area will be 2(42) + 2(18) + 2(21) = 84 + 36 + 42 = 162 square meters.

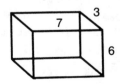

16. (C) If the average of 9 numbers is 7, then the sum of these numbers must be 9 × 7, or 63.

    If the average of 7 numbers is 9, then the sum of these numbers must be 7 × 9, or 63.

    The sum of all 16 numbers must be 63 + 63, or 126.

    Hence the average of all 16 numbers must be

    $$126 \div 16 = \frac{126}{16} = 7\frac{14}{16} = 7\frac{7}{8}$$

    Notice answers (A) and (E) are not reasonable.

17. (D) Only the 19 cannot be weighed. To get 13, place 10 and 4 on one side and the 1 on the other. To get the 15, place the 10, 4, and 1 on one side. To get the 17, place the 10 and 7 on one side. To get the 21, place the 10, 7, and 4 on one side.

18. (B) Since 100 plus 120 is 220, there must be 20 students that study both languages. Thus, of the 100 who study French, 80 do not study Spanish. 80 is 40% of the total of 200.

19. (C) The total price of toy A is $5.0227 [$2.5796 + $2.4431], and the total price of toy B is $5.0080 [$2.5768 + $2.4312]. Toy A exceeds toy B by $0.0147; therefore 10,000 of each must be manufactured to have a $147.00 difference.

20. (A) Ratio of diameters = ratio of radii

    $$\frac{d_1}{d_2} = \frac{r_1}{r_2} = \frac{30}{100} = 3/10$$

    Ratio of area = (ratio of radii)^2

    $$\frac{A_1}{A_2} = \left(\frac{r_1}{r_2}\right)^2$$

    $$\frac{A_1}{A_2} = 9/100$$

    Hence the area of circle R is 9/100, or 9%, of the area of circle S.

SECTION VII: DATA SUFFICIENCY

1. **(C)** Statement (1) implies that the three cameras sell for a total price of $3 \times \$172 = \$516$. Statement (2) implies that two of the cameras each sell for $\frac{1}{2}(\$332) = \$166$. The third camera must sell for $\$516 - \$332 = \$184$.

2. **(E)** The area of the right triangle equals half the product of the two legs, AE and CE. The length of AE is given (1). But point E is not on the circle, so CE is less than $\frac{1}{2}$ (BD), the diameter (2). Lacking the length of CE, one cannot calculate the area.

3. **(B)** Statement (1) reveals a product, not a quotient. However, dividing both sides of equation (2) by $6/m$ demonstrates that $n/m = 1/6$.

4. **(E)** The second statement means that the Emporium sold a total of 2568 shoes. You cannot assume from the first statement that one-quarter of those shoes were black, because some shoes are neither black nor brown.

5. **(D)** This problem may be solved swiftly with knowledge of the principle that for quadrilaterals of equal area, the square has the shortest perimeter. Then the farmer would need less fencing for the stubbier configuration, approaching a square. Statement (2) yields that information immediately. Since the area of 3000 equals the length times the width, statement (1) implies that lot X would be 75×40 and lot Y would be 60×50. From either statement, lot Y would have the shorter perimeter.

6. **(C)** From the first statement, David has 6 sisters and brothers (he is the seventh child). Combining that datum with the second statement, he must have 4 sisters and 2 brothers.

7. **(D)** If $b < a$, statement (1), then $(a - b) > 0$ and, for any c, $(a - b)^c$ is positive. Incidentally, if $c = 0$, the entire exponential quantity equals 1, by definition. Also, if $c = 2a$, statement (2), then c is an even integer and the entire exponential quantity is positive, even if $(a - b)$ is negative.

8. **(C)** Since the compass directions are at right angles, the distance can be computed from the Pythagorean theorem, providing Otto's and Anna's positions at 4 P.M. are known. Otto will be 24 miles west of the origin. Anna will be 10 miles south and 20 miles west of the origin. Relative to

Otto, Anna is 10 miles south and 4 miles east at 4 P.M. It is helpful to sketch a map in a problem involving positions.

9. (C) The problem may be solved utilizing both statements. Emily and Joan's joint rate of counting is 1/26 of the books per hour. If e is Emily's rate, then Joan's rate is 2e, twice as fast. The individual rates sum to the joint rate:

$$2e + e = \frac{1}{26}$$

$$e = \frac{1}{78} \quad \text{Emily's rate}$$

$$2e = \frac{1}{39} \quad \text{Joan's rate}$$

Because rates are the reciprocals of the times, *and conversely*, it would take Joan 39 hours (the reciprocal of her rate) to tally the books alone.

10. (C) You must know that December has 31 days. (For the GMAT, you should know the number of days in each month of the year.) Therefore, December has 4 weeks and 3 extra days. For the 7 days of the week, 4 occur 4 times and the other 3 occur 5 times. Since there are only 2 days between Saturday (statement 2) and Tuesday (statement 1), there must be 4 Sundays and Mondays that month.

11. (E) Neither statement permits the calculation of $x + y + z$. Especially, the second statement cannot be inverted to obtain 9/4, for the summation of fractions requires a common denominator:

$$\frac{yz + xz + xy}{xyz} = \frac{4}{9}$$

12. (D) From the first statement, $x = y = 47°$, for vertical angles are equal. From the second statement, the interior angle adjacent to z is 70°, because that angle and z sum to a straight angle. Since the interior angles of a triangle add to 180°, you can write the equation $x + 63° + 70° = 180°$, permitting the determination of x.

13. (D) The diagonal through the center of a cube, from one corner to the opposite corner, may be found with the Pythagorean theorem providing that the length of the cube's edge is known. Statement (1) implies that the edge is $4.24/\sqrt{2}$ centimeters. Moreover, since the surface area (2) is 6 faces, each face has an area of $54/6 = 9$ cm², and so the edge is $\sqrt{9} = 3$ cm.

14. **(B)** The two temperature scales have identical values when °H = °W. Substituting into the second statement, °H = 0.6(°H − 20). That equation can be solved for the one variable. The two temperature scales coincide at −30°.

15. **(A)** Let's symbolize the first number as f and the second as s. The main clause of the first sentence of the question yields the equation $f = 5 + \frac{1}{2}s$, and statement (1) is the equation $f = s - 1$. Those two linear equations with two unknowns can be solved for both the first number ($f = 11$) and the second number ($s = 12$).

16. **(E)** The question cannot be answered, even with both statements, because any burnt-out bulb could have its switch either ON or OFF.

17. **(C)** To solve the problem, it is necessary to know the *total* number of beverage cans manufactured in both 1975 and 1980. Graph (1) has the data for aluminum cans and graph (2) has the data for steel cans. The data from the two graphs must be added together.

18. **(A)** From statement (1), $3c$ and $8d^3$ have opposite signs. Hence c and d^3 have opposite signs. With the odd exponent, the sign of d will be the same as d^3. So statement (1) is sufficient to answer the question, even though the answer is "no."

19. **(B)** The amount of wallpaper can be measured in square feet, the area of the two largest walls. Each large wall has an area equal to the length of the room times the height of the room. The total amount of wallpaper required is $2 \times 24 \times 9 = 432$ square feet.

20. **(B)** The month is uniquely determined only if there were no deposits or withdrawals from the account, else any month is possible. With the restriction, the account exceeded $1100 first on October 31st, when the interest credited brought the account up to $1104.62.

21. **(C)** The question can be answered with both pieces of information. With $x < y$ and $y < 0$, then $(x - y)$ is negative. With $y < 0$ and $z < 0$, then the product yz is positive. Given both statements, $(x - y)$ is less than yz.

22. **(E)** The information is insufficient to determine the number of workers at the plant. Statement (1) is inadequate without the average salary of the remaining workers. Statement (2) is inadequate because the extra

employees may not earn the same average salary as the original employees.

23. (C) In the rectangle, $\overline{BA} = \overline{CD}$ = 3 inches. So two sides of right triangle BAE are known and the length of side AE can be found with the Pythagorean theorem to be 4 inches. As point E is the midpoint of $\overline{AD}$, the length of the rectangle is twice $\overline{AE}$, or 8 inches. The area of the right triangle BCD is half the product of the sides adjacent to the right angle:

$$A = \tfrac{1}{2}bh = \tfrac{1}{2}(8)(3) = 12 \text{ in}^2$$

24. (D) Substituting n = 3 into the equation m = n + 2, it is found that m = 5. That value can be substituted into the quadratic expression:

$$m^2 - 4m + 4 = (5)^2 - 4(5) + 4 = 9$$

Since $n^2 = 400$, then n = 20 or -20.

Substituting in each one gives the following:

$$n = 20, \text{ and } m = n + 2$$

So   m = 22

Now $m^2 - 4m + 4 = (22)^2 - 4(22) + 4 = 484 - 88 + 4 = 400$

$$n = -20, \text{ and } m = n + 2$$

So   m = -18

Now $m^2 - 4m + 4 = (-18)^2 - 4(-18) + 4 = 324 + 72 + 4 = 400$

25. (E) The question is indeterminate because many different combinations of the two cone prices can sum to $209.15. The question could be answered if you also knew *either* the number of Generous cones *or* the number of all cones.

PRACTICE TEST 2

Section I: Reading Comprehension—30 Minutes; 25 Questions
Section II: Problem Solving—30 Minutes; 20 Questions
Section III: Data Sufficiency—30 Minutes; 25 Questions
Section IV: Sentence Correction—30 Minutes; 25 Questions
Section V: Problem Solving—30 Minutes; 20 Questions
Section VI: Problem Solving—30 Minutes; 20 Questions
Section VII: Sentence Correction—30 Minutes; 25 Questions

ANSWER SHEET FOR PRACTICE TEST 2
(Remove This Sheet and Use It to Mark Your Answers)

SECTION I	SECTION II	SECTION III

SECTION I

1 Ⓐ Ⓑ Ⓒ Ⓓ Ⓔ
2 Ⓐ Ⓑ Ⓒ Ⓓ Ⓔ
3 Ⓐ Ⓑ Ⓒ Ⓓ Ⓔ
4 Ⓐ Ⓑ Ⓒ Ⓓ Ⓔ
5 Ⓐ Ⓑ Ⓒ Ⓓ Ⓔ
6 Ⓐ Ⓑ Ⓒ Ⓓ Ⓔ
7 Ⓐ Ⓑ Ⓒ Ⓓ Ⓔ
8 Ⓐ Ⓑ Ⓒ Ⓓ Ⓔ
9 Ⓐ Ⓑ Ⓒ Ⓓ Ⓔ
10 Ⓐ Ⓑ Ⓒ Ⓓ Ⓔ
11 Ⓐ Ⓑ Ⓒ Ⓓ Ⓔ
12 Ⓐ Ⓑ Ⓒ Ⓓ Ⓔ
13 Ⓐ Ⓑ Ⓒ Ⓓ Ⓔ
14 Ⓐ Ⓑ Ⓒ Ⓓ Ⓔ
15 Ⓐ Ⓑ Ⓒ Ⓓ Ⓔ
16 Ⓐ Ⓑ Ⓒ Ⓓ Ⓔ
17 Ⓐ Ⓑ Ⓒ Ⓓ Ⓔ
18 Ⓐ Ⓑ Ⓒ Ⓓ Ⓔ
19 Ⓐ Ⓑ Ⓒ Ⓓ Ⓔ
20 Ⓐ Ⓑ Ⓒ Ⓓ Ⓔ
21 Ⓐ Ⓑ Ⓒ Ⓓ Ⓔ
22 Ⓐ Ⓑ Ⓒ Ⓓ Ⓔ
23 Ⓐ Ⓑ Ⓒ Ⓓ Ⓔ
24 Ⓐ Ⓑ Ⓒ Ⓓ Ⓔ
25 Ⓐ Ⓑ Ⓒ Ⓓ Ⓔ

SECTION II

1 Ⓐ Ⓑ Ⓒ Ⓓ Ⓔ
2 Ⓐ Ⓑ Ⓒ Ⓓ Ⓔ
3 Ⓐ Ⓑ Ⓒ Ⓓ Ⓔ
4 Ⓐ Ⓑ Ⓒ Ⓓ Ⓔ
5 Ⓐ Ⓑ Ⓒ Ⓓ Ⓔ
6 Ⓐ Ⓑ Ⓒ Ⓓ Ⓔ
7 Ⓐ Ⓑ Ⓒ Ⓓ Ⓔ
8 Ⓐ Ⓑ Ⓒ Ⓓ Ⓔ
9 Ⓐ Ⓑ Ⓒ Ⓓ Ⓔ
10 Ⓐ Ⓑ Ⓒ Ⓓ Ⓔ
11 Ⓐ Ⓑ Ⓒ Ⓓ Ⓔ
12 Ⓐ Ⓑ Ⓒ Ⓓ Ⓔ
13 Ⓐ Ⓑ Ⓒ Ⓓ Ⓔ
14 Ⓐ Ⓑ Ⓒ Ⓓ Ⓔ
15 Ⓐ Ⓑ Ⓒ Ⓓ Ⓔ
16 Ⓐ Ⓑ Ⓒ Ⓓ Ⓔ
17 Ⓐ Ⓑ Ⓒ Ⓓ Ⓔ
18 Ⓐ Ⓑ Ⓒ Ⓓ Ⓔ
19 Ⓐ Ⓑ Ⓒ Ⓓ Ⓔ
20 Ⓐ Ⓑ Ⓒ Ⓓ Ⓔ

SECTION III

1 Ⓐ Ⓑ Ⓒ Ⓓ Ⓔ
2 Ⓐ Ⓑ Ⓒ Ⓓ Ⓔ
3 Ⓐ Ⓑ Ⓒ Ⓓ Ⓔ
4 Ⓐ Ⓑ Ⓒ Ⓓ Ⓔ
5 Ⓐ Ⓑ Ⓒ Ⓓ Ⓔ
6 Ⓐ Ⓑ Ⓒ Ⓓ Ⓔ
7 Ⓐ Ⓑ Ⓒ Ⓓ Ⓔ
8 Ⓐ Ⓑ Ⓒ Ⓓ Ⓔ
9 Ⓐ Ⓑ Ⓒ Ⓓ Ⓔ
10 Ⓐ Ⓑ Ⓒ Ⓓ Ⓔ
11 Ⓐ Ⓑ Ⓒ Ⓓ Ⓔ
12 Ⓐ Ⓑ Ⓒ Ⓓ Ⓔ
13 Ⓐ Ⓑ Ⓒ Ⓓ Ⓔ
14 Ⓐ Ⓑ Ⓒ Ⓓ Ⓔ
15 Ⓐ Ⓑ Ⓒ Ⓓ Ⓔ
16 Ⓐ Ⓑ Ⓒ Ⓓ Ⓔ
17 Ⓐ Ⓑ Ⓒ Ⓓ Ⓔ
18 Ⓐ Ⓑ Ⓒ Ⓓ Ⓔ
19 Ⓐ Ⓑ Ⓒ Ⓓ Ⓔ
20 Ⓐ Ⓑ Ⓒ Ⓓ Ⓔ
21 Ⓐ Ⓑ Ⓒ Ⓓ Ⓔ
22 Ⓐ Ⓑ Ⓒ Ⓓ Ⓔ
23 Ⓐ Ⓑ Ⓒ Ⓓ Ⓔ
24 Ⓐ Ⓑ Ⓒ Ⓓ Ⓔ
25 Ⓐ Ⓑ Ⓒ Ⓓ Ⓔ

ANSWER SHEET FOR PRACTICE TEST 2
(Remove This Sheet and Use It to Mark Your Answers)

SECTION IV	SECTION V	SECTION VI	SECTION VII
1 Ⓐ Ⓑ Ⓒ Ⓓ Ⓔ	1 Ⓐ Ⓑ Ⓒ Ⓓ Ⓔ	1 Ⓐ Ⓑ Ⓒ Ⓓ Ⓔ	1 Ⓐ Ⓑ Ⓒ Ⓓ Ⓔ
2 Ⓐ Ⓑ Ⓒ Ⓓ Ⓔ	2 Ⓐ Ⓑ Ⓒ Ⓓ Ⓔ	2 Ⓐ Ⓑ Ⓒ Ⓓ Ⓔ	2 Ⓐ Ⓑ Ⓒ Ⓓ Ⓔ
3 Ⓐ Ⓑ Ⓒ Ⓓ Ⓔ	3 Ⓐ Ⓑ Ⓒ Ⓓ Ⓔ	3 Ⓐ Ⓑ Ⓒ Ⓓ Ⓔ	3 Ⓐ Ⓑ Ⓒ Ⓓ Ⓔ
4 Ⓐ Ⓑ Ⓒ Ⓓ Ⓔ	4 Ⓐ Ⓑ Ⓒ Ⓓ Ⓔ	4 Ⓐ Ⓑ Ⓒ Ⓓ Ⓔ	4 Ⓐ Ⓑ Ⓒ Ⓓ Ⓔ
5 Ⓐ Ⓑ Ⓒ Ⓓ Ⓔ	5 Ⓐ Ⓑ Ⓒ Ⓓ Ⓔ	5 Ⓐ Ⓑ Ⓒ Ⓓ Ⓔ	5 Ⓐ Ⓑ Ⓒ Ⓓ Ⓔ
6 Ⓐ Ⓑ Ⓒ Ⓓ Ⓔ	6 Ⓐ Ⓑ Ⓒ Ⓓ Ⓔ	6 Ⓐ Ⓑ Ⓒ Ⓓ Ⓔ	6 Ⓐ Ⓑ Ⓒ Ⓓ Ⓔ
7 Ⓐ Ⓑ Ⓒ Ⓓ Ⓔ	7 Ⓐ Ⓑ Ⓒ Ⓓ Ⓔ	7 Ⓐ Ⓑ Ⓒ Ⓓ Ⓔ	7 Ⓐ Ⓑ Ⓒ Ⓓ Ⓔ
8 Ⓐ Ⓑ Ⓒ Ⓓ Ⓔ	8 Ⓐ Ⓑ Ⓒ Ⓓ Ⓔ	8 Ⓐ Ⓑ Ⓒ Ⓓ Ⓔ	8 Ⓐ Ⓑ Ⓒ Ⓓ Ⓔ
9 Ⓐ Ⓑ Ⓒ Ⓓ Ⓔ	9 Ⓐ Ⓑ Ⓒ Ⓓ Ⓔ	9 Ⓐ Ⓑ Ⓒ Ⓓ Ⓔ	9 Ⓐ Ⓑ Ⓒ Ⓓ Ⓔ
10 Ⓐ Ⓑ Ⓒ Ⓓ Ⓔ	10 Ⓐ Ⓑ Ⓒ Ⓓ Ⓔ	10 Ⓐ Ⓑ Ⓒ Ⓓ Ⓔ	10 Ⓐ Ⓑ Ⓒ Ⓓ Ⓔ
11 Ⓐ Ⓑ Ⓒ Ⓓ Ⓔ	11 Ⓐ Ⓑ Ⓒ Ⓓ Ⓔ	11 Ⓐ Ⓑ Ⓒ Ⓓ Ⓔ	11 Ⓐ Ⓑ Ⓒ Ⓓ Ⓔ
12 Ⓐ Ⓑ Ⓒ Ⓓ Ⓔ	12 Ⓐ Ⓑ Ⓒ Ⓓ Ⓔ	12 Ⓐ Ⓑ Ⓒ Ⓓ Ⓔ	12 Ⓐ Ⓑ Ⓒ Ⓓ Ⓔ
13 Ⓐ Ⓑ Ⓒ Ⓓ Ⓔ	13 Ⓐ Ⓑ Ⓒ Ⓓ Ⓔ	13 Ⓐ Ⓑ Ⓒ Ⓓ Ⓔ	13 Ⓐ Ⓑ Ⓒ Ⓓ Ⓔ
14 Ⓐ Ⓑ Ⓒ Ⓓ Ⓔ	14 Ⓐ Ⓑ Ⓒ Ⓓ Ⓔ	14 Ⓐ Ⓑ Ⓒ Ⓓ Ⓔ	14 Ⓐ Ⓑ Ⓒ Ⓓ Ⓔ
15 Ⓐ Ⓑ Ⓒ Ⓓ Ⓔ	15 Ⓐ Ⓑ Ⓒ Ⓓ Ⓔ	15 Ⓐ Ⓑ Ⓒ Ⓓ Ⓔ	15 Ⓐ Ⓑ Ⓒ Ⓓ Ⓔ
16 Ⓐ Ⓑ Ⓒ Ⓓ Ⓔ	16 Ⓐ Ⓑ Ⓒ Ⓓ Ⓔ	16 Ⓐ Ⓑ Ⓒ Ⓓ Ⓔ	16 Ⓐ Ⓑ Ⓒ Ⓓ Ⓔ
17 Ⓐ Ⓑ Ⓒ Ⓓ Ⓔ	17 Ⓐ Ⓑ Ⓒ Ⓓ Ⓔ	17 Ⓐ Ⓑ Ⓒ Ⓓ Ⓔ	17 Ⓐ Ⓑ Ⓒ Ⓓ Ⓔ
18 Ⓐ Ⓑ Ⓒ Ⓓ Ⓔ	18 Ⓐ Ⓑ Ⓒ Ⓓ Ⓔ	18 Ⓐ Ⓑ Ⓒ Ⓓ Ⓔ	18 Ⓐ Ⓑ Ⓒ Ⓓ Ⓔ
19 Ⓐ Ⓑ Ⓒ Ⓓ Ⓔ	19 Ⓐ Ⓑ Ⓒ Ⓓ Ⓔ	19 Ⓐ Ⓑ Ⓒ Ⓓ Ⓔ	19 Ⓐ Ⓑ Ⓒ Ⓓ Ⓔ
20 Ⓐ Ⓑ Ⓒ Ⓓ Ⓔ	20 Ⓐ Ⓑ Ⓒ Ⓓ Ⓔ	20 Ⓐ Ⓑ Ⓒ Ⓓ Ⓔ	20 Ⓐ Ⓑ Ⓒ Ⓓ Ⓔ
21 Ⓐ Ⓑ Ⓒ Ⓓ Ⓔ			21 Ⓐ Ⓑ Ⓒ Ⓓ Ⓔ
22 Ⓐ Ⓑ Ⓒ Ⓓ Ⓔ			22 Ⓐ Ⓑ Ⓒ Ⓓ Ⓔ
23 Ⓐ Ⓑ Ⓒ Ⓓ Ⓔ			23 Ⓐ Ⓑ Ⓒ Ⓓ Ⓔ
24 Ⓐ Ⓑ Ⓒ Ⓓ Ⓔ			24 Ⓐ Ⓑ Ⓒ Ⓓ Ⓔ
25 Ⓐ Ⓑ Ⓒ Ⓓ Ⓔ			25 Ⓐ Ⓑ Ⓒ Ⓓ Ⓔ

SECTION I: READING COMPREHENSION

Time: 30 Minutes
25 Questions

DIRECTIONS

Each passage in this group is followed by questions based on its content. After reading a passage, choose the best answer to each question and blacken the corresponding space on the answer sheet. Answer all questions following a passage on the basis of what is *stated* or *implied* in that passage. You may refer back to the passage.

Concerning the origin of the soul Augustine's view differs from that of the Greek philosophers. He does not believe that souls are eternal or that they have an existence prior to their union with the body. He holds that souls are created by God, although it is not entirely clear whether he means that a soul is created simultaneously with the birth of each infant or the soul of the newborn child is generated from the souls of the parents at the same time when the new body is developed. In either case it is the creative activity of God that is involved. Although the souls do not exist prior to their union with the body, they will survive the death of the physical body, in which case they will again be united with some other type of body, the nature of which we do not know. It is in this sense only that Augustine believes in the immortality of the soul. His argument in support of this belief is similar to the one used by Plato. Because the soul is capable of knowing truth which is eternal it must possess qualities that are more than merely temporal.

Souls are free insofar as they have the power to choose between right and wrong courses of action. Hence man is to some degree at least responsible for his fate. He cannot place the blame for his sins on God, nature, or even Satan as the Manicheans were inclined to do. The responsibility lies in himself. The temptations are there through no fault of his own but yielding to these temptations is another matter and one for which he can justly be blamed. The nature of man's freedom was, however, a very difficult one for him to explain and he was never able to do so without becoming involved in inconsistencies. One of the reasons for this was his belief in predestination along with the idea that God knows what man will do in the future.

Although man was created in the image of God and without any evil being present in this nature, he now finds himself in a miserable predicament. As Augustine contemplates his own nature as well as that of his fellow men he sees wickedness and corruption on every hand. Man is a sinful creature and there is nothing that is wholly good about him. How did this come about? The answer is to be found in original sin which mankind inherited from Adam. In what sense can it be said that Adam's descendants are responsible for what he did long ago? It is in this connection that Augustine makes use of the Platonic relationship between the universal and the individual. If Adam is regarded as a particular human being it would make no sense at all to blame his descendants for the mistakes that he made. But Adam is interpreted to mean the universal man rather than a particular individual. Since the universal necessarily includes all of the particulars belonging to the class they are involved in whatever the universal does.

The total corruption of human nature as taught by Augustine did not mean that man is incapable of doing any good deeds. It meant that each part of his nature is infected with an evil tendency. In contrast to the Greek notion of a good mind and an evil body, he held that both mind and body had been made corrupt as a result of the fall. This corruption is made manifest in the lusts of the flesh and also in the activities of the mind. So far as the mind is concerned the evil tendency is present in both the intellect and in the will. In the intellect it is expressed in the sin of pride and in the will there is the inclination to follow that which is pleasant at the moment rather than to obey the demands of reason.

1. According to Augustine, one of the symptoms of human corruption is
   (A) man's exclusive pursuit of pleasure
   (B) man's periodic attempts to do good deeds
   (C) man's refusal to connect the universal with the particular
   (D) Adam
   (E) Eve

2. Augustine thinks that the soul is
   (A) eternal   (D) transient
   (B) eternal, but not immortal   (E) capable of sin
   (C) immortal, but not eternal

3. Augustine could not declare man to be wholly free because
   (A) man is shackled by Adam's sin
   (B) God knows man's every move before it is made
   (C) the question of freedom is a political one
   (D) he himself was not free
   (E) anything that is free is not worth much

4. According to the passage, the desires of the flesh are controlled by
   - (A) Augustine's theory
   - (B) the intellect
   - (C) God
   - (D) the will
   - (E) none of these

5. Pride is a function of
   - (A) Augustine's theory
   - (B) the intellect
   - (C) God
   - (D) the soul
   - (E) the will

The Nellie, a cruising yawl, swung to her anchor without a flutter of the sails, and was at rest. The flood had made, the wind was nearly calm, and being bound down the river, the only thing for it was to come to and wait for the turn of the tide.

The sea-reach of the Thames stretched before us like the beginning of an interminable waterway. In the offing the sea and the sky were welded together without a joint, and in the luminous space the tanned sails of the barges drifting up with the tide seemed to stand still in red clusters of canvas sharply peaked, with gleams of varnished sprits. A haze rested on the low shores that ran out to sea in vanishing flatness. The air was dark above Gravesend, and farther back still seemed condensed into a mournful gloom, brooding motionless over the biggest, and the greatest, town on earth.

The Director of Companies was our captain and our host. We four affectionately watched his back as he stood in the bows looking to seaward. On the whole river there was nothing that looked half so nautical. He resembled a pilot, which to a seaman is trustworthiness personified. It was difficult to realize his work was not out there in the luminous estuary, but behind him, within the brooding gloom.

Between us there was, as I have already said somewhere, the bond of the sea. Besides holding our hearts together through long periods of separation, it had the effect of making us tolerant of each other's yarns—and even convictions. The Lawyer—the best of old fellows—had, because of his many years and many virtues, the only cushion on deck, and was lying on the only rug. The Accountant had brought out already a box of dominoes, and was toying architecturally with the bones. Marlow sat cross-legged right aft, leaning against the mizzen-mast. He had sunken cheeks, a yellow complexion, a straight back, an ascetic aspect, and, with his arms dropped, the palms of hands outwards, resembled an idol. The Director, satisfied the anchor had good hold, made his way aft and sat down amongst us. We exchanged a few words lazily. Afterwards there was silence on board the yacht. For some reason or other we did not begin that game of dominoes. We felt meditative, and fit for nothing but placid staring. The day was ending in a serenity of still and exquisite brilliance. The water shone pacifically; the sky, without a speck, was a benign immensity of unstained light; the very mist on the Essex marsh was like a gauzy and radiant fabric, hung from the wooded rises inland, and draping the low shores in diaphanous folds. Only the gloom to the west, brooding over the upper reaches, became more sombre every minute, as if angered by the approach of the sun.

And at last, in its curved and imperceptible fall, the sun sank low, and from glowing white changed to a dull red without rays and without heat, as if about to go out suddenly, stricken to death by the touch of that gloom brooding over a crowd of men.

6. The last paragraph describes
    (A) man's destruction of the sun
    (B) a sunrise
    (C) a change of seasons
    (D) a sunset
    (E) the death of a crowd of men

7. How many men are aboard the *Nellie*?
    (A) four   (D) cannot be determined
    (B) five   (E) more than five
    (C) three

8. In paragraph 4, "bones" is another word for
    (A) the architecture of the accountant's hands
    (B) the skeletons which emerge at sunset
    (C) Marlow
    (D) the planks which make up the deck
    (E) dominoes

9. The author implies that each of the passengers is a former
    (A) seaman
    (B) storyteller
    (C) idol
    (D) pilot
    (E) personification of trustworthiness

10. The *Nellie* is
    (A) not moving
    (B) fluttering
    (C) stretching down the interminable waterway
    (D) becoming increasingly gloomy
    (E) a government vessel

Economic growth involves both benefits and costs. The desirability of increasing production has frequently been challenged in recent years, and some have even maintained that economic growth is merely a quantitative enlargement that has no human meaning or value. However, economic growth is an increase in the capacity to produce goods and services that people want. Since the product of economic growth can be measured by its value to someone, it is important to ask whose standard of valuation counts.

In the United States, the value of a product is what purchasers pay for it. This is determined by the purchasers' preferences combined with conditions of supply, which in turn reflect various other factors, such as natural and technological circumstances at any given time and the preferences of those who supply capital and labor. The value by which we measure a product synthesizes all these factors. Gross National Product (GNP) is the market value of the nation's total output of goods and services.

Gross National Product is not a perfect measure of all the activities involved in economic output. It does not account for deteriorations or improvements in the environment, even when they are incidental results of the production process. On the other hand, it does not count as "product" many benefits provided as side effects of the economic process; it does not include productive but unpaid work (such as that done by a housewife); and it does not reckon with such other factors as the burdensomeness of work, the length of the work week, and so forth.

Nonetheless, the GNP concept makes an important contribution to our understanding of how the economy is working. While it is not a complete measure of economic productivity and even less so of "welfare," the level and rate of increase of the GNP are clearly and positively associated with what most people throughout the world see as an improvement in the quality of life.

Although there has been much soul-searching about the role of increasing material affluence in the good life, it seems quite certain that most Americans prefer a rapidly growing GNP and its consequences. This does not mean that growth of the GNP is an absolute that must be furthered at all costs. Growth of the GNP has its costs, and beyond a certain point they are not worth paying. Moreover, people want things that are not measured in the GNP. Still, while human values and conditions of life change, and might conceivably make the social cost of a rising GNP seem too high, it is likely that we would still be concerned about the growth of our nation's GNP.

In any case, since there is little evidence of a decline in the value assigned to economic output as a whole, the factors that influence our capacity to produce remain of great importance. In the long run, the same factors result in a growing GNP and in other social benefits: size and competence of population, state of knowledge, amount of capital, and the effectiveness with which these are combined and utilized.

The average rate of economic growth in the United States has been exceptionally high. In the mid-nineteenth century, per capita real incomes in this country and in the industralized countries of Europe were roughly equal. In mid-twentieth century, however, real per capita income in the United States was double that in the advanced countries of Europe, and in the 1970s the growth of real per capita income in the United States is expected to surpass the historical average. This will result mainly from an unusually rapid growth in the size of the labor force relative to the population as a whole. It is uncertain, however, whether this will lead to increases in the rate of individual productivity.

A country's annual outflow of goods and services depends on these three factors:

1. The quantity and quality of the factors of production.
2. The efficiency with which these factors are used.
3. The extent of utilization of the potential capacity of the economy.

Within this framework it is possible to point out both the shortcomings and the advantages of developed and developing nations in the growth race.

11. The United States GNP is more than double that of the advanced European countries; this does not necessarily mean that
    (A) the average rate of economic growth in the U.S. has been high
    (B) the U.S. output of goods and services exceeds that of European countries
    (C) the U.S. enjoys greater material affluence than the European countries
    (D) European households are maintained less efficiently than American households
    (E) European countries have a lower GNP than does the U.S.

12. Someone opposed to furthering growth of the GNP might instead favor
    (A) a longer work week
    (B) both benefits and costs
    (C) material growth
    (D) development of native lands
    (E) an emphasis on the spiritual growth of American citizens

13. We might assume that the author favors continuing growth of the GNP because
    (A) although he mentions that the GNP has its costs, he does not list those costs
    (B) he is not a housewife
    (C) he is unlike most people throughout the world
    (D) he does not believe in perfect measures of economic growth
    (E) he prefers things as they were in the 19th century

14. Those who decide the value of a product are
    (A) the GNP   (D) its inventors
    (B) economic theorists   (E) its purchasers
    (C) its naysayers

15. The factor which does not influence the growth of the GNP is
    (A) the condition of the population
    (B) the American dependence upon soul-searching
    (C) the capital available in the country
    (D) knowledge related to production of goods and services
    (E) the efficiency of the production process

Today the study of language in our schools is somewhat confused. It is the most traditional of scholastic subjects being taught in a time when many of our traditions no longer fit our needs. You to whom these pages are addressed speak English and are therefore in a worse case than any other literate people.

People pondering the origin of language for the first time usually arrive at the conclusion that it developed gradually as a system of conventionalized grunts, hisses, and cries and must have been a very simple affair in the beginning. But when we observe the language behavior of what we regard as primitive cultures, we find it strikingly elaborate and complicated. Stefansson, the explorer, said that "In order to get along reasonably well an Eskimo must have at the tip of his tongue a vocabulary of more than 10,000 words, much larger than the active vocabulary of an average businessman who speaks English. Moreover these Eskimo words are far more highly inflected than those of any of the well-known European languages, for a single noun can be spoken or written in several hundred different forms, each having a precise meaning different from that of any other. The forms of the verbs are even more numerous. The Eskimo language is, therefore, one of the most difficult in the world to learn, with the result that almost no traders or explorers have even tried to learn it. Consequently there has grown up, in intercourse between Eskimos and whites, a jargon similar to the pidgin English used in China, with a vocabulary of from 300 to 600 uninflected words, most of them derived from Eskimo but some derived from English, Danish, Spanish, Hawaiian and other languages. It is this jargon which is usually referred to by travelers as 'the Eskimo language.'"[1] And Professor Thalbitzer of Copenhagen, who did take the trouble to learn Eskimo, seems to endorse the explorer's view when he writes: "The language is polysynthetic. The grammar is extremely rich in flexional forms, the conjugation of a common verb being served by about 350 suffixes, equivalent to personal pronouns and verb endings. For the declension of a noun there are 150 suffixes (for dual and plural, local cases, and possessive flexion). The demonstrative pronouns have a separate flexion. The derivative endings effective in the vocabulary and the construction of sentences or sentence-like words amount to at least 250. Notwithstanding all these constructive peculiarities, the grammatical and synthetic system is remarkably concise and, in its own way, logical."[2]

[1] *The Encyclopaedia Britannica,* Fourteenth Edition, Vol. 8, p. 709.
[2] Ibid., p. 707.

16. The size of the Eskimo language spoken by most whites is
    (A) spoken in England, Denmark, Spain, and Hawaii
    (B) less than the size of the language spoken by Eskimos
    (C) highly inflected
    (D) inestimable
    (E) irrelevant

17. Some of the evidence about language in the passage is taken from the observations of
    (A) linguists   (D) an explorer
    (B) Eskimos   (E) primitive cultures
    (C) businessmen

18. The passage implies that a "traditional" course in today's schools would be
    (A) Advances in Biology: The Creation of Artificial Life
    (B) Social Revolution in America
    (C) The History of the English Language
    (D) Television and Its Impact
    (E) Disco Dancing as Psychotherapy

19. According to the passage, the language of primitive cultures was
    (A) nonexistent
    (B) only spoken by Eskimos
    (C) monosyllabic
    (D) simpleminded
    (E) elaborate and complicated

20. The author's overall point is that
    (A) primitive languages may be large, complex, and complicated
    (B) primitive languages may be large, complex, and logical.
    (C) primitive languages may be large, old, and logical
    (D) primitive languages may be similar to pidgin English
    (E) primitive languages tell us little about the origin of language

21. In this passage, the word "inflection" means
    (A) the suffixes added on to a verb or noun
    (B) a sophisticated pidgin English
    (C) a conventionalized system of grunts and hisses
    (D) inflicted
    (E) changes in the form and meaning of a word

Geologic processes have not necessarily been uniform in time. Glaciation, for example, has been spasmodic, occurring only at rare intervals during the past. Mountains have been formed at different times in different places and have been unequally spaced in their origin and distribution. The relative arrangement of land and sea has varied considerably, so that maps of the continents would continually be different but not in predictable fashion. The evolution of life has been one-directional and its results cannot be anticipated. Thus, geology has been described as "the historical science." But the principles of cause and effect have been dependable, so that miracles and catastrophes need not be required to account for geologic features. Sudden and drastic events are not ruled out, however, so long as they take place in a natural fashion.

The original meanings of the names given to the intervals of geologic time have been modified, so that they no longer carry much of their original (mostly geographic) significance. Thus, Devonian rocks were first studied in Devonshire, and the Cretaceous rocks were often chalky (crete means chalk) where originally described. The nature of the fossil record is now given chief emphasis. Eras (representing the main chapters of earth history) are subdivided into periods, and these into epochs.

Formations are named after a type locality, which is where they were first described. Thus, the famous St. Peter sandstone was named for a town in Minnesota. Formations may be divided into members, or they may be combined into groups; members and groups are also given names. Formations are usually sedimentary rocks, but igneous and metamorphic bodies may be similarly named (such as the Pikes Peak granite). The boundary between two beds (strata) is called the bedding plane. The formations of a given locality can be charted as a columnar section, in which the older rock is drawn beneath the younger one as in the normal sequence in the earth.

The original position of bedded rocks (which are always deposited nearly flat) can be determined by such features as mud cracks, ripple marks, raindrop impressions, and the gas cavities in lava. These features show which side of the rock was up and which was down, for some of them occur only at the top or are different at the top.

Parallel strata that are separated by an interval of lost time make up a disconformity. If rocks of two different types (igneous, sedimentary, or metamorphic) are in such contact, the structure is called a nonconformity. When the lower beds were tilted before the upper ones were put down, an angular unconformity resulted.

Rock layers can sometimes be correlated by observing them over a considerable distance, as along a canyon wall, such as across the Grand Canyon. Some rocks appear similar in composition, texture, color, or other features over a wide distance. The more distinctive a bed is, the farther it can be traced with confidence; red standstone and gray shale, for instance, are often ordinary looking for there are many rocks like them.

22. The passage suggests that the most regular feature of the earth's surface is
   (A) the predictable occurrences of glaciation
   (B) the ratio between land and sea
   (C) its irregularity
   (D) its seacoasts
   (E) its mountains

23. Epochs of geologic time were sometimes named after
   (A) a study site
   (B) a characteristic of a type of rock
   (C) an ancient god
   (D) (A) and (B)
   (E) (B) and (C)

24. According to the passage, the turned-up side of a bedded rock might retain
    (A) chalkiness
    (B) its original hardness
    (C) its original shape
    (D) raindrop impressions
    (E) an ancient fossil

25. Igneous, sedimentary, and metamorphic are terms distinguishing
    (A) formations of different types
    (B) bedding positions
    (C) rocks of different ages
    (D) red sandstone from gray shale
    (E) the age of rocks

STOP. IF YOU FINISH BEFORE TIME IS CALLED, CHECK YOUR WORK ON THIS SECTION ONLY. DO NOT WORK ON ANY OTHER SECTION IN THE TEST.

SECTION II: PROBLEM SOLVING

Time: 30 Minutes
20 Questions

DIRECTIONS

In this section solve each problem, using any available space on the page for scratchwork. Then indicate the *best* answer in the appropriate space on the answer sheet.

1. A man walks from B to C, a distance of x miles, at 8 miles per hour and returns at 12 miles per hour. What is his average speed?
   (A) 10 mph   (B) 9.6 mph   (C) 8.8 mph   (D) 8.4 mph
   (E) cannot be determined from the information given

2. During one season, a tennis team won 21 matches and lost 30% of their matches. What was the number of matches that the team lost?
   (A) 70   (B) 30   (C) 9   (D) 7   (E) 5

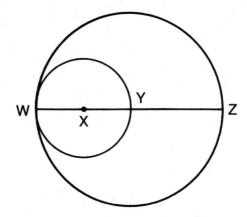

3. In the figure, X and Y are the centers of the two circles. If the area of the larger circle is 144π, what is the area of the smaller circle?
   (A) 72π (B) 36π (C) 24π (D) 12π
   (E) cannot be determined

4. A girl runs k miles in n hours. How many miles will she run in x hours at the same rate?
   (A) knx   (B) $\dfrac{k}{n}$ (C) $\dfrac{kx}{n}$ (D) kx   (E) $\dfrac{kn}{x}$

160

5. If 20% of a class averages 80% on a test, 50% of the class averages 60% on the test, and the remainder of the class averages 40% on the test, what is the overall class average?
(A) 80% (B) 74% (C) 58% (D) 56% (E) none of these

6. If m and n are integers and $\sqrt{mn} = 10$, which of the following cannot be a value of m + n?
(A) 25   (B) 29   (C) 50   (D) 52   (E) 101

Houses sold in one year

Age	Number
1–2	1200
3–4	1570
5–6	1630
7–8	1440
9–10	1720

7. According to the chart, how many more houses from 5 to 10 years old were sold than those 4 to 8 years old?
(A) 2455 (B) 1570 (C) 150 (D) 130 (E) cannot be determined

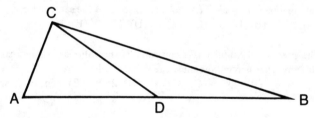

8. In the figure, AB = BC, CD = BD, and angle CAD = 70°. Therefore, what is the measure of angle ADC?
(A) 50° (B) 60° (C) 70° (D) 80° (E) cannot be determined

9. If x, y, and z are consecutive positive integers greater than 1, not necessarily in that order, then which of the following is (are) true?

I. x > z   III. yz > xz
II. x + y > z   IV. xy > y + z

(A) I   (B) II   (C) II and III   (D) III and IV
(E) II and IV

10. At a party there were 5 times as many females as males. There were 3 times as many adults as children. Which of the following could not be the number of people at the party?
    (A) 384   (B) 258   (C) 216   (D) 120   (E) 72

11. If electricity costs x cents per kilowatt hour for the first 30 kilowatt hours and y cents per kilowatt hour for each additional kilowatt hour, what is the cost of z kilowatt hours (z > 30)?
    (A) 30 (x − y) + yz   (B) 30y − 30x + yz   (C) 30 (x − y + z)
    (D) (z − 30)x + 30y   (E) 30x + (y − 30)z

12. Pete has some apples. He sold 40% more than he ate. If he sold 70 apples, how many did he eat?
    (A) 90   (B) 50   (C) 42   (D) 28   (E) 6

13. If a 32-inch chord is drawn in a circle of radius 20 inches, how far is the chord from the center of the circle?
    (A) 4 inches   (B) 6 inches   (C) 8 inches
    (D) 10 inches   (E) 12 inches

14. A drawer contains red socks, black socks, and white socks. What is the least number of socks that must be taken out of the drawer to be sure of having 4 pairs of socks? (A pair is two socks of the same color.)
    (A) 8   (B) 10   (C) 12   (D) 14   (E) 16

15. The product of x and y is a constant. If the value of x is increased by 50%, by what percentage must the value of y be decreased?
    (A) 50%   (B) 40%   (C) 33⅓%   (D) 25%   (E) none of these

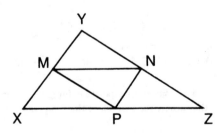

16. In △ XYZ, points M, N, and P are midpoints. If XY = 10, YZ = 15, and XZ = 17, what is the perimeter of △ MNP?
    (A) 10⅔   (B) 14   (C) 16   (D) 21   (E) cannot be determined

17. There are 36 students in a certain geometry class. If two-thirds of the students are boys and three-fourths of the boys are under six feet tall, how many boys in the class are under six feet tall?

(A) 6   (B) 12   (C) 18   (D) 24   (E) 27

18. The current in a river is 4 mph. A boat can travel 20 mph in still water. How far up the river can the boat travel if the round trip is to take 10 hours?

(A) 69 miles   (B) 88 miles   (C) 96 miles
(D) 100 miles   (E) 112 miles

19. In a triangle, the ratio of two angles is 5:2, and the third angle is equal to the difference between the other two. Find the number of degrees in the smallest angle.

(A) 18   (B) 25²⁄₇   (C) 25⁵⁄₇   (D) 36   (E) cannot be determined

20. Macey is three times as old as Mike. In 8 years, she will be twice as old as Mike. How old was Macey 3 years ago?

(A) 5   (B) 8   (C) 21   (D) 24   (E) 30

STOP. IF YOU FINISH BEFORE TIME IS CALLED, CHECK YOUR WORK ON THIS SECTION ONLY. DO NOT WORK ON ANY OTHER SECTION IN THE TEST.

SECTION III: DATA SUFFICIENCY

Time: 30 Minutes
25 Questions

DIRECTIONS

Each of the problems below consists of a question and two statements, labeled (1) and (2), in which certain data are given. You must decide whether the data given in the statements are *sufficient* to answer the question. Using the data given in the statements *plus* your knowledge of mathematics and everyday facts (such as the number of days in July or the meaning of *counterclockwise*), you are to blacken space

- (A) if statement (1) ALONE is sufficient, but statement (2) alone is not sufficient to answer the question asked;
- (B) if statement (2) ALONE is sufficient, but statement (1) alone is not sufficient to answer the question asked;
- (C) if BOTH statements (1) and (2) TOGETHER are sufficient to answer the question asked, but NEITHER statement ALONE is sufficient;
- (D) if EACH statement ALONE is sufficient to answer the question asked;
- (E) if statements (1) and (2) TOGETHER are NOT sufficient to answer the question asked, and additional data specific to the problem are needed.

1. Which is the tallest of four men?
   (1) Jim is shorter than Steve.
   (2) Mark and Steve are shorter than Walter.

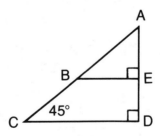

2. What is the ratio of the area of quadrilateral BCDE to the area of triangle ABE?
   (1) BC = ½ AC
   (2) Angle CBE = 135°

3. Assuming that neither m nor n is zero, is the product m^2n positive?
   (1) $m > 0$
   (2) $n > 0$

4. What was the percentage increase of Mr. Doolittle's rent?
   (1) His rent was raised $45.
   (2) He now pays $315 per month.

5. Where is the center of a circle on the xy plane?
   (1) The circle passes through both the origin and (0,7).
   (2) The diameter equals 10.

6. What is the average of ten numbers?
   (1) Nine of the numbers sum to 45.
   (2) One of the numbers is 15.

7. What is the area of a rectangular field?
   (1) The diagonal is twice the width.
   (2) The length is 173 feet.

8. Given $2m^2 + n^2 = 27$, what is the value of m?
   (1) n is positive.
   (2) $m = n$

9. How far is Sacramento from Los Angeles?
   (1) A car that obtains 28 miles per gallon drove the distance on exactly one tank of gasoline.
   (2) Another car averaged 50 miles per hour and arrived in 8 hours.

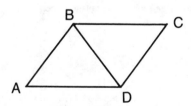

10. In rhombus ABCD, what is angle BCD?
    (1) $BC = BD$
    (2) Angle $BDA = 60°$

11. Is the product xy > 27?
    (1) $2 < x < 5$
    (2) $6 > y$

12. What is the value of a one-inch cube of expensium?
    (1) Expensium is being quoted at $886 per troy ounce.
    (2) The cube weighs 12.3 troy ounces.

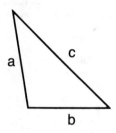

13. What is the length of side c?
    (1) $a = 6$
    (2) $b = 7$

14. Is x greater than y?
    (1) $x = \sqrt{3}$
    (2) y is a prime number.

15. Three spies Ex, Why, and Zee together know 19 different secrets. There is no overlap of information. How many secrets does Why know?
    (1) Ex knows one more than Why and twice as many as Zee.
    (2) Why knows three more secrets than Zee.

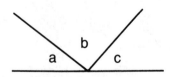

16. How many degrees is angle c?
    (1) b is a right angle.
    (2) $a + b = 131°$

17. The positive integer C is a perfect cube; what is its value?
    (1) $30 < C < 100$
    (2) C is an even number.

18. How much gross profit did White Store make during its Great Refrigerator Sale?
    (1) The store sold 112 refrigerators for $33,060.
    (2) The refrigerators cost White an average of $186.

19. What is the volume of a cylindrical can?
    (1) The radius of the can is 3 inches.
    (2) The area of the bottom is 9π square inches.

20. What is the value of $x^3 - 2x^2 + 7$?
    (1) $3x^3 - x = 2$
    (2) $x^5 = 1$

21. What is Toni's typing speed in words per minute?
    (1) She completed a report of 3150 words in one hour.
    (2) The report had 7 pages, each averaging 450 words.

22. Which is greater, ef or fg?
    (1) $e > g$
    (2) $f^2 = eg$

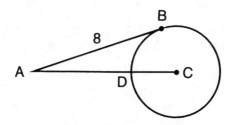

23. Given that AB is tangent to the circle with center C, what is the length of the circle's radius?
    (1) $AD = 4$
    (2) $AC = 10$

24. If gasoline costs $1.09 per gallon and alcohol costs $1.81, what fraction of each would be used to make Gasohol 99?
    (1) The mixture is predominantly gasoline.
    (2) A gallon of Gasohol 99 costs $1.22.

25. What is the value of $(u + v)$?
    (1) $2w - 7 = 0$
    (2) $u + v - 3w = 11$

STOP. IF YOU FINISH BEFORE TIME IS CALLED, CHECK YOUR WORK ON THIS SECTION ONLY. DO NOT WORK ON ANY OTHER SECTION IN THE TEST.

SECTION IV: SENTENCE CORRECTION

Time: 30 Minutes
25 Questions

DIRECTIONS

Some part of each sentence below is underlined; sometimes the whole sentence is underlined. Five choices for rephrasing the underlined part follow each sentence; the first choice (A) repeats the original, and the other four are different. If choice (A) seems better than the alternatives, choose answer (A); if not, choose one of the others.

For each sentence, consider the requirements of standard written English. Your choice should be a correct and effective expression, not awkward or ambiguous. Focus on grammar, word choice, sentence construction, and punctuation. If a choice changes the meaning of the original sentence, do not select it.

1. To enjoy exploring marine life in general, and so that they could learn in particular about the ways in which certain sea animals possess "human" traits, the university's school of oceanography offered supervised summer field trips for the elementary school children in the area.
   - (A) To enjoy exploring marine life in general, and so that they could learn in particular about the ways in which certain sea animals possess "human" traits
   - (B) To stress the enjoyment of marine life in general, and particularly the ways in which certain sea animals are "human"
   - (C) In order to teach young people about the "human" traits of certain sea animals, and to provide them an opportunity to enjoy marine exploration in general
   - (D) Because marine life in general shares certain "human" traits
   - (E) From general marine life to the specifically "human" possessions of sea animals

2. Although he is liable to make political enemies with the decision, the President will propose severe tax cuts that may both stimulate business and reduce the availability of home loans.
   - (A) liable to
   - (B) liable from
   - (C) able to
   - (D) of a mind to
   - (E) acknowledging his liability to

169

3. Success in school, according to many of the more cynical critics of public education, is like playing marbles: distinguished achievement depends not upon talent but upon luck.
   (A) Success in school, according to many of the more cynical critics of public education, is like playing marbles:
   (B) Criticizing success in public education cynically, may compare successful schooling to a successful marble game:
   (C) School is a game of marbles, according to many of the more cynical critics of public education
   (D) The more cynical critics of public education say that success in school is like playing marbles:
   (E) The more cynical critics of public education say that succeeding in school is like playing marbles:

4. The defendant's refusal to discuss his whereabouts completely convinced the jury of his guilt, even though so many other facts surrounding the crime indicated not only that he was entirely innocent but also that he had been "framed" by members of a local syndicate.
   (A) The defendant's refusal to discuss his whereabouts completely convinced the jury of his guilt
   (B) Refusing to completely discuss the defendant's whereabouts, the jury was completely convinced of his guilt
   (C) The defendant's refusal to completely discuss his whereabouts convinced the jury of his guilt
   (D) The defendant's refusal to discuss his complete whereabouts convinced the jury that he was guilty
   (E) Guilty in the eyes of the jury because his whereabouts had not been completely discussed

5. By composing at the typewriter, the poetry of this century often illustrates a more purposeful alignment of lines and letters made possible by the typewriter itself.
   (A) By composing at the typewriter, the poetry of this century often illustrates a more purposeful alignment of lines and letters made possible by the typewriter itself.
   (B) The poets of this century who compose at the typewriter often use that machine to arrange lines and letters more purposefully.
   (C) The typewriters of the poets of this century align lines and letters more purposefully.
   (D) With the typewriter as their means of composition, the poets of this century often align lines and letters more purposefully than the poets before the typewriter.
   (E) With the more purposeful alignment of lines and letters, the poets of this century rely on the typewriter often.

6. Because nuclear weapons have been scorned by so many liberal activists with the power to destroy the world, both of the superpowers have begun to consider both the limitation and the reduction of their arsenals.

   (A) Because nuclear weapons have been scorned by so many liberal activists with the power to destroy the world

   (B) World-destroying nuclear weapons have been scorned by many liberal activists

   (C) With the power to destroy the world, liberal activists have scorned nuclear weapons

   (D) Because nuclear weapons with the power to destroy the world have been scorned by so many liberal activists

   (E) Liberal activists scorning nuclear weapons

7. To the behalf of many citizens who believe that some criminal statutes are unfair to the victims of crime, legislators in California drafted a "Victim's Bill of Rights" law, which passed handily in the election.

   (A) To the behalf of many citizens who believe that some criminal statutes are unfair to the victims of crime

   (B) Listening for many citizens' belief that criminal statutes are unfair to the victims of crime

   (C) With the belief of their citizens that the victims of crime are unfairly served by some criminal statutes

   (D) On the behalf of many citizens who believe that some criminal statutes are unfair to the victims of crime

   (E) To believe on the behalf of many citizens about criminal statutes that are unfair to crime victims

8. The typical holiday shopper, although seduced by row upon row of novelty gifts, tend to purchase more practical items these days because he or she realizes that frivolous gadgets are often cheaply made.

   (A) The typical holiday shopper, although seduced by row upon row of novelty gifts, tend to purchase more practical

   (B) As a typical holiday shopper, the tendency to purchase row upon row of novelty gifts is won over by the purchase of more practical

   (C) Typically, the holiday shopper who is attracted to novelty gifts tends to remain practical with

   (D) The typical holiday shopper, although seduced by row upon row of novelty gifts, tends to purchase more practical

   (E) The typical holiday shopper, although seduced by row upon row of novelty gifts, tends to purchase the most practical

9. The most recent National Conference of Mathematics Teachers addressed the problem of convincing students who rely on calculators that the ability to calculate mentally or with pencil and paper is important.
   (A) The most recent National Conference of Mathematics Teachers addressed the problem of convincing students who
   (B) The most recent problem faced by the National Conference of Mathematics Teachers was convincing students who
   (C) The most recent National Conference of Mathematics Teachers addressed the problem of convincing students whom
   (D) Most recently, the National Conference of Mathematics Teachers addressed the problem of convincing students who
   (E) The most recent National Conference of Mathematics Teachers addressed those students who

10. Understanding the droning lecturer with comprehension required the intense concentration of the class members present in the lecture hall, all of whom were students.
    (A) Understanding the droning lecturer with comprehension required the intense concentration of the class members present in the lecture hall, all of whom were students.
    (B) Comprehending the droning lecturer with the intense concentration of the class members present.
    (C) To understand the droning lecturer, the students had to concentrate intensely.
    (D) As the lecturer droned on, the students found themselves required to concentrate in order to understand.
    (E) The students listening to the lecturer, who was droning, increased their comprehension by concentrating.

11. Movie critics Gene Siskel and Roger Ebert often praise distinguished performances even when they are new to the screen.
    (A) Movie critics Gene Siskel and Roger Ebert often praise distinguished performances even when they are new to the screen.
    (B) Movie critics Gene Siskel and Roger Ebert, praising distinguished performances that are new to the screen.
    (C) Even distinguished performances that are new to the screen are praised by movie critics Gene Siskel and Roger Ebert.
    (D) Movie critics Gene Siskel and Roger Ebert often praise distinguished performances, even those by actors new to the screen.
    (E) With distinguished performances in mind, movie critics Gene Siskel and Roger Ebert often praise even new screen actors.

12. In *Charlotte's Web,* Wilbur is awarded a blue ribbon not because his appearance is superior to the other pigs but also with reference to the belief that he possesses some sort of "supernatural" power.

 (A) his appearance is superior to the other pigs but also with reference to the belief that he possesses

 (B) he looked better than the other pigs but because he was thought to possess

 (C) of his superior appearance but as far as the belief that he possessed

 (D) he looks better than that of the other pigs but because of a belief in supernatural power

 (E) he looks better than the other pigs but because he is thought to possess

13. Clarity and brilliance, in addition to enjoying the beauty: these are the qualities of a beautiful diamond and along with it a beautiful painting.

 (A) Clarity and brilliance, in addition to enjoying the beauty: these are the qualities of a beautiful diamond and along with it a beautiful painting.

 (B) Clarity, brilliance, and beauty: these are the qualities of a beautiful diamond as well as a beautiful painting.

 (C) To be clear, brilliant, and beautiful is to be either a beautiful diamond or a beautiful painting.

 (D) Diamonds and paintings give out clarity, brilliance, and beauty.

 (E) Where there are clarity and brilliance and beauty there are the qualities of not only a beautiful diamond but also a beautiful painting.

14. So many of us bemoan our lack of foresight, by complaining that if we would have bought property twenty years ago, we could have taken advantage of the recent real estate boom.

 (A) , by complaining that if we would have bought property twenty years ago, we could have taken advantage of the recent real estate boom

 (B) , looking backward to a potential property purchase twenty years ago and wishing we had done so for present purposes

 (C) : with real estate available so cheaply twenty years ago, the advantages of the recent boom would be ours for the asking

 (D) , complaining that if we had bought property twenty years ago, we could have taken advantage of the recent real estate boom

 (E) ; the complaint being our lack of purchasing property twenty years ago and the consequent absence of profit in the recent real estate boom

15. According to legend, while working as an engineer, a train collided with Casey Jones and killed him, but he remains with us as part of a rich American folk history of songs and legends.
    - (A) According to legend, while working as an engineer, a train collided with Casey Jones and killed him
    - (B) The legendary engineer Casey Jones experienced a collision with another train on the job that killed him
    - (C) Engineer Casey Jones was killed when his train collided with another
    - (D) Driving the engine, another train killed Casey Jones
    - (E) An engineer's work brought Casey Jones to his death when he was hit by a train while working

16. With the advent of sound, many stars of silent films found themselves unable to adapt to the "talkies" because their speaking voices were either unattractive or their acting consisted of only exaggerated pantomime.
    - (A) because their speaking voices were either unattractive or their acting consisted of only exaggerated pantomime
    - (B) because of their voices either being unattractive or their acting being exaggerated pantomime
    - (C) with their unattractive voices and exaggerated pantomime
    - (D) because of their unattractive voices or exaggerated pantomime that didn't require sound
    - (E) because either their voices were unattractive or their acting was only exaggerated pantomime

17. According to statistics, one in every two marriages ends in divorce, most often involving married couples not wealthy enought to "buy" each other's love.
    - (A) According to statistics, one in every two marriages ends in divorce, most often involving married couples not wealthy enough to "buy" each other's love.
    - (B) Statistically, fifty percent of marriages are divorces, often caused by people not wealthy enough to "buy" each other's love.
    - (C) According to statistics, half of all marriages end in divorce, often because the partners are not wealthy enough to "buy" each other's love.
    - (D) Statistics tell half of all marriages that they will end in divorce, often because the partners are not wealthy enough to "buy" each other's love.
    - (E) Those who cannot "buy" each other's love are destined for divorce in at least half the cases, according to statistics.

18. The All-Star Game signals the middle of the baseball season and reminds the losing teams that the time for them to improve their playing is running out.
    (A) The All-Star Game signals the middle of the baseball season
    (B) With double significance, the All-Star Game occurs midway through
    (C) The baseball season is divided in half by the All-Star Game
    (D) The baseball All-Star Game signals the middle of the season
    (E) With the All-Star Game, half the season is over

19. Not gaining sufficient legislative approval, thousands of women vowed to keep the Equal Rights Amendment alive by continuing their protests.
    (A) Not gaining sufficient legislative approval, thousands of women vowed to keep the Equal Rights Amendment alive by continuing their protests.
    (B) Not gaining sufficient legislative approval, the Equal Rights Amendment had thousands of women vowing to keep it alive with their protests.
    (C) Thousands of women vowed to keep the Equal Rights Amendment alive in spite of failure to gain legislative approval.
    (D) After the Equal Rights Amendment did not gain sufficient legislative approval, thousands of women vowed to keep it alive by continuing their protests.
    (E) Not gaining sufficient legislative approval, protests continued by women who vowed to keep the Equal Rights Amendment alive.

20. Recounting a painful childhood experience, the woman remembered that her father was very angry when she failed the fifth grade because she could see him shaking with anger.
    (A) Recounting a painful childhood experience, the woman remembered that her father was very angry when she failed the fifth grade because she could see him shaking with anger.
    (B) Recounting a painful childhood experience, the woman remembered that her father was shaking with anger when she failed the fifth grade.
    (C) Painfully, the woman remembered when she failed the fifth grade and when her father was shaking with anger.
    (D) The failure of the fifth grade and her father's anger were painful for the woman recounting the experience.
    (E) The woman described her father's shaking with anger when he learned that she had failed the fifth grade.

21. The <u>principle reason for the British invasion was because</u> the sovereignty of British territory had been challenged.
    (A) The principle reason for the British invasion was because
    (B) The principle reason for the British invasion was that
    (C) The principal reason for the British invasion was that
    (D) The British invaded because
    (E) Principally, the British staged an invasion because

22. The <u>state governor understood that if he did not sign the new budget quick, the state</u> might begin the new fiscal year not only with a significant deficit but also with no budgetary guidelines for lessening that deficit.
    (A) The state governor understood that if he did not sign the state budget quick, the state
    (B) Not signing the new state budget quickly, the governor knew that the state
    (C) Without a quick signing, the state governor new that as far as the budget was concerned, the state
    (D) The state governor understood that if he did not sign the new budget quickly, the state
    (E) The governor understood that if he did not sign the budget and sign it quickly, that the effects of that action might cause the state to

23. <u>Reading modern novels continually reminds many people</u> that we live in an age of lost faith and growing anxiety.
    (A) Reading modern novels continually reminds many people
    (B) Reading modern novels frequently reminds many people
    (C) Those who read modern novels continually realize
    (D) Those who continually read modern novels realize
    (E) The reading of modern novels is what continually reminds many people

24. Most citizens of nineteenth-century London believed that remaining respectable was more important and more difficult than <u>to question</u> the virtues of the age.
    (A) to question
    (B) questioning
    (C) the question of
    (D) a question over
    (E) all

25. If all the local candidates would have participated in the debate, the voters would have a better understanding of the contending points of view.

    (A) If all the local candidates would have participated in the debate
    (B) If all the candidates had engaged in local debate
    (C) If all the local candidates had participated in the debate
    (D) Debating as they should have
    (E) After a debate

STOP. IF YOU FINISH BEFORE TIME IS CALLED, CHECK YOUR WORK ON THIS SECTION ONLY. DO NOT WORK ON ANY OTHER SECTION IN THE TEST.

SECTION V: PROBLEM SOLVING

Time: 30 Minutes
20 Questions

DIRECTIONS

In this section solve each problem, using any available space on the page for scratchwork. Then indicate the *best* answer in the appropriate space on the answer sheet.

1. A small college reduced its faculty by approximately 13 percent to 195 professors. What was the original number of faculty members?
   (A) 220   (B) 224   (C) 230   (D) 236   (E) 242

2. If $g < 0$ and $f \neq 0$, which of these four expressions must have a positive sign?

   I. gf
   II. g^2f
   III. gf^2
   IV. $(gf)^2$

   (A) I and III   (D) II and IV
   (B) I and IV   (E) IV only
   (C) II and III

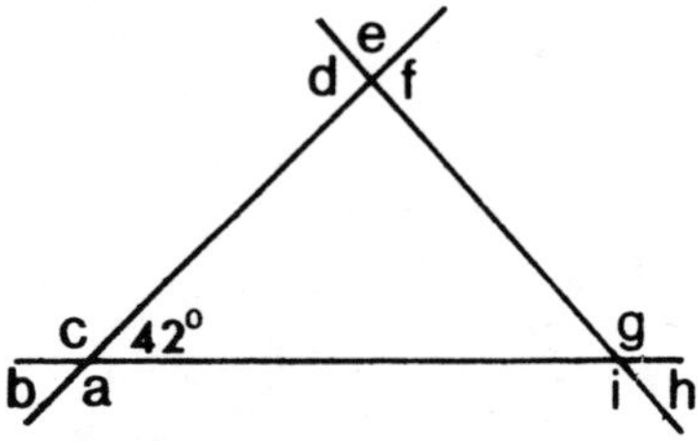

3. In the figure above, what is the sum of the nine angles labeled with letters?
   (A) 138°   (D) 900°
   (B) 378°   (E) indeterminate
   (C) 678°

4. Three factories of Conglomerate Corporation are capable of manufacturing hubcaps. Two of the factories can each produce 100,000 hubcaps in 15 days. The third factory can produce hubcaps 30% faster. How many days would it take to produce a million hubcaps with all three factories working simultaneously?

(A) 38   (B) 42   (C) 46   (D) 50   (E) 54

5. The three digits of a number add to 11. The number is evenly divisible by 5. The first digit is double the second digit. What is the product of the three digits?

(A) 40   (B) 72   (C) 78   (D) 88   (E) 125

6. Two airplanes take off from one airfield at noon. One flies eastward at 200 miles per hour while the other flies northeastward at 283 miles per hour. How many miles apart are the airplanes at 2 P.M.?

(A) 166   (B) 332   (C) 400   (D) 483   (E) 566

7. Which of the five choices is equivalent to the expression

$$\frac{x - 4}{2x^2 - 10x + 8}?$$

(A) $\dfrac{1}{2x^2 - 9x}$ (D) $\dfrac{1}{2x}$

(B) $\dfrac{1}{2x^2 - 9x + 4}$ (E) $\dfrac{1}{2x - 2}$

(C) $\dfrac{1}{2x + 4}$

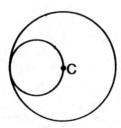

8. In the figure above, point C is the center of the larger circle. What is the ratio of the area of the crescent to the area of the small circle?

(A) 2   (B) 2.4   (C) 3   (D) 3.25   (E) 4

9. A woman has three blouses of different colors, three skirts of different colors, and two different pairs of shoes. She refuses to wear her pink blouse with her green skirt. How many different blouse-skirt-shoe combinations could she wear?

(A) 8   (B) 12   (C) 16   (D) 17   (E) 18

10. Given the two equations $3r + s = 17$ and $r + 2s = 9$, by how much does r exceed s?

(A) 3   (B) 4   (C) 5   (D) 6   (E) 7

Questions 11 to 13 refer to the flow chart of steel making on the following page. The numbers indicate the relative weights of material at the various stages. At some stages, the relative weight exceeds 2000 due to recycling.

11. During the steel-making process, what is the ratio of molten steel to molten iron?

(A) 0.9   (B) 1.0   (C) 1.1   (D) 1.3   (E) 1.5

12. In steel making, what percentage of molten iron ends up as finished shapes?

(A) 83   (B) 86   (C) 89   (D) 92   (E) 95

13. During steel making, what percentage of all scrap is used to feed electric-arc furnaces?

(A) 17   (B) 23   (C) 33   (D) 67   (E) 75

14. The first five numbers in a regular sequence are 4, 10, 22, 46, and 94. What is the next number in the sequence?

(A) 142   (B) 154   (C) 176   (D) 182   (E) 190

15. Approximately how many cubic feet of water are needed to fill a circular swimming pool that is 50 feet across and 8 feet deep?

(A) 400   (D) 20,000
(B) 6000   (E) 42,000
(C) 16,000

16. An incredible punch is composed of buttermilk, orange juice, and brandy. How many pints of orange juice are required to make $7\frac{1}{2}$ gallons of punch containing twice as much buttermilk as orange juice and three times as much orange juice as brandy?

(A) 16   (B) 18   (C) 20   (D) 22   (E) 24

The Steel-Making Process

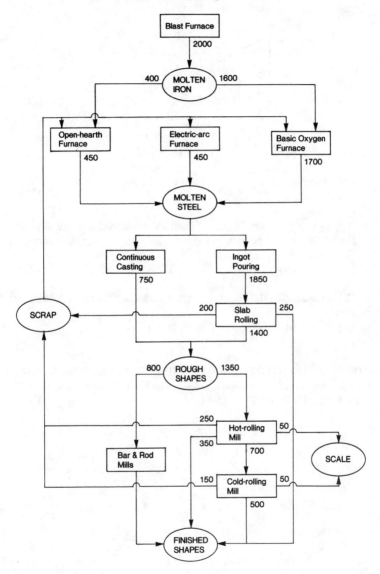

17. If x = 6 and y = −2, what is the value of $(x - 2y)^y$?
    (A) −100   (B) 0.01   (C) 0.25   (D) 4   (E) 8

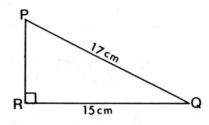

18. What is the perimeter of right triangle PQR?
    (A) 39 cm   (D) 42 cm
    (B) 40 cm   (E) 43 cm
    (C) 41 cm

19. A ferry can transport 78 tons of vehicles. Automobiles range in weight
    from 1800 to 3200 pounds. What is the greatest number of automobiles
    that can be loaded onto the ferry?
    (A) 23   (B) 41   (C) 48   (D) 62   (E) 86

20. Given the exponential quantities m = 8^5 and n = 2^{12}, what is the quotient
    m/n?
    (A) 6   (B) 6^{-7} (C) 7^{-6} (D) 8   (E) 16

STOP. IF YOU FINISH BEFORE TIME IS CALLED, CHECK YOUR
WORK ON THIS SECTION ONLY. DO NOT WORK ON ANY
OTHER SECTION IN THE TEST.

SECTION VI: PROBLEM SOLVING

Time: 30 Minutes
20 Questions

DIRECTIONS

In this section solve each problem, using any available space on the page for scratchwork. Then indicate the *best* answer in the appropriate space on the answer sheet.

1. Simplify: $2 + \cfrac{1}{2 + \cfrac{1}{2 + \frac{1}{2}}}$

(A) 29/12   (B) 12/5   (C) 70/29   (D) 2⅜   (E) 12/29

2. If 5 machines can produce 20 units in 10 hours, how long would it take 20 machines to produce 100 units?
(A) 50 hours   (B) 40 hours   (C) 12.5 hours   (D) 12 hours
(E) 8 hours

3. Five A's and two B's exactly balance six B's and five C's. One A and four C's exactly balance two A's and four B's. Express the weight of A in terms of C.
(A) (3/2) C   (B) (6/5) C   (C) (5/6) C   (D) (2/3) C
(E) (1/2) C

4. If paint costs $3.20 per quart, and a quart covers 20 square feet, how much will it cost to paint the outside of a cube 10 feet on each edge?
(A) $1.60   (B) $16.00   (C) $96.00   (D) $108.00
(E) none of these

5. A bookseller sells his books at a 20% markup in price. If he sells a book for $12.00, how much did he pay for it?
(A) $14.40   (B) $14.00   (C) $10.00   (D) $9.60
(E) $5.00

6. If $x = \dfrac{1 + y}{y}$, then $y =$

(A) $\dfrac{1}{x - 1}$ (B) $\dfrac{1}{x + 1}$ (C) $\dfrac{1 + x}{x}$ (D) $\dfrac{1 - x}{x}$ (E) x

183

7. While traveling from city A to city B, Sharon and Andy average 50 miles per hour. For the return trip, they average 40 miles per hour. What was their average speed for the round trip?
   (A) 45 mph   (B) more than 45 mph   (C) less than 45 mph
   (D) cannot be determined   (E) depends on the distance traveled

8. Machine A can do a certain job in 8 hours. Machine B can do the same job in 10 hours. Machine C can do the same job in 12 hours. All three machines start the job at 9:00 A.M. Machine A breaks down at 11:00 A.M., and the other two machines finish the job. Approximately what time will the job be finished?
   (A) 12:00   (B) 12:30   (C) 1:00   (D) 1:30   (E) 2:00

Questions 9–11 refer to the chart.

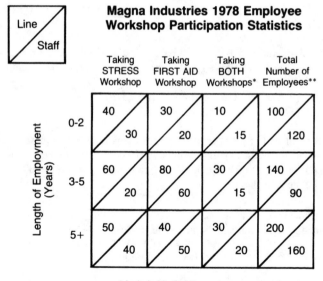

Magna Industries 1978 Employee Workshop Participation Statistics

Line / Staff

Length of Employment (Years)		Taking STRESS Workshop	Taking FIRST AID Workshop	Taking BOTH Workshops*	Total Number of Employees**
0-2	Line	40	30	10	100
	Staff	30	20	15	120
3-5	Line	60	80	30	140
	Staff	20	60	15	90
5+	Line	50	40	30	200
	Staff	40	50	20	160

* Included in first two columns.
** Including nonparticipants in workshop.

9. What is the number of line employees with 3 to 5 years of employment not taking the First Aid workshop?
   (A) 20   (B) 60   (C) 80   (D) 140   (E) 190

10. What is the number of employees with 0 to 2 years of employment taking only one of the workshops?
    (A) 25   (B) 70   (C) 80   (D) 120   (E) none of these

11. Approximately what percent of the employees with 5 or more years employment are not taking either workshop?
    (A) 86%   (B) 64%   (C) 50%   (D) 14%   (E) 7%

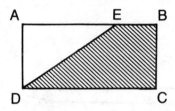

12. Find the area of the shaded portion of this rectangle, given that AD = 6, CD = 8, AE = x
    (A) 48 − 3x   (B) 48 + 3x   (C) 3x + 16   (D) 24 − 3x
    (E) 24 + 3x

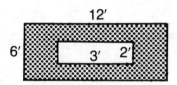

13. How many 2-inch by 3-inch rectangular tiles are required to tile this shaded region?
    (A) less than 10   (B) 10–100   (C) 101–1000
    (D) 1001–1500   (E) 1500+

14. If the radius of a circle is decreased 20%, what happens to the area?
    (A) 10% decrease   (B) 20% decrease   (C) 36% decrease
    (D) 40% decrease   (E) none of these

15. Two quarts containing 2/3 water and 1/3 formula are mixed with three quarts containing 3/8 water and 5/8 formula. Approximately what percent of the combined five quart mixture is water?
    (A) 40%   (B) 45%   (C) 50%   (D) 55%   (E) 60%

Questions 16–17 refer to the graph.

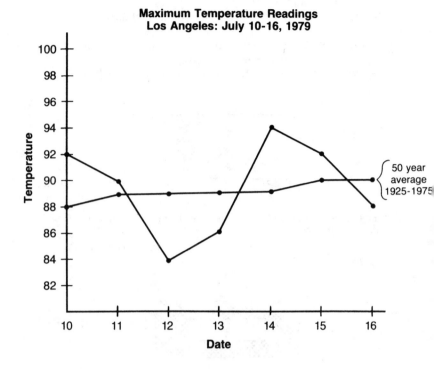

Maximum Temperature Readings
Los Angeles: July 10-16, 1979

50 year
average
1925-1975

16. Of the seven days shown, about what percent of the days did the maximum temperature exceed the average temperature?
    (A) 3%   (B) 4%   (C) 43%   (D) 57%   (E) 93%

17. What was the percent increase in the maximum temperature from July 12 to July 14, 1979?
    (A) 10%   (B) 10.6%   (C) 11.9%
    (D) cannot be determined   (E) none of these

18. An empty fuel tank is filled with brand Z gasoline. When the tank is half empty, it is filled with brand Y gasoline. When the tank is half empty again, it is filled with brand Z gasoline. When the tank is half empty again, it is filled with brand Y gasoline. At this time, what percent of the gasoline in the tank is brand Z?
    (A) 50%   (B) 40%   (C) 37.5%   (D) 33⅓%   (E) 25%

19. To rent an office, each member of a club must pay n dollars. If two more
    members join the club, the per-member payment would be reduced by
    two dollars. Which of the following could be the number of members
    currently in the club?

    I. 16   II. 27   III. 36

    (A) I   (B) I and III   (C) II and III   (D) II
    (E) I, II, and III

20. What is the area of a square that has a diagonal of length $\sqrt{10}$?
    (A) 5   (B) 10   (C) 20   (D) 40   (E) none of these

STOP. IF YOU FINISH BEFORE TIME IS CALLED, CHECK YOUR
WORK ON THIS SECTION ONLY. DO NOT WORK ON ANY
OTHER SECTION IN THE TEST.

SECTION VII: SENTENCE CORRECTION

Time: 30 Minutes
25 Questions
DIRECTIONS

Some part of each sentence below is underlined; sometimes the whole sentence is underlined. Five choices for rephrasing the underlined part follow each sentence; the first choice (A) repeats the original, and the other four are different. If choice (A) seems better than the alternatives, choose answer (A); if not, choose one of the others.

For each sentence, consider the requirements of standard written English. Your choice should be a correct and effective expression, not awkward or ambiguous. Focus on grammar, word choice, sentence construction, and punctuation. If a choice changes the meaning of the original sentence, do not select it.

1. In the early fourteenth century, almost 200 years before Columbus reached the West Indies, and 250 years before the Reformation, <u>Europe had been Catholic and the Church continued to influence virtually every phase of human life.</u>
   (A) Europe had been Catholic and the Church continued to influence virtually every phase of human life
   (B) the Catholic Church continued to influence every phase of human life
   (C) the Europe that had been Catholic was still influenced in virtually every phase of human life by the Church
   (D) Europe was Catholic and the Church influenced virtually every phase of human life
   (E) every phase of human life bore traces of the European influence of the Catholic Church

2. Although the Contadora group of Central America has completed <u>their meeting that address the political tensions in that area,</u> no easing of tensions has resulted.
   (A) their meeting that address the political tensions in that area
   (B) their meeting that addresses the political tensions in that area
   (C) its meeting that address the political tensions for that area
   (D) its meeting that addresses the political tensions with that area in mind
   (E) its meeting that addresses the political tensions in that area

3. In the 1950s, toy stores sold thousands of play replicas of a gun popularized by the *Wyatt Earp* television series, the "Buntline Special," a long-barreled six-gun named after the legendary Ned Buntline.

   (A) In the 1950s, toy stores sold thousands of play replicas of a gun popularized by the *Wyatt Earp* television series
   (B) Popularized by the 1950s *Wyatt Earp* television series, toy stores sold thousands of play replicas of a gun
   (C) In the 1950s, the *Wyatt Earp* television series popularized thousands of play replicas of a gun sold in toy stores
   (D) A play replica of a gun popularized by the *Wyatt Earp* television series, which sold thousands in toy stores in the 1950s
   (E) As toy stores sold thousands of the 1950s replicas of a gun popularized by the *Wyatt Earp* television series

4. The more the union stubbornly refused to budge from its original demand for a 20% across-the-board salary increase, the more the district administration reiterated its original proposal of a mere 1% raise.

   (A) the more the district administration reiterated its original proposal of a mere 1% raise
   (B) the district administration's original proposal for a mere 1% raise was reiterated all the more
   (C) proposing its original and mere 1% raise was the district administration's response, more and more
   (D) the district administration reiterated its proposal of a mere 1% raise
   (E) the more the district administration's original proposal of a mere 1% raise was reiterated

5. During the literary renaissance of the 1920s, a large number of new writers—William Faulkner, Ernest Hemingway, John Dos Passos, and F. Scott Fitzgerald—sought to record the inner life of Americans and to scrutinize the American dream, the dream that anyone can earn his own fortune and live happily ever after through hard work, which had become tarnished.

   (A) the dream that anyone can earn his own fortune and live happily ever after through hard work, which had become tarnished
   (B) the tarnished dream that anyone can make his own fortune and live happily ever after through hard work
   (C) the tarnished dream that anyone can, through hard work, make his own fortune and live happily ever after
   (D) the dream that anyone can earn his own fortune and live happily ever after, though tarnished, through hard work
   (E) that making one's own fortune and living happily ever after, through hard work, had become tarnished

6. To bring to an end the 1984 Olympics, the festivities were highlighted by the arrival of an "alien" spaceship that hovered mysteriously over the Coliseum, to the amazement and delight of thousands of spectators.

   (A) To bring to an end the 1984 Olympics, the festivities were highlighted

   (B) The festivities to bring to an end to the 1984 Olympics were highlighted

   (C) With the festivities that ended the 1984 Olympics highlighted

   (D) Festive highlights brought an end to the 1984 Olympics

   (E) The festive conclusion of the 1984 Olympics was highlighted

7. Homer's *Odyssey* is often dramatized as a series of hairbreadth escapes from terrible monsters and vengeful gods, and while those episodes are exciting and important literary achievements, they stand apart from the poem's extensive attention to domestic life, to domestic values, and to a hero whose most important achievement is the reestablishment of his home and family.

   (A) and while those episodes are exciting and important literary achievements

   (B) and although in fact these episodes are exciting, important achievements in literature

   (C) and while an exciting and important literary achievement

   (D) and those episodes are exciting and important literary achievements

   (E) and with those episodes as exciting and important literary achievements

8. Public enthusiasm that had been growing for airline travel, still in its infancy, when Amelia Earhart's plane disappeared in the 1930s, diminished for awhile; however, today fear of flying is rare.

   (A) Public enthusiasm that had been growing for airline travel, still in its infancy, when Amelia Earhart's plane disappeared in the 1930s, diminished for awhile

   (B) Public enthusiasm that had been growing for airline travel, still in its infancy when Amelia Earhart's plane disappeared in the 1930s, diminished for awhile

   (C) Growing public enthusiasm for airline travel, still in its infancy, diminished for awhile after Amelia Earhart's plane disappeared in the 1930s

   (D) When Amelia Earhart's plan disappeared in the 1930s, growing public enthusiasm for airline travel, still in its infancy, diminished for awhile

   (E) After Amelia Earhart's plane disappeared in the 1930s, the enthusiasm that had been growing for airline travel in its infancy diminished for awhile

9. Much like Macbeth when he interprets the witches' prophecies all too literally, <u>the mysterious harpooner who Ahab takes aboard the *Pequod* has the captain accepting his strange prophecies without questioning their hidden meaning.</u>

 (A) the mysterious harpooner who Ahab takes aboard the *Pequod* has the captain accepting his strange prophecies without questioning their hidden meaning

 (B) the strange prohpecies of the mysterious harpooner he has taken aboard the *Pequod* are accepted by Ahab without questioning their hidden meaning

 (C) the mysterious harpooner whom Ahab takes aboard the *Pequod* has the captain accepting his strange prophecies without questioning their hidden meaning

 (D) Ahab accepts the strange prophecy of the mysterious harpooner whom he has taken aboard the *Pequod,* without questioning their hidden meaning

 (E) Ahab accepts the strange prophecies of the mysterious harpooner he has taken aboard the *Pequod,* without questioning their hidden meaning

10. <u>The recent decrease in the prime interest rate</u> has encouraged some economists and worried others, who recall all too vividly the skyrocketing rates and consequent economic stagnation of the late 1970s.

 (A) The recent decrease in the prime interest rate

 (B) Decreasing recently, the prime interest rate

 (C) The recent rate of decrease in prime interest

 (D) The prime interest rate, recently decreased,

 (E) The recently decreasing prime interest rate

11. Golding's most famous novel concerns little boys, <u>once a well-behaved and civilized group, whose</u> resort to murder and savagery during their brief time on a tropical island without adult supervision.

 (A) once a well-behaved and civilized group, whose

 (B) once well-behaved and civilized, who

 (C) once a well-behaved and civilized herd, who

 (D) once civilized and well-behaved, whose

 (E) behaved and civilized, who

12. When reading some of the most rich and beautiful speeches in Shake-speare's *Romeo and Juliet,* <u>when one stresses the singsong cadence of iambic pentameter, the lines take on an almost simpleminded, childish quality</u>.

(A) when one stresses the singsong cadence of iambic pentameter, the lines take on an almost simpleminded, childish quality

(B) stressing the singsong cadence of iambic pentameter gives the lines an almost simpleminded, childish quality

(C) if one stresses the singsong cadence of iambic pentameter, it gives the lines an almost simpleminded, childish quality

(D) the simpleminded, childish quality of some lines results from the songsong cadence of iambic pentameter

(E) the singsong cadence of iambic pentameter, sounds almost sim-pleminded and childish

13. The weather in San Diego, California, is temperate for most of the year, and although the air is not so clean as it used to be, it has remained virtually smog free through recent years of rapid industrial growth, <u>unlike most urban areas in southern California</u>.

(A) unlike most urban areas in southern California

(B) unlike the air in most southern California urban areas

(C) unlike other southern California air

(D) unlike southern California urban areas

(E) in contrast to the smog condition elsewhere in urban southern California

14. Brokers who offer foreign cars on the "gray market," thus bypassing the car dealer by shipping directly from the manufacturer to the waiting consumer at the dock, claim that their purpose is not to cheat dealerships out of a profit, but rather <u>to provide the consumer with the finest value for his dollar</u>.

(A) to provide the consumer with the finest value for his dollar

(B) the provision of the finest value for the dollar

(C) providing the finest values for consumer dollars

(D) that they have an obligation to give consumers value for their dollars

(E) to deliver value for the dollar

15. Two recent statements on the tenure of university professors offer conflicting points of view: those which say that lifetime tenure ensures academic freedom and those which say that lifetime tenure encourages professional laziness and irresponsibility.
    (A) those which say that lifetime tenure ensures academic freedom and those which say that lifetime tenure encourages professional laziness and irresponsibility
    (B) some declare that lifetime tenure ensures academic freedom, and others say that it encourages professional laziness and irresponsibility
    (C) saying that lifetime tenure either ensures academic freedom or encourages irresponsible laziness
    (D) one emphasizes the academic freedom that tenure ensures, and one stresses the professional laziness and irresponsibility it encourages
    (E) advocacies of academic freedom and warnings about professional laziness and irresponsibility

16. With an explosive capacity that can devastate life and property for a radius of hundreds of miles, proponents of peace from several Western bloc countries met to discuss the continuing manufacture and deployment of nuclear warheads.
    (A) With an explosive capacity that can devastate life and property for a radius of hundreds of miles, proponents of peace from several Western bloc countries met to discuss the continuing manufacture and deployment of nuclear warheads.
    (B) Proponents of peace from several Western bloc countries with an explosive capacity that can devastate life and property for a radius of hundreds of miles met to discuss the continuing manufacture and deployment of nuclear warheads.
    (C) Meeting to discuss the continuing manufacture and deployment of nuclear warheads with an explosive capacity that can devastate life and property for a radius of hundreds of miles were several Western bloc countries.
    (D) Proponents of peace from several Western bloc countries met to discuss the continuing manufacture and deployment of nuclear warheads that can devastate life and property with an explosive capacity for a radius of hundreds of miles.
    (E) Proponents of peace from several Western bloc countries met to discuss the continuing manufacture and deployment of nuclear warheads with an explosive capacity that can devastate life and property for a radius of hundreds of miles.

17. During the French Revolution, especially the Reign of Terror, citizens whom the government suspected of treasonous tendencies were eventually put to death by Monsieur Sanson, the infamous executioner who supervised the killing of hundreds at the guillotine.
    (A) citizens whom the government suspected of treasonous tendencies were eventually put to death
    (B) citizens of which the government had suspicions were eventually put to death
    (C) suspicious citizens were eventually killed
    (D) citizens who the government suspected of treason were eventually put to death
    (E) the citizenry under suspicion were eventually put to death

18. Irregardless of the "new modernism" in literature, which produces novels which often read like the diaries of madmen, most readers still prefer a conventional plot and simple style.
    (A) Irregardless of the "new modernism" in literature, which produces
    (B) Irregardless of the "new modernism" in literature, which produced
    (C) Regardless, the "new modernism" in literature, which produces
    (D) Regardless of the "new modernism" in literature, which produces
    (E) Regardless of the "new modernism" in literature, which produce

19. During the last century, whaling voyages departed regularly from the New England states, and because each voyage normally extends for years, the hold was packed with supplies before a whaling ship set sail.
    (A) and because each voyage normally extends for years
    (B) and because each trip was long
    (C) and because each voyage normally extended for years
    (D) and while these were long trips
    (E) and because the voyage had lasted for years

20. As he looked out on an expanse that seemed empty of gods or goddesses, Odysseus must certainly have felt abondoned by the rulers on Olympus.
    (A) As he looked out on an expanse that seemed empty of gods or goddesses
    (B) As he looked out on an empty expanse of gods and goddesses
    (C) With no gods or goddesses as he looked out on the empty expanse
    (D) Facing the empty expanse of gods and goddesses
    (E) As he looked out on an expanse that seemed empty of either a god or a goddess

21. Arms talks <u>from Geneva between China, the United States, the Soviet Union, and other nations may be even more effecting than many world leaders think they would be.</u>
    - (A) from Geneva between China, the United States, the Soviet Union, and other nations may be even more effecting than many world leaders think they would be
    - (B) in Geneva between China, the United States, the Soviet Union, and other nations may be even more effective than many world leaders suppose
    - (C) in Geneva between China, the United States, the Soviet Union, and other nations may be even more affecting than many world leaders think they will be
    - (D) in Geneva among China, the United States, the Soviet Union, and other nations may be even more effective than many world leaders expect
    - (E) between China, the United States, the Soviet Union, and other nations in Geneva may be even more effective than many world leaders believe

22. If Swift's *Gulliver's Travels* <u>attracts less of a readership than he did in the eighteenth century,</u> perhaps the reason is that modern readers do not know enough political history to appreciate the satire.
    - (A) attracts less of a readership than he did in the eighteenth century
    - (B) attracts less readers than the eighteenth century did
    - (C) attracts fewer readers than it did in the eighteenth century
    - (D) attracts fewer readers than he did in the eighteenth century
    - (E) attract less reading than it did in the eighteenth century

23. <u>Proposing that inordinate government spending was causative of the high deficit, the president presented a budget</u> that maintained relatively high defense expenditures while it reduced funding for certain social programs which, the administration argued, were receiving sufficient support from the private sector.
    - (A) Proposing that inordinate government spending was causative of the high deficit, the president presented a budget
    - (B) Proposing that government spending causes deficits, the president presented a budget
    - (C) With a proposal that inordinate government spending was causative of the high deficit, the president presented a budget
    - (D) The president presented a budget proposal that inordinate government spending was causative of the high deficit
    - (E) Proposing that inordinate government spending caused the high deficit, the president presented a budget

24. Acknowledging the volunteers' giving of a great deal of their time to
    canvas the neighborhood and collect donations from the neighbors, the
    chairman of the local United Way expressed his sincere gratitude.
    (A) Acknowledging the volunteers' giving of a great deal of their time to
        canvas the neighborhood and collect donations from the neighbors,
        the chairman of the local United Way expressed his sincere
        gratitude.
    (B) Acknowledging the time spent by neighborhood volunteers to
        canvas and to collect neighborhood donations, the chairman of the
        local United Way expressed his sincere gratitude.
    (C) With sincere gratitude, the chairman of the local United Way
        expressed his acknowledgment of the neighborhood donations can-
        vased and collected on the volunteers' time.
    (D) The chairman of the local United Way offered sincere thanks to the
        volunteers who gave so much time to canvasing the neighborhood to
        collect donations.
    (E) The chairman of the local United Way thanked the neighborhood
        volunteers, sincerely.

25. A diagonal line connecting two corners of a rectangle is also the
    hypotenuse of each of two right triangles contained within the rectangle,
    which is longer than any of the sides.
    (A) which is longer than any of the sides
    (B) and the line is longer than any of the sides
    (C) which is longer than the sides
    (D) that is longer than any of the sides
    (E) that is longer than any of the other sides

STOP. IF YOU FINISH BEFORE TIME IS CALLED, CHECK YOUR
WORK ON THIS SECTION ONLY. DO NOT WORK ON ANY
OTHER SECTION IN THE TEST.

ANSWER KEY FOR PRACTICE TEST 2

Section I Reading Comprehension	Section II Problem Solving	Section III Data Sufficiency
1. A	1. B	1. C
2. C	2. C	2. A
3. B	3. B	3. B
4. E	4. C	4. C
5. B	5. C	5. E
6. D	6. C	6. E
7. B	7. E	7. C
8. E	8. D	8. C
9. A	9. B	9. B
10. A	10. B	10. D
11. D	11. A	11. E
12. E	12. B	12. C
13. A	13. E	13. E
14. E	14. B	14. C
15. B	15. C	15. A
16. B	16. D	16. B
17. D	17. C	17. A
18. C	18. C	18. C
19. E	19. D	19. E
20. B	20. C	20. B
21. E		21. A
22. C		22. E
23. D		23. D
24. D		24. B
25. C		25. C

ANSWER KEY FOR PRACTICE TEST 2

Section IV Sentence Correction	Section V Problem Solving	Section VI Problem Solving	Section VII Sentence Correction
1. C	1. B	1. A	1. D
2. A	2. E	2. C	2. E
3. E	3. D	3. A	3. A
4. C	4. C	4. C	4. A
5. B	5. A	5. C	5. C
6. D	6. C	6. A	6. E
7. D	7. E	7. C	7. A
8. D	8. C	8. C	8. C
9. A	9. C	9. B	9. E
10. C	10. A	10. B	10. A
11. D	11. D	11. B	11. B
12. E	12. E	12. A	12. B
13. B	13. E	13. E	13. B
14. D	14. E	14. C	14. A
15. C	15. C	15. C	15. D
16. E	16. B	16. D	16. E
17. C	17. B	17. C	17. A
18. A	18. B	18. C	18. D
19. D	19. E	19. E	19. C
20. E	20. D	20. A	20. A
21. C			21. D
22. D			22. C
23. D			23. E
24. B			24. D
25. C			25. B

HOW TO SCORE YOUR EXAM

1. Add the total number of correct responses for each section.
2. Add the total number of incorrect responses (only those attempted or marked in) for each section.
3. The total number of incorrect responses should be divided by 4, giving the adjustment factor.
4. Subtract this adjustment factor from the total number of correct responses to obtain a raw score.
5. This score is then scaled from 200 to 800.

Example:
A. If the total number of correct answers was 100 out of a possible 205.
B. And 60 problems were attempted but missed.
C. Dividing the 60 by 4 gives an adjustment factor of 15.
D. Subtracting this adjustment factor of 15 from the original 100 correct gives a raw score of 85.
E. This raw score is then scaled to a range of 200 to 800.

ANALYZING YOUR TEST RESULTS

The charts on the following pages should be used to carefully analyze your results and spot your strengths and weaknesses. The complete process of analyzing each subject area and each individual problem should be completed for each Practice Test. These results should then be reexamined for trends in types of errors (repeated errors) or poor results in specific subject areas. THIS REEXAMINATION AND ANALYSIS IS OF TREMENDOUS IMPORTANCE TO YOU IN ASSURING MAXIMUM TEST PREPARATION BENEFIT.

PRACTICE TEST 2: ANALYSIS SHEET

	Possible	Completed	Right	Wrong
Section I: Reading Comprehension	25			
Section II: Problem Solving	20			
Section III: Data Sufficiency	25			
Section IV: Sentence Correction	25			
Section V: Problem Solving	20			
Section VI: Problem Solving	20			
Section VII: Sentence Correction	25			
OVERALL TOTALS	160			

WHY?????????????????????????????????

ANALYSIS—TALLY SHEET FOR PROBLEMS MISSED

One of the most important parts of test preparation is analyzing WHY! you missed a problem so that you can reduce the number of mistakes. Now that you have taken the practice test and corrected your answers, carefully tally your mistakes by marking them in the proper column.

	REASON FOR MISTAKE			
	Total Missed	Simple Mistake	Misread Problem	Lack of Knowledge
Section I: Reading Comprehension				
Section II: Problem Solving				
Section III: Data Sufficiency				
Section IV: Sentence Correction				
Section V: Problem Solving				
Section VI: Problem Solving				
Section VII: Sentence Correction				
OVERALL TOTALS				

Reviewing the above data should help you determine WHY you are missing certain problems. Now that you have pinpointed the type of error, take the next practice test and focus on avoiding your most common type.

COMPLETE ANSWERS AND EXPLANATIONS FOR PRACTICE TEST 2

SECTION I: READING COMPREHENSION

1. (A) The fourth paragraph describes Augustine's ideas about man's evil tendency, which contributes to the "corruption of human nature." This evil tendency is associated "in the will" with "the inclination to follow that which is pleasant." Adam (D) and Eve (E) became corrupt, but they cannot be described as "symptoms" because they are people.

2. (C) Paragraph 1 says that Augustine does not "believe that souls are eternal," and later states that souls are immortal, that "they will survive the death of the physical body." (E) is incorrect because it is the intellect and the will which are capable of sin, not the soul (see paragraph 4).

3. (B) Paragraph 2 states that one of the difficulties Augustine had explaining "the nature of man's freedom" involved "the idea that God knows what man will do in the future." (A) is correct according to certain religions, but is not stated in the passage as an obstacle to man's freedom.

4. (E) According to the passage (paragraph 4) the intellect and the will (B and D) are parts of the mind, not the flesh. (A) and (C) are obviously inconsistent with the passage.

5. (B) Paragraph 4 says, "In the intellect it [the evil tendency] is expressed in the sin of pride."

6. (D) Although the paragraph compares the sunset to a death, it simply and explicitly states, "the sun sank low." If anything is responsible for this imagined "death," it is the "gloom" which surrounds the big town in the west.

7. (B) The five men are the Director of Companies (captain), the Lawyer, the Accountant, Marlow, and the narrator.

8. (E) "The bones" seems to refer to something just mentioned, and it is *dominoes* that were just mentioned.

9. (A) In paragraph 4 the author says, "Between us there was . . . the bond of the sea."

10. (A) The first sentence tells us that the *Nellie* "was at rest."

11. (D) Choices (A), (B), and (C) are all necessary results of a high U.S. GNP. But, as paragraph 3 states, the GNP does not measure "productive but unpaid work" such as keeping house; so a lower European GNP tells us nothing about how their households are maintained.

12. (E) Since the GNP measures material growth an alternative type of growth would be nonmaterial growth, of which spiritual growth is one type.

13. (A) In a fifth paragraph the author states, "Growth of the GNP has its costs," but without emphasizing those costs he soon concludes that "while . . . the social cost of a rising GNP seem[s] too high, it is likely that we would still be concerned about the growth of the nation's GNP." In other words, he deemphasizes the negative effects of a growing GNP in order to emphasize people's general appreciation of such growth. Choices (B), (C), (D), and (E) are simply not true according to the passage.

14. (E) The second paragraph says that "the value of a product is what purchasers pay for it." The other factors which may help determine value are not listed as choices.

15. (B) Choices (A), (C), (D), and (E) are all listed as growth factors in the passage (paragraphs 6–8).

16. (B) Only answers (B), (D), and (E) could refer to *size*. (B) summarizes the information of paragraph 2, which tells us that an Eskimo's vocabulary is over 10,000 words, whereas the conversation between Eskimos and whites is made up of 300 to 600 words—less than one-tenth of the real Eskimo vocabulary.

17. (D) "Stefansson, the explorer," makes an observation about Eskimo language in the second paragraph.

18. (C) The passage says that language "is the most traditional of scholastic subjects." The only choice directly involving language is (C). And all of the other choices are very untraditional.

19. (E) This is directly stated in paragraph 2.

20. (B) Choice (E) contradicts the passage's extensive concentration on primitive language. (D) contradicts paragraph 2, where pidgin English is compared to a kind of Eskimo jargon different from native Eskimo. (C) and (A) each contain an unnecessary repetition: *primitive* and *old* are repetitious in (C); *complex* and *complicated* are repetitious in (A).

21. (E) Inflections are changes in the form and meaning of a word by adding prefixes and suffixes or merely changing the structure. (A) is too specific, while (B), (C), and (D) are clearly wrong by the passage.

22. (C) The first sentence of the passage says, "Geologic processes have not necessarily been uniform in time," and the paragraph goes on to describe the *irregular* features of the earth's surface.

23. **(D)** Paragraph 2 says that Devonian rocks were named after a study site—Devonshire—and that Cretaceous rocks were named so because of their characteristic chalkiness.

24. **(D)** Raindrop impressions are one of the features which show which side of a bedded rock was turned up, according to paragraph 4.

25. **(C)** This is stated in paragraph 5.

SECTION II: PROBLEM SOLVING

1. **(B)** Average speed is total distance/total time. The total distance is 2x. Time going is x/8. Time coming back is x/12. Thus average speed is

$$\frac{2x}{x/8 + x/12} = \frac{2x}{3x/24 + 2x/24}$$

$$= \frac{2x}{5x/24} = \frac{2x}{1} \cdot \frac{24}{5x} = \frac{48}{5} = 9.6$$

Notice answers (C), (D), and (E) were not reasonable.

2. **(C)** Since 21 is 70% of the total, the total must be 30. Thus the team lost 9 matches.

21 = 70% of x
21 = .7x
$^{21}/_{.7}$ = x
30 = x
30 − 21 = 9

Notice answers (A) and (B) are not reasonable.

3. **(B)** Area of larger circle = 144π

Since area = πr^2, then

$\pi r^2 = 144\pi$
$r^2 = 144$
$r = 12$

Radius of larger circle = 12
Diameter of smaller circle = 12
Radius of smaller circle = 6
Area of smaller circle = πr^2
$\qquad\qquad\qquad\qquad = \pi(6)^2$
$\qquad\qquad\qquad\qquad = 36\pi$

4. **(C)** Distance = rate × time

d = rt $\qquad\qquad$ Hence d = rt

k = rn $\qquad\qquad$ $d = \left(\frac{k}{n}\right) \cdot (x) = \frac{kx}{n}$

$r = \frac{k}{n}$ miles per hour

5. (C) We look at total percentage points.

   (20)(80) + (50)(60) + (30)(40) = 5800 = 58%

   Notice answers (A) and (B) are not reasonable.

6. (C) Since $\sqrt{mn}$ = 10, mm = 100, and the possible values for m and n would be: 1 and 100, 2 and 50, 4 and 25, 5 and 20, 10 and 10. Since none of these combinations yield m + n = 50, choice (C) is correct.

7. (E) Since the chart does not distinguish how many houses are 3 years old or 4 years old, the answer cannot be determined.

8. (D) Since AB = BC, angle CAD is equal to angle ACB (isosceles triangle ABC). Thus angle ACB is also 70°. This makes angle B equal to 40° (180° in a triangle). Also angle BCD equals 40° (same reason as above). Thus angle ADC equals 80° (external angle theorem: external angle of a triangle is equal to the sum of the opposite two angles).

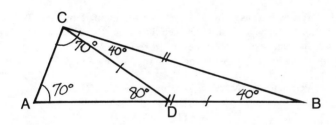

9. (B) Adding any two of three consecutive positive integers greater than 1, will always be greater than the other integer, therefore II is true. The others cannot be determined, as they depend on values and/or the order of x, y, and z.

10. (B) From the first sentence, we see that the total number of persons at the party must be divisible by 6 (5:1). From the second sentence, the total must be divisible by 4 (3:1). Thus, the total must be a number divisible by both 6 and 4; such a number would be divisible by 12. The only number given that is not divisible by 12 is 258.

11. (A) From the given information, it costs 30x for the first 30 kilowatt hours. Thus z − 30 kilowatt hours remain at y cents per kilowatt hour. Thus 30x + (z − 30)y = (30x) − (30y) + yz = 30(x − y) + yz.

12. (B) Let x = number of apples Peter ate. Thus x + .4x = 1.4x is the number of apples Peter sold. Thus 1.4x = 70; x = 70/1.4, or 50.
Notice answers (A), (D), and (E) are not reasonable.

13. (E) From the figure, we use the Pythagorean theorem and find the missing side, x, is 12 inches. Thus, (E) is correct.

$a^2 + b^2 = c^2$
$16^2 + x^2 = 20^2$
$256 + x^2 = 400$
$x^2 = 400 - 256$
$x^2 = 144$
$x = 12$

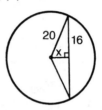

14. (B) If only 9 were picked out, it is possible to get 3 of each color. Thus the 10th is necessary to be sure of 4 pairs.

15. (C) If x is increased by 50%, we can represent it by $\frac{3}{2}$ x. We must multiply this by $\frac{2}{3}$ y in order to keep the product equal to xy. Since $\frac{2}{3}$ is a $\frac{1}{3}$ reduction, answer (C) is the correct response.
You could have also tried using some values for x and y.

16. (D) Perimeter of ΔMNP = $\frac{1}{2}$ (perimeter of ΔXYZ)
          = $\frac{1}{2}$ (XY + YZ + XZ)
          = $\frac{1}{2}$ (10 + 15 + 17)
          = $\frac{1}{2}$ (42)
Perimeter of ΔMNP = 21

17. (C) Since two-thirds of the students are boys, we have $\frac{2}{3}$ (36) = 24 boys in the class.
Out of the 24 boys in the class, three-fourths of them are under six feet tall or
$\frac{3}{4}$ (24) = 18 boys under six feet tall.

18. (C) We can set up the following chart

	D	=	R	×	T
Up	D		16		$\frac{D}{16}$
Down	D		24		$\frac{D}{24}$

Since the time is 10 hours for the whole trip,

$$\frac{D}{16} + \frac{D}{24} = 10 \quad \text{Multiply by 48,} \quad 3D + 2D = 480$$

$$5D = 480$$
$$D = 96$$

19. (D) Let

$5x$ = first angle
$2x$ = second angle
$5x - 2x = 3x$ = third angle

Since the sum of the angles in any triangle is 180°, we have

$5x + 2x + 3x = 180°$
$\qquad\qquad 10x = 180°$
$\qquad\qquad\quad x = 18°$
Hence $\qquad 5x = 90°$
$\qquad\qquad 2x = 36°$
$\qquad\qquad 3x = 54°$

The smallest angle will have a measure of 36°.

20. (C) Let x be Mike's age. Thus, 3x is Macey's age. Thus $3x + 8 = 2(x + 8)$, $3x + 8 = 2x + 16$. Thus x = 8. Therefore, 3x = 24. Thus Macey is 24. Thus, 21, three years ago.
Notice you could have worked from the answers.

SECTION III: DATA SUFFICIENCY

1. (C) From both statements, Jim must also be shorter than Walter, who is taller than any of the other men.

2. (A) Area BCDE equals triangle ACD minus triangle ABE. From the sketch it is clear that the two triangles are similar, as their respective sides are parallel. From (1) we see that the base and height of ABE are half those of ACD, hence the area of ABE is one-quarter that of ACD. Consequently, the area BCDE is three times the area of ABE.

3. (B) Whether m is positive or negative, m^2 must be positive. So the sign of n determines the sign of the product.

4. (C) His initial rent was $315 − $45 = $270, so the increase was 45 divided by 270 equals 16.7%.

5. (E) The first statement lists two points through which the circle passes, but many circles could pass through any two points. Knowing the diameter would still not yield a unique circle.

6. (E) To calculate the average, we require the sum of the ten numbers. Statement (1) offers the sum of nine. We do not know whether the number cited in (2) is or is not one of those nine.

7. (C) The first statement implies that the diagonal divides the field into two 30°–60° right triangles, with sides in the ratio $1:2:\sqrt{3}$. Employing that ratio to find the width with a length of 173 feet, the width equals 100 feet. Then the area equals 17,300 square feet.

8. (C) From the second statement, $3m^2 = 27$, $m^2 = 9$, and $m = \pm 3$. But from both statements, since n is positive, so must be m.

9. (B) Statement (1) lacks the capacity of the tank. But from (2) and the formula d = rt you can compute the distance to be 400 miles.

10. (D) The definition of a rhombus stipulates the equality of its four sides. The first statement reveals that the two triangles are equilateral, so all the angles must be 60°. From the second statement, CBD = 60° (by alternate interior angles); triangle BCD is isosceles with BC = CD (from the definition of a rhombus), so angle BDC = CBD = 60°; subtracting those angles from 180° leaves 60° for angle BCD.

11. **(E)** From (1), $x < 5$, and from (2), $y < 6$, so $xy < 30$. Hence the product may or may not exceed 27.

12. **(C)** Multiplying both facts yields a value of $10,898.

13. **(E)** The Pythagorean theorem, $a^2 + b^2 = c^2$, can only be employed for a triangle known to have a right angle.

14. **(C)** The smallest prime is 2, which exceeds $\sqrt{3}$ (approximately 1.73). Consequently, x is less than y.

15. **(A)** The first statement translates to $Y = X - 1$ and $Z = \frac{1}{2}X$. Given that $X + Y + Z = 19$, substitution yields $X + X - 1 + \frac{1}{2}X = 19$, so $X = 8$. From (1), $Y = 7$ and $Z = 4$.

16. **(B)** Since the three angles sum to a straight angle, $c = 180° - 131° = 49°$.

17. **(A)** The first five perfect cubes are 1, 8, 27, 64, and 125. Therefore $C = 64$.

18. **(C)** From the second statement, the refrigerators cost $112 \times \$186 = \$20,832$. Subtraction from the sale revenue in (1) leaves a gross profit of $12,228.

19. **(E)** Volume is the product of three dimensions. For the can, volume equals its base area (two dimensional) times its height; but the height is not stated.

20. **(B)** We cannot solve the first equation by elementary methods. The second equation implies $x = 1$. Hence $x^3 - 2x^2 + 7 = 6$.

21. **(A)** From (1), Toni types $3150/60 = 52\frac{1}{2}$ words per minute.

22. **(E)** From (2), the product eg is positive, hence e and g have the same sign: f could be either positive or negative. Assume all three numbers are positive, and from (1) $ef > eg$. However, if we assume e and g are positive but f is negative, then from (1) $ef < eg$. The contradiction makes the problem indeterminate.

23. **(D)** The radius BC must be perpendicular to the tangent AB, so ABC is a right triangle. The second statement implies it is a 6-8-10 right

triangle, so the radius is 6. We can solve from the first statement with the Pythagorean theorem:

$(AC)^2 = (AB)^2 + (BC)^2$
$(4 + r)^2 = 8^2 + r^2$
$16 + 8r + r^2 = 64 + r^2$
$r = {}^{48}\!/_8 = 6$

24. **(B)** Let g be the fraction of gasoline. Then the fraction of alcohol is $1 - g$. So for the mixture, $1.09g + 1.81(1 - g) = 1.22$, and we can solve for $g = 0.82$. Gasohol 99 is 82% gasoline and 18% alcohol.

25. **(C)** From the first statement, $w = 3\frac{1}{2}$. Substituting that into (2) yields $u + v - 3 \cdot 3\frac{1}{2} = 11$, which can be solved for $(u + v) = 21\frac{1}{2}$.

SECTION IV: SENTENCE CORRECTION

1. (C) Along with having inconsistent verb tense and wordiness problems, the original sentence illustrates a long dangling modifier. The underlined portion seems to modify *the university's school of oceanography* and thereby seems to say that the *school* is enjoying *exploring marine life,* etc. Only (C) offers an introductory phrase that is both correct and unambiguous. (B) and (D), although grammatically correct, significantly change the intended meaning of the original sentence.

2. (A) The original is better than any of the alternatives.

3. (E) The original sentence contains a subtle error in faulty parallelism. The items compared—*success in school* and *playing marbles*—become parallel if *success* is changed to *succeeding.* (E) makes this necessary change and also brings the compared items closer together in order to further clarify their relationship.

4. (C) The original sentence contains a squinting modifier; it is unclear whether *completely* refers to *discuss* or to *convince.* Either reference is possible. Only (C) clarifies the reference with a construction that is both grammatical and logical.

5. (B) The introductory phrase is a dangling modifier and makes the sentence seem to say that the poetry is composing at the typewriter. Choice (B) makes it clear that the poets do the composing and does so without significantly altering the meaning of the original.

6. (D) A misplaced modifier here makes it seem that liberal activists have *the power to destroy the world.* Choice (D) logically links nuclear weapons with the power to destroy the world. Although choice (B) is somewhat clearer than the original, it creates a clause incompatible with the rest of the sentence.

7. (D) *To the behalf* is not idiomatic. Choice (D) corrects this error and does not make additional, unnecessary changes, as do the other choices.

8. (D) In the original, the subject, *shopper,* does not agree with the verb, *tend.* Choice (D) corrects this error without making additional, unnecessary changes.

9. (A) The original is more correct, clear, and logical than any of the other choices.

10. (C) The original is extremely wordy, filled with repetitious phrases (for instance, *understanding . . . with comprehension* and *class members . . . were students*). All choices except (C) retain some of the original wordiness or are grammatically unacceptable.

11. (D) The pronoun *they* is not used clearly in the original; it is illogical to conclude that *they* refers to *distinguished performances* because all performances are *new to the screen*. (Each performance is done only once even though it may be shown many times.) New *performers* (as opposed to veteran actors) may be new to the screen, however, and the use of *actors* in choice (D) provides this clear, logical reference.

12. (E) The conventions of standard written English dictate that *but also* be preceded by *not only,* which is not the case in the original here. Additionally, the underlined portion illogically compares *appearance* to *other pigs* and relies on a vague, wordy phrase, *with reference to the belief.* Choice (E) remedies all of these problems by simplifying the structure and clarifying the diction. (B) is not a good choice because it employs the past tense. The original is in present tense, and there is no reason to change it because present tense is appropriate when one discusses "timeless" works of art and literature.

13. (B) Two major errors weaken the original. (1) Faulty parallelism— *enjoying the beauty* is not parallel in structure with *clarity* and *brilliance.* (2) Vague wordiness—*and along with it* might suggest that the diamond and the painting are being perceived together, but the more logical meaning is that they are phenomena that are generally similar to one another. (B) is syntactically and logically correct and retains the intended meaning of the original.

14. (D) The use of *would have* and *could have* as the main verbs here does not clearly indicate that buying property twenty years ago is a much earlier action; the verb *had* makes clear the distinction between distant past and recent past. Choice (D) supplies the appropriate verb and eliminates the unnecessary *by.*

15. (C) The original is constructed so that *a train* seems to be *working as an engineer.* Also, the phrase *according to legend* repeats information supplied later in the sentence. Choice (C) is both economical and clearly constructed.

16. (E) *Either* is misplaced in the original so that it does not refer to *voices* as well as *acting.* (E) corrects this error, eliminates the repetitious term *speaking,* and changes *consisted of* to *was* to produce a more economical, parallel structure.

17. (C) The original is not the best choice here because it is not as economical and clear as (C). Each of the other choices is either too wordy, vague, or illogical.

18. (A) The original is perfectly clear and correct, and none of the other choices is an improvement.

19. (D) The introductory phrase is a dangling modifier, making it seem as if the *women* did not gain legislative approval. Only choice (D) both clarifies the relationship between the Equal Rights Amendment and legislative approval and indicates that the failure of the amendment precedes the protests logically and chronologically.

20. (E) The original suggests that she failed the fifth grade possibly because of her father's shaking. (B) is clearer in this respect, but somewhat repetitious with its use of both *recounting* and *remembered*. Choice (E) is the clearest and most economical of the choices. The fact that such an experience would be painful is obvious, and since the experience happened in fifth grade, it is clearly a childhood experience. The sentence is not harmed by the lack of these details.

21. (C) The original contains two errors: *principle* (fundamental truth) is incorrect usage, and *reason . . . was because* is a redundant phrase. Only choice (C) corrects both of these errors and retains the full meaning of the original.

22. (D) In the original sentence, the adjective *quick* is used incorrectly to modify an *action,* signing. Actions are modified by adverbs—in this case, *quickly.* This is the only necessary change.

23. (D) *Continually* is a squinting modifier, unclear because it may refer to either *reading* or *reminds.* Choice (D) clarifies its reference. Choice (E) is vague and wordy.

24. (B) *To question* is not parallel with *remaining;* only (B) corrects this problem.

25. (C) In order to indicate that participation in the debate precedes voter understanding, the verb *had* must replace *would have.* None of the other choices retains the original meaning clearly and fully.

SECTION V: PROBLEM SOLVING

1. **(B)** Since the reduction was approximately 13 percent, the 195 professors are 87 percent of the original number.

$$195 = .87n$$

$$n = \frac{195}{.87} \simeq 224$$

2. **(E)** Since g is negative and f may be negative, it is necessary to square each of the two parameters to be assured of obtaining a positive expression. Note that $(gf)^2 = g^2f^2$.

3. **(D)** The four angles around each point of intersection sum to 360°, a complete revolution. The twelve angles in the figure must sum to 3 × 360° = 1080°. Three of the angles are the interior angles of a triangle, so the nine lettered angles equal 1080° − 180° = 900°. The 42° angle was merely a distraction.

4. **(C)** Let's calculate the rates of production per day. Two of the factories each make 100,000/15 ≃ 6667 hubcaps per day. The third plant makes 1.3 × 6667 ≃ 8667 hubcaps per day. The total production rate is 8667 + 2(6667) = 22,001 hubcaps per day. At that rate it would take 45.5 days to produce a million hubcaps.

5. **(A)** Since the number is divisible by 5, it must end with a 0 or 5. Because the first digit is double the second, the first two digits of the number must be 21, 42, 63, or 84. The only combination that adds to 11 is 425. The product of those digits is 4 × 2 × 5 = 40.

6. **(C)** It is helpful to sketch a map of the positions. You should know that the northeast direction is 45° north of east, bisecting the north and east directions. After two hours the airplanes are at the arrowheads on the map. Since $566 = 400\sqrt{2}$, they are at two corners of a 45° right triangle. At that time, the airplanes are 400 miles apart.

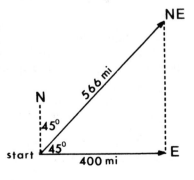

7. (E) Since the five choices all have a numerator of 1, the denominator of the correct choice times $(x - 4)$ will equal $(2x^2 - 10x + 8)$. That denominator may be found by dividing polynomials:

$$
\begin{array}{r}
2x - 2 \qquad \leftarrow \textit{denominator of answer} \\
x - 4\overline{\smash{\big)}\ 2x^2 - 10x + 8} \\
\underline{2x^2 - 8x} \\
- 2x + 8 \\
\underline{- 2x + 8}
\end{array}
$$

8. (C) The radius of the large circle equals the diameter of the small circle, so the radius of the large circle is twice the radius of the small circle. Area is proportional to the square of the radius, so the large circle has an area $2^2 = 4$ times that of the small circle. If the small circle is $\frac{1}{4}$ of the large circle, then the crescent area is $\frac{3}{4}$ of the large circle. The crescent and small circle are in the ratio $(\frac{3}{4})/(\frac{1}{4}) = 3$.

9. (C) The maximum number of dress combinations is $3 \times 3 \times 2 = 18$. However, because the woman won't wear her pink blouse and green skirt with either of the two pairs of shoes, two of the combinations are excluded. She could wear $18 - 2 = 16$ different combinations.

10. (A) You must solve the two simultaneous linear equations for both variables.

$$
\begin{array}{rcl}
3r + s & = & 17 \qquad \text{The first equation} \\
-3r - 6s & = & -27 \qquad \text{The second equation times } -3 \\
\hline
-5s & = & -10 \qquad \text{Adding two equations} \\
s & = & 2 \qquad \text{Solution for s} \\
3r + 2 & = & 17 \qquad \text{Substituting into the first equation} \\
3r & = & 15 \\
r & = & 5 \qquad \text{Solution for r}
\end{array}
$$

So r exceeds s by 3.

11. (D) On the flow chart, molten steel equals $450 + 450 + 1700 = 2600$ and molten iron equals 2000. Thus the ratio of steel to iron is $2600/2000 = 1.3$. The relative weight of steel exceeds the initial blast furnace output of 2000 because some scrap is recycled through the furnaces.

12. (E) The finished shapes have a relative weight of 1900 from four sources: bar and rod mills (800), hot-rolling mill (350), cold-rolling mill

(500), and slab rolling plant (250). Notice that the sole other endpoint for the flow chart is waste scale (100) from the mills. On any flow chart, the initial quantity (2000) equals the sum of the final quantities (1900 + 100).

13. (E) The total weight of scrap is 600, from the slab rolling plant (200), the hot-rolling mill (250), and the cold-rolling mill (150). That scrap feeds the furnaces in these amounts: open-hearth (50), electric-arc (450), and basic oxygen (100). The electric-arc furnaces receive 450/600 = 75 percent of all scrap.

14. (E) The given sequence more than doubles at each step, so it is fundamentally a geometric (multiplicative) sequence rather than an arithmetic (additive) sequence. Each term is two more than double the preceding term. The next number in the sequence would be 2 + 2(94) = 190.

15. (C) The volume of the swimming pool equals its area time its depth. The circular area has a radius of 25 feet.

$$V = \pi r^2 h = 3.14(25)^2(8) = 15,700$$

That volume is closest to choice (C).

16. (B) Since there are 8 pints per gallon, the volume of punch is 60 pints. If we call the amount of orange juice J, then the amount of buttermilk is 2J and the amount of brandy is J/3. All the ingredients add to 60 pints.

$$J + 2J + J/3 = 60$$

$$\frac{3J + 6J + J}{3} = 60$$

$$3J + 6J + J = 180$$

$$10J = 180$$

$$J = 18 \text{ pints of orange juice}$$

17. (B) Substituting for x and y, the expression is

$$(6 - 2(-2))^{-2}$$

$$= (6 + 4)^{-2} = (10)^{-2}$$

$$= \frac{1}{(10)^2} = \frac{1}{100} = 0.01$$

18. **(B)** The third side of the right triangle can be found using the Pythagorean theorem.

$$a^2 + b^2 = c^2$$

$$a^2 + (15)^2 = (17)^2$$

$$a^2 + 225 = 289$$

$$a^2 = 64$$

$$a = 8$$

The perimeter is the sum of the three sides of the triangle.

$$8 + 15 + 17 = 40 \text{ cm}$$

19. **(E)** The ferry can transport the maximum number of cars when they are all the minimum weight, 1800 pounds. Each of those cars weighs $1800/2000 = 0.9$ tons. The number of those automobiles that can be transported by the ferry is its capacity divided by the weight of one car: $78/0.9 = 86.67$ automobiles.

20. **(D)** Exponential quantities can be readily divided (or multiplied) if they have the same base. To convert m from base-8 to base-2, consider that $8 = 2^3$. Therefore, $m = 8^5 = (2^3)^5 = 2^{15}$.

$$\frac{m}{n} = \frac{2^{15}}{2^{12}} = 2^3 = 8$$

If two exponential quantities have the same base, they may be divided by subtracting the exponent of the denominator from the exponent of the numerator.

SECTION VI: PROBLEM SOLVING

1. (A) Start at the lower right, add the whole number 2 with the fraction. Change to an improper fraction, invert, and continue.

2. (C) If 5 machines can produce 20 units in 10 hours, then 20 machines can produce 80 units in 10 hours. Since 100 is 25% more than 80, the correct answer is 25% more than 10, or 12.5 hours.

3. (A) Set up two equations.

$$5A + 2B = 6B + 5C \qquad 1A + 4C = 2A + 4B$$
$$5A = 4B + 5C \qquad\quad 4C = A + 4B$$
$$4C - A = 4B$$

Substitute $4C - A$ for $4B$ in the other equation.

$$5A = 4C - A + 5C$$
$$6A = 9C$$
$$A = (9/6)C$$
$$= (3/2)C$$

4. (C) The six faces of the cube each have an area of $10 \times 10 = 100$ square feet. That is a total of 600 square feet. Since it takes one quart for each 20 square feet, you need 30 quarts. Take $30 \times \$3.20 = \$96.00$

5. (C) If x represents the cost of the book, then we have the following equation:

$$x + .20x = \$12.00$$
$$1.2x = \$12.00$$
$$x = \$10.00$$

6. (A) We solve for y as follows:

$$x = \frac{1 + y}{y}$$
$$xy = 1 + y$$
$$xy - y = 1$$
$$y(x - 1) = 1$$
$$y = \frac{1}{x - 1}$$

7. (C) Since more time was spent traveling at 40 mph, the average will be closer to 40 than to 50.

8. (C) Since machine A worked for 2 hours and could do the entire job in 8 hours, machine A must have done $\frac{1}{4}$ of the job. We have the following formula in which the value of x represents the time actually worked.

$$\overset{A}{2/8} + \overset{B}{x/10} + \overset{C}{x/12} = 1$$

$$x/10 + x/12 = 3/4$$
$$6x + 5x = 45$$
$$11x = 45$$
$$x = 4\frac{1}{11}$$

9:00 A.M. + $4\frac{1}{11}$ hours $\simeq$ 1:00 P.M.

9. (B) There are 140 line employees with 3 to 5 years of employment. There are 80 of them taking the First Aid workshop. Thus, $140 - 80 = 60$.

10. (B) For the line employees, since 10 are taking both, there are 30 who are taking only the Stress workshop, and 20 who are taking only the First Aid workshop. For the staff employees, since 15 are taking both workshops, there are 15 taking only the Stress workshop and 5 taking only the First Aid workshop. Thus, 30 plus 20 plus 15 plus 5 equals 70.

11. (B) For the line employees, there are 30 taking both workshops, 20 taking only the Stress workshop, and 10 taking only the First Aid workshop. For the staff employees, there are 20 taking both, 20 taking only the Stress workshop, and 30 taking only the First Aid workshop. Thus, 130 are taking at least one workshop. Therefore 230 out of 360 are not taking a workshop, or 64%.

12. (A) The shaded area is the difference between the entire rectangle (with an area of $6 \times 8 = 48$) and the white triangle (with an area of $(6 \times x)/2 = 3x$). Thus, $48 - 3x$.

13. (E) First find the area of the shaded region. The difference of the outer rectangle ($6 \times 12 = 72$) and the inner rectangle ($2 \times 3 = 6$) is 66 square feet. Since it takes 24 2-inch by 3-inch tiles to cover one square foot, the correct answer is $24 \times 66 = 1584$.

14. (C) If the radius of a circle is 1 and it is reduced by 20%, it becomes .8. Since the area formula squares the radius, the original factor remains 1, but the new factor becomes .64 which is a 36% decrease.

15. (C) Looking at the water, we have 2/3 of 2 quarts = 4/3 quarts, and 3/8 of 3 quarts = 9/8 quarts. These add together to give 2 11/24 which is very close to 50% of 5 quarts.

16. (D) There were 4 days where the maximum temperature exceeded the average, thus 4/7 is approximately 57%.

17. (C) The increase was 94 − 84 = 10. The percent increase is found by dividing the increase by the *original* or *from* amount. Thus 10/84 = 11.9%

18. (C) We can tabulate the data:

	part of tank brand Z	part of tank brand Y
after first fill up	1	0
before second fill up	½	0
after second fill up	½	½
before third fill up	¼	¼
after third fill up	¾	¼
before fourth fill up	⅜	⅛
after fourth fill up	⅜	⅝

Since the tank is now full, ⅜, or 37.5% is brand Z.

19. (E) Any number of members is possible as long as the number of dollars per member is two more than the number of members.

20. (A) From the relationship that exists in a right triangle, we see that the sides of the square must equal the square root of 5. Thus the area of the square is 5.

SECTION VII: SENTENCE CORRECTION

1. (D) The verbs are the problem in the original underlined portion. The context supplied by the rest of the sentence suggests that the verbs should be simple past tense, both of them indicating what *was* true *in* the fourteenth century. As it stands, the underlined portion is internally contradictory. It states that Europe *had been* Catholic, implying that the region is no longer Catholic, but also states that Catholic influence *continued*. Choice (D) corrects this grammatical/logical problem while retaining the original intended meaning. Choices (B) and (E) are grammatically correct but omit information contained in the original sentence.

2. (E) Both *group* and *meeting* are singular, so the singular pronoun *its* and the singular verb *addresses* must be used. The agreement is correct in choice (D), but *with that area in mind* is needlessly wordy.

3. (A) Although choice (A) is perhaps not the best choice one can imagine, it is decidedly the best choice of the five offered here. *"Buntline Special"* should be placed as close to *gun* as possible. In choice (B), the opening phrase modifies *toy stores,* not *gun,* and the phrase *the 1950s* now modifies the *television series* instead of *sold.* Choice (C) also misplaces the phrase *in the 1950s.* Choices (D) and (E) are sentence fragments.

4. (A) The original underlined portion is the most clear and correct choice, resulting in a balanced sentence, with the structure of the second half (that is, the underlined portion) parallel to the structure of the first half: *the more* . . . subject . . . active verb. Choices (B), (C), and (D) omit *the more.* In choice (E), the verb is passive.

5. (C) The original version is confusing because the clause *which had become tarnished* is awkwardly separated from *dream* and the prepositional phrase *through hard work* is awkwardly separated from the verb it modifies, *earn.* In choices (B), (D), and (E), the prepositional phrase is misplaced.

6. (E) This is the most direct, clear, and economical choice that retains the essential meaning of the original underlined portion. Compared to choice (E), both (A) and (B) are wordy. Choice (C) is a sentence fragment, and (D) distorts the meaning.

7. (A) The original underlined portion is the best choice. Choice (B) is wordy, (C) introduces an agreement error, (D) introduces a comma error, and (E), by omitting the *while,* changes the meaning.

8. (C) The best choice here arranges the parts of the sentence in the most direct and clear way by keeping the modifiers as close as possible to the words they modify. In addition, choice (C) replaces *when* with a more appropriate and logical term, *after*.

9. (E) The underlined portion must name Ahab immediately in order to clarify the comparison between Ahab and Macbeth. It is Ahab, *not* the *harpooner,* choices (A) or (C), not the *prophecies,* choice (B), who is *much like Macbeth.* Choice (D) has the right structure but has an agreement error in *prophecy* and *their.*

10. (A) None of the alternate choices is more direct and clear than the original underlined portion. Since it is the *decrease* that has encouraged some economists, not the *rate,* choices (B), (C), (D), and (E) all change the meaning of the sentence.

11. (B) Choice (B) is grammatically correct and economical. In choice (C), *herd* introduces a meaning not in the original, while choice (E) omits details. Choices (A) and (D) are sentence fragments.

12. (B) Choice (B) is the most economical and clear version of the original. Choices (A) and (C) are wordy, containing the unnecessary phrases *when one* and *if one.* Choices (D) and (E) omit the notion of stressing and so change the meaning.

13. (B) The original underlined portion presents an illogical comparison, of *areas* to the topic of the first part of the sentence, *air.* Only choice (B) clarifies the air to air comparison, without the inappropriate wordiness of choice (E).

14. (A) The original underlined portion is the best choice. It maintains parallel structure with *to provide.* Each of the other choices makes unnecessary changes in grammar and syntax that do not improve the original.

15. (D) In the original underlined portion, *those* is incorrect. To express respectively two singular points of view, the noun or pronoun which refers to each must be singular; *those* is, of course, plural. Only choice (D) provides a clearly singular reference, *one,* for each viewpoint.

16. (E) The introductory phrase in the original (preceding the comma) properly modifies warheads. Only choice (E) makes this necessary change while retaining the intended meaning of the original.

17. **(A)** The original underlined portion is the best choice. *Whom* is used correctly, as the object of *suspected*. Each of the other choices omits or changes this correct pronoun unnecessarily or changes the meaning of the original.

18. **(D)** *Irregardless* is nonstandard usage. Apart from this error, the original underlined portion is correct and clear. To make sense, choice (C) would require the preposition *of*. Choice (E) contains an agreement error.

19. **(C)** The original underlined portion contains a verb tense error. *Extends* (A) and *has lasted* (E) are inconsistent with the past tense established through the rest of the sentence. Choice (C) supplies the simple past tense, *extended,* that agrees with the other verbs in the sentence. Choices (B) and (D), while grammatically correct, substitute the vaguer *long* for the phrase *for years*.

20. **(A)** It is an expanse, empty of gods, not an empty expanse of gods—choices (B) and (D). Choice (E) is needlessly wordy and (C) distorts the meaning.

21. **(D)** There are several errors in the original version that must be corrected: the preposition *in* for *from*, the adjective *effective* for *effecting*, and the preposition *among* for *between*.

22. **(C)** *Fewer readers* is more economical than choice (A). *Less* in choice (B) is incorrect when the noun (*readers*) can be numbered (for example: fewer gallons, less gasoline; fewer dollars, less money). Since the pronoun refers to the book, not to the author, *it,* not *he,* is correct. Choice (E) incorrectly uses the plural *attract*—*Gulliver's Travels* is the name of a book and is singular.

23. **(E)** *Caused* is better than the wordy and pretentious phrase *was causative of* in choices (A), (C), and (D). Choice (B) omits two adjectives and unnecessarily changes the tense in *causes*.

24. **(D)** The original underlined sentence as well as choices (B) and (C) are unnecessarily wordy. Choice (D) is an efficient, direct, and clear expression that retains the meaning of the original. Choice (E) leaves out essential information from the original.

25. **(B)** Though choice (B) requires more words, it is the only version that avoids the ambiguous pronouns—*which* in choices (A) and (C) and *that* in choices (D) and (E)—which seem at first to refer to *rectangle*.

PRACTICE TEST 3

Section I: Critical Reasoning—30 Minutes; 25 Questions
Section II: Problem Solving—30 Minutes; 20 Questions
Section III: Data Sufficiency—30 Minutes; 25 Questions
Section IV: Sentence Correction—30 Minutes; 25 Questions
Section V: Problem Solving—30 Minutes; 20 Questions
Section VI: Reading Comprehension—30 Minutes; 25 Questions
Section VII: Problem Solving—30 Minutes; 20 Questions

ANSWER SHEET FOR PRACTICE TEST 3
(Remove This Sheet and Use It to Mark Your Answers)

SECTION I   SECTION II   SECTION III

SECTION I	SECTION II	SECTION III
1 Ⓐ Ⓑ Ⓒ Ⓓ Ⓔ	1 Ⓐ Ⓑ Ⓒ Ⓓ Ⓔ	1 Ⓐ Ⓑ Ⓒ Ⓓ Ⓔ
2 Ⓐ Ⓑ Ⓒ Ⓓ Ⓔ	2 Ⓐ Ⓑ Ⓒ Ⓓ Ⓔ	2 Ⓐ Ⓑ Ⓒ Ⓓ Ⓔ
3 Ⓐ Ⓑ Ⓒ Ⓓ Ⓔ	3 Ⓐ Ⓑ Ⓒ Ⓓ Ⓔ	3 Ⓐ Ⓑ Ⓒ Ⓓ Ⓔ
4 Ⓐ Ⓑ Ⓒ Ⓓ Ⓔ	4 Ⓐ Ⓑ Ⓒ Ⓓ Ⓔ	4 Ⓐ Ⓑ Ⓒ Ⓓ Ⓔ
5 Ⓐ Ⓑ Ⓒ Ⓓ Ⓔ	5 Ⓐ Ⓑ Ⓒ Ⓓ Ⓔ	5 Ⓐ Ⓑ Ⓒ Ⓓ Ⓔ
6 Ⓐ Ⓑ Ⓒ Ⓓ Ⓔ	6 Ⓐ Ⓑ Ⓒ Ⓓ Ⓔ	6 Ⓐ Ⓑ Ⓒ Ⓓ Ⓔ
7 Ⓐ Ⓑ Ⓒ Ⓓ Ⓔ	7 Ⓐ Ⓑ Ⓒ Ⓓ Ⓔ	7 Ⓐ Ⓑ Ⓒ Ⓓ Ⓔ
8 Ⓐ Ⓑ Ⓒ Ⓓ Ⓔ	8 Ⓐ Ⓑ Ⓒ Ⓓ Ⓔ	8 Ⓐ Ⓑ Ⓒ Ⓓ Ⓔ
9 Ⓐ Ⓑ Ⓒ Ⓓ Ⓔ	9 Ⓐ Ⓑ Ⓒ Ⓓ Ⓔ	9 Ⓐ Ⓑ Ⓒ Ⓓ Ⓔ
10 Ⓐ Ⓑ Ⓒ Ⓓ Ⓔ	10 Ⓐ Ⓑ Ⓒ Ⓓ Ⓔ	10 Ⓐ Ⓑ Ⓒ Ⓓ Ⓔ
11 Ⓐ Ⓑ Ⓒ Ⓓ Ⓔ	11 Ⓐ Ⓑ Ⓒ Ⓓ Ⓔ	11 Ⓐ Ⓑ Ⓒ Ⓓ Ⓔ
12 Ⓐ Ⓑ Ⓒ Ⓓ Ⓔ	12 Ⓐ Ⓑ Ⓒ Ⓓ Ⓔ	12 Ⓐ Ⓑ Ⓒ Ⓓ Ⓔ
13 Ⓐ Ⓑ Ⓒ Ⓓ Ⓔ	13 Ⓐ Ⓑ Ⓒ Ⓓ Ⓔ	13 Ⓐ Ⓑ Ⓒ Ⓓ Ⓔ
14 Ⓐ Ⓑ Ⓒ Ⓓ Ⓔ	14 Ⓐ Ⓑ Ⓒ Ⓓ Ⓔ	14 Ⓐ Ⓑ Ⓒ Ⓓ Ⓔ
15 Ⓐ Ⓑ Ⓒ Ⓓ Ⓔ	15 Ⓐ Ⓑ Ⓒ Ⓓ Ⓔ	15 Ⓐ Ⓑ Ⓒ Ⓓ Ⓔ
16 Ⓐ Ⓑ Ⓒ Ⓓ Ⓔ	16 Ⓐ Ⓑ Ⓒ Ⓓ Ⓔ	16 Ⓐ Ⓑ Ⓒ Ⓓ Ⓔ
17 Ⓐ Ⓑ Ⓒ Ⓓ Ⓔ	17 Ⓐ Ⓑ Ⓒ Ⓓ Ⓔ	17 Ⓐ Ⓑ Ⓒ Ⓓ Ⓔ
18 Ⓐ Ⓑ Ⓒ Ⓓ Ⓔ	18 Ⓐ Ⓑ Ⓒ Ⓓ Ⓔ	18 Ⓐ Ⓑ Ⓒ Ⓓ Ⓔ
19 Ⓐ Ⓑ Ⓒ Ⓓ Ⓔ	19 Ⓐ Ⓑ Ⓒ Ⓓ Ⓔ	19 Ⓐ Ⓑ Ⓒ Ⓓ Ⓔ
20 Ⓐ Ⓑ Ⓒ Ⓓ Ⓔ	20 Ⓐ Ⓑ Ⓒ Ⓓ Ⓔ	20 Ⓐ Ⓑ Ⓒ Ⓓ Ⓔ
21 Ⓐ Ⓑ Ⓒ Ⓓ Ⓔ		21 Ⓐ Ⓑ Ⓒ Ⓓ Ⓔ
22 Ⓐ Ⓑ Ⓒ Ⓓ Ⓔ		22 Ⓐ Ⓑ Ⓒ Ⓓ Ⓔ
23 Ⓐ Ⓑ Ⓒ Ⓓ Ⓔ		23 Ⓐ Ⓑ Ⓒ Ⓓ Ⓔ
24 Ⓐ Ⓑ Ⓒ Ⓓ Ⓔ		24 Ⓐ Ⓑ Ⓒ Ⓓ Ⓔ
25 Ⓐ Ⓑ Ⓒ Ⓓ Ⓔ		25 Ⓐ Ⓑ Ⓒ Ⓓ Ⓔ

ANSWER SHEET FOR PRACTICE TEST 3
(Remove This Sheet and Use It to Mark Your Answers)

SECTION IV

1 Ⓐ Ⓑ Ⓒ Ⓓ Ⓔ
2 Ⓐ Ⓑ Ⓒ Ⓓ Ⓔ
3 Ⓐ Ⓑ Ⓒ Ⓓ Ⓔ
4 Ⓐ Ⓑ Ⓒ Ⓓ Ⓔ
5 Ⓐ Ⓑ Ⓒ Ⓓ Ⓔ
6 Ⓐ Ⓑ Ⓒ Ⓓ Ⓔ
7 Ⓐ Ⓑ Ⓒ Ⓓ Ⓔ
8 Ⓐ Ⓑ Ⓒ Ⓓ Ⓔ
9 Ⓐ Ⓑ Ⓒ Ⓓ Ⓔ
10 Ⓐ Ⓑ Ⓒ Ⓓ Ⓔ
11 Ⓐ Ⓑ Ⓒ Ⓓ Ⓔ
12 Ⓐ Ⓑ Ⓒ Ⓓ Ⓔ
13 Ⓐ Ⓑ Ⓒ Ⓓ Ⓔ
14 Ⓐ Ⓑ Ⓒ Ⓓ Ⓔ
15 Ⓐ Ⓑ Ⓒ Ⓓ Ⓔ
16 Ⓐ Ⓑ Ⓒ Ⓓ Ⓔ
17 Ⓐ Ⓑ Ⓒ Ⓓ Ⓔ
18 Ⓐ Ⓑ Ⓒ Ⓓ Ⓔ
19 Ⓐ Ⓑ Ⓒ Ⓓ Ⓔ
20 Ⓐ Ⓑ Ⓒ Ⓓ Ⓔ
21 Ⓐ Ⓑ Ⓒ Ⓓ Ⓔ
22 Ⓐ Ⓑ Ⓒ Ⓓ Ⓔ
23 Ⓐ Ⓑ Ⓒ Ⓓ Ⓔ
24 Ⓐ Ⓑ Ⓒ Ⓓ Ⓔ
25 Ⓐ Ⓑ Ⓒ Ⓓ Ⓔ

SECTION V

1 Ⓐ Ⓑ Ⓒ Ⓓ Ⓔ
2 Ⓐ Ⓑ Ⓒ Ⓓ Ⓔ
3 Ⓐ Ⓑ Ⓒ Ⓓ Ⓔ
4 Ⓐ Ⓑ Ⓒ Ⓓ Ⓔ
5 Ⓐ Ⓑ Ⓒ Ⓓ Ⓔ
6 Ⓐ Ⓑ Ⓒ Ⓓ Ⓔ
7 Ⓐ Ⓑ Ⓒ Ⓓ Ⓔ
8 Ⓐ Ⓑ Ⓒ Ⓓ Ⓔ
9 Ⓐ Ⓑ Ⓒ Ⓓ Ⓔ
10 Ⓐ Ⓑ Ⓒ Ⓓ Ⓔ
11 Ⓐ Ⓑ Ⓒ Ⓓ Ⓔ
12 Ⓐ Ⓑ Ⓒ Ⓓ Ⓔ
13 Ⓐ Ⓑ Ⓒ Ⓓ Ⓔ
14 Ⓐ Ⓑ Ⓒ Ⓓ Ⓔ
15 Ⓐ Ⓑ Ⓒ Ⓓ Ⓔ
16 Ⓐ Ⓑ Ⓒ Ⓓ Ⓔ
17 Ⓐ Ⓑ Ⓒ Ⓓ Ⓔ
18 Ⓐ Ⓑ Ⓒ Ⓓ Ⓔ
19 Ⓐ Ⓑ Ⓒ Ⓓ Ⓔ
20 Ⓐ Ⓑ Ⓒ Ⓓ Ⓔ

SECTION VI

1 Ⓐ Ⓑ Ⓒ Ⓓ Ⓔ
2 Ⓐ Ⓑ Ⓒ Ⓓ Ⓔ
3 Ⓐ Ⓑ Ⓒ Ⓓ Ⓔ
4 Ⓐ Ⓑ Ⓒ Ⓓ Ⓔ
5 Ⓐ Ⓑ Ⓒ Ⓓ Ⓔ
6 Ⓐ Ⓑ Ⓒ Ⓓ Ⓔ
7 Ⓐ Ⓑ Ⓒ Ⓓ Ⓔ
8 Ⓐ Ⓑ Ⓒ Ⓓ Ⓔ
9 Ⓐ Ⓑ Ⓒ Ⓓ Ⓔ
10 Ⓐ Ⓑ Ⓒ Ⓓ Ⓔ
11 Ⓐ Ⓑ Ⓒ Ⓓ Ⓔ
12 Ⓐ Ⓑ Ⓒ Ⓓ Ⓔ
13 Ⓐ Ⓑ Ⓒ Ⓓ Ⓔ
14 Ⓐ Ⓑ Ⓒ Ⓓ Ⓔ
15 Ⓐ Ⓑ Ⓒ Ⓓ Ⓔ
16 Ⓐ Ⓑ Ⓒ Ⓓ Ⓔ
17 Ⓐ Ⓑ Ⓒ Ⓓ Ⓔ
18 Ⓐ Ⓑ Ⓒ Ⓓ Ⓔ
19 Ⓐ Ⓑ Ⓒ Ⓓ Ⓔ
20 Ⓐ Ⓑ Ⓒ Ⓓ Ⓔ
21 Ⓐ Ⓑ Ⓒ Ⓓ Ⓔ
22 Ⓐ Ⓑ Ⓒ Ⓓ Ⓔ
23 Ⓐ Ⓑ Ⓒ Ⓓ Ⓔ
24 Ⓐ Ⓑ Ⓒ Ⓓ Ⓔ
25 Ⓐ Ⓑ Ⓒ Ⓓ Ⓔ

SECTION VII

1 Ⓐ Ⓑ Ⓒ Ⓓ Ⓔ
2 Ⓐ Ⓑ Ⓒ Ⓓ Ⓔ
3 Ⓐ Ⓑ Ⓒ Ⓓ Ⓔ
4 Ⓐ Ⓑ Ⓒ Ⓓ Ⓔ
5 Ⓐ Ⓑ Ⓒ Ⓓ Ⓔ
6 Ⓐ Ⓑ Ⓒ Ⓓ Ⓔ
7 Ⓐ Ⓑ Ⓒ Ⓓ Ⓔ
8 Ⓐ Ⓑ Ⓒ Ⓓ Ⓔ
9 Ⓐ Ⓑ Ⓒ Ⓓ Ⓔ
10 Ⓐ Ⓑ Ⓒ Ⓓ Ⓔ
11 Ⓐ Ⓑ Ⓒ Ⓓ Ⓔ
12 Ⓐ Ⓑ Ⓒ Ⓓ Ⓔ
13 Ⓐ Ⓑ Ⓒ Ⓓ Ⓔ
14 Ⓐ Ⓑ Ⓒ Ⓓ Ⓔ
15 Ⓐ Ⓑ Ⓒ Ⓓ Ⓔ
16 Ⓐ Ⓑ Ⓒ Ⓓ Ⓔ
17 Ⓐ Ⓑ Ⓒ Ⓓ Ⓔ
18 Ⓐ Ⓑ Ⓒ Ⓓ Ⓔ
19 Ⓐ Ⓑ Ⓒ Ⓓ Ⓔ
20 Ⓐ Ⓑ Ⓒ Ⓓ Ⓔ

SECTION I: CRITICAL REASONING

Time: 30 Minutes
25 Questions

DIRECTIONS

You will be presented with brief passages or statements and will be required to evaluate their reasoning. In each case, select the best answer choice, even though more than one choice may present a possible answer. Choices which are unreasonable or incompatible with common-sense standards should be eliminated.

Aristotle said that art represents "general truths" about human nature. Our city councilman is arguing in favor of the artistry—a giant mural in front of a Jeep dealership, portraying a variety of four-wheel-drive vehicles. He cites Aristotle's conception of art as his support.

1. The passage above raises which of the following questions?
   (A) Can a city councilman understand Aristotle?
   (B) Which general truths about human nature does a four-wheel-drive mural *not* represent?
   (C) Could Aristotle have predicted a modern society filled with sophisticated machines?
   (D) To what extent are four-wheel-drive vehicles representative of a general advance in modern technology?
   (E) What "general truth" about human nature does a mural of four-wheel-drive vehicles represent?

2. *Speaker 1:* The holy passion of friendship is of so sweet and steady and loyal and enduring a nature that it will last through a whole lifetime.
   Speaker 2: If not asked to lend money.

   The two speakers represent which of the following contrasting attitudes?
   (A) faith and despair
   (B) idealism and cynicism
   (C) idealism and optimism
   (D) socialism and capitalism
   (E) friendship and enmity

In 1933, a new industrial code was established to fix a minimum wage of 40 cents an hour in the United States.

3. The above statement suggests which of the following maxims, or proverbs?
   (A) You can fool some of the people some of the time.
   (B) Don't count your chickens before they hatch.
   (C) Times change.
   (D) There's a sucker born every minute.
   (E) Power to the people.

Unfortunately, only 11 percent of the driving public uses regular seat belts. Automatic restraints are the answer, and the quicker they are required, the sooner highways deaths will be reduced.

4. The author's conclusion is based upon which of the following assumptions?
   (A) Only 11 percent of the driving public cares about passengers' lives.
   (B) The use of restraints reduces highway deaths.
   (C) Regular seat belts are inadequate safety devices.
   (D) It is unfortunate that 89 percent of the driving public does not use regular seat belts.
   (E) Highway deaths occur often enough so that reducing them is a necessity.

Questions 5 and 6 refer to the following passage

The heart and soul of our business is credibility. We get that credibility and respect, and the power that goes with it, only by being a socially and professionally responsible agent for the public. In some ways we journalists have to have the same attitude to news as an employee of a bank has to money—it isn't ours. We're handling it on behalf of other people, so it cannot be converted to our own use. If we do, it's embezzlement.

5. Which of the following criticisms would most weaken the comparison between journalists and bank employees?
   (A) Different newspapers print different news, just as different banks hold assets from various sources.
   (B) Journalists are necessarily more creative individuals than bank employees.
   (C) The heart and soul of the banking business is money, not credibility.
   (D) A bank teller need not be credible, just responsible.
   (E) Embezzlement is properly a crime against the bank, not against the depositors.

6. The first sentence makes a point with which the following techniques?
   (A) metaphor
   (B) sarcasm
   (C) parody
   (D) overstatement
   (E) statistical support

The value of a close examination of the circumstances of an aircraft accident lies not only in fixing blame but in learning lessons.

7. The above statement fits most logically into which of the following types of passages?
   (A) a survey of the "scapegoat phenomenon" in modern society
   (B) an argument in favor of including specific details in any academic essay
   (C) an argument against the usefulness of the National Transportation Safety Board
   (D) a brief history of aeronautics
   (E) a description of the causes of a particular aircraft accident

Consumers are not so easily manipulated as they are often painted. They may know what they want, and what they want may be greatly different from what other people believe they need.

8. Which of the following statements, if true, most weakens the above argument?
   (A) Most people continue to buy the same brand of a product year after year.
   (B) Companies that advertise the most sell the most products.
   (C) Store shelves packed with a variety of different brands have the potential to confuse the consumer.
   (D) Most consumers know which brand they are going to buy before entering a store.
   (E) People who shop with others rarely argue with their companions.

Questions 9 and 10 refer to the following passage

The last census showed a sharp rise during the 1970s in the number of Americans living together as unmarried couples, but a more recent increase in the marriage rate in 1981 suggests that matrimony will make a comeback in the 1980s.

9. Which of the following best refutes the argument above?
   (A) One of the causes of more marriages is that the large population resulting from a baby boom is just now reaching marriageable age.
   (B) Although information about the 1981 marriage rate is not complete, most analysts consider it to be reliable.
   (C) Many of those marrying in 1981 were couples who had lived together during the 1970s.
   (D) The number of Americans living together did not rise at a consistent rate during the 1970s.
   (E) The marriage rate increased dramatically in 1971 and fell even more dramatically in following years.

10. With which of the following would the author be likely to agree?
    (A) Americans should not live together as unmarried couples.
    (B) Matrimony is preferable to living together.
    (C) Economic circumstances have made matrimony attractive as a way of paying less income tax.
    (D) The attitudes of young people in the 1980s are altogether different from the attitudes of young people in the 1970s.
    (E) Prevailing attitudes toward marriage tend to persist for more than one year.

The shortsightedness of our government and our scientists has virtually nullified all of their great discoveries because of their failure to consider the environmental impact. The situation is far from hopeless, but our government agencies must become better watchdogs.

11. This argument fails to place any blame on

    I. consumers who prefer new technology to clean air
    II. the ability of government to actually police industry
    III. legal loopholes which allow industry abuse of government regulations

    (A) I only
    (B) II only
    (C) III only
    (D) I, II, and III
    (E) I and III

Voltaire once said, "Common sense is not so common."

12. Which of the following most nearly parallels Voltaire's statement?
    (A) God must have loved the common man; he certainly made enough of them.
    (B) The common good is not necessarily best for everyone.
    (C) Jumbo shrimp may not actually be very big.
    (D) Good people may not necessarily have good sense.
    (E) Truth serum cannot contain the truth.

Questions 13 and 14 refer to the following passage

The department store owned by my competitor sells green necklaces that glow in the dark. Only those customers of mine wearing those necklaces must be giving business to the competition.

13. The conclusion could best be strengthened by
    (A) deleting *that glow in the dark*
    (B) changing *sells* to *has sold*
    (C) changing *the competition* to *my competitor*
    (D) inserting *only* as the first word in sentence one
    (E) changing *wearing* to *owning*

14. The author foolishly assumes that
    (A) the customers might find the necklaces attractive
    (B) customers are not buying other products from the competition
    (C) customers will wear the necklaces in daylight
    (D) a department store should not sell necklaces
    (E) the competition is outselling the author

15. Which of the following most logically completes the passage at the blank below?

    Several of the survivors discussed their dilemma. They could remain on the island and attempt to survive as best they knew how. Or they could attempt to escape, using the resources available to them. None of the group wished to venture away from their uncertain sanctuary, but all of them knew that help would be a long time coming. Their discussions were thus _____ .

    (A) futile, arbitrary, and capricious
    (B) limited by their imagination and resolve
    (C) dampened by a sense of impending doom
    (D) possible, but by no means successful
    (E) courageous and honorable

Questions 16 and 17 refer to the following letter

To the Chairman:

    At the October 7th meeting it was decided that no two officers would hold positions on the same committee. It has recently come to my attention that both Charles S. Smith and Arnold Krunkle will be serving in some capacity on the Building and Maintenance Committee, and both have been nominated for officer status. As you know, this is in direct disregard for the rules as voted by the membership last October 7th. I would hope that sufficient action be taken by the Disciplinary Committee (on which committee both of the above are members) so that this problem will be remedied.

Sincerely,
Irving H. Fortnash

16. Which of the following is the essential flaw that the writer of the letter fails to notice?
    (A) Smith and Krunkle are already serving together on the Disciplinary Committee.
    (B) The Chairman has no power in the matter.
    (C) The membership cannot pass rules limiting members.
    (D) Smith and Krunkle are not yet officers.
    (E) Building and Maintenance is actually two committees.

17. Which of the following most completely and reasonably describes actions that may occur in the near future?
    (A) Fortnash resigns his membership.
    (B) Either Smith or Krunkle resigns his membership.
    (C) Krunkle resigns his committee post on the Building and Maintenance Committee.
    (D) Smith resigns his position on the Building and Maintenance Committee.
    (E) One of the two (Smith or Krunkle) resigns his position on the Building and Maintenance Committee, and the other resigns his position on the Disciplinary Committee.

Flamo Lighters when you need them! Always reliable, always dependable. In all weather, with ten-year guarantee. Don't get caught without a light—keep a Flamo in your pocket wherever you go!

18. All of the following are claims made or implied by Flamo Lighters *except*
    (A) convenience
    (B) dependability
    (C) longevity
    (D) winter-proof
    (E) all-purpose

Questions 19 through 21 refer to the following statements

(A) The skating team of Roscoe and Nordoff is obviously the best. They are more graceful and more pleasing to the eye than any of the other skaters.
(B) Newspaper reporters have a commitment to report only the truth. Since only the truth may be printed, reporters must seek it out.
(C) And who can argue that winning the war against poverty isn't foremost? It is the terrible affliction of our time.
(D) All records of births, deaths, and marriages are doubtful, since all these records are open to question.
(E) The quality of American goods far surpasses any of the imports; after all, we pay far less money for Japanese televisions.

19. Which statement supports its conclusion by using a subjective basis of comparison?

20. Which statement uses a probable irrelevancy to support its point?

21. Which statement supports itself by redundancy?

All race-car lovers enjoy classical music.
No backgammon players enjoy classical music.
All those who enjoy classical music also enjoy fine wine.

22. If each of the above statements is true, which of the following must also be true?
   (A) Everyone who plays backgammon enjoys fine wine.
   (B) No one who enjoys fine wine plays backgammon.
   (C) No backgammon players are race-car lovers.
   (D) No backgammon players enjoy fine wine.
   (E) No race-car lover enjoys fine wine.

Questions 23 though 25 refer to the following passage

   It has been proven that the "lie detector" can be fooled. If one is truly unaware that one is lying, when in fact one is, then the "lie detector" is worthless.

23. The author of this argument implies that
   (A) the lie detector is a useless device
   (B) a good liar can fool the device
   (C) a lie detector is often inaccurate
   (D) the lie detector is sometimes worthless
   (E) no one can fool the lie detector all of the time

24. This argument would be strenthened most by
   (A) demonstrating that one's awareness of truth or falsity is always undetectable
   (B) showing that the "truth" of any statement always relies on a subjective assessment
   (C) citing evidence that there are other means of measuring truth which are consistently less reliable than the lie detector
   (D) citing the number of cases in which the lie detector mistook falsehood for truth
   (E) claiming that ordinary, unbiased people are the best "lie detectors"

25. Without contradicting his or her own statements, the author might present which of the following arguments as a strong point in favor of the lie detector?
    (A) The methodology used by investigative critics of the lie detector is itself highly flawed.
    (B) Law-enforcement agencies have purchased too many detectors to abandon them now.
    (C) Circumstantial evidence might be more useful in a criminal case than is personal testimony.
    (D) The very threat of a lie-detector test has led a significant number of criminals to confess.
    (E) People are never "truly aware" that they are lying.

STOP. IF YOU FINISH BEFORE TIME IS CALLED. CHECK YOUR WORK ON THIS SECTION ONLY. DO NOT WORK ON ANY OTHER SECTION IN THE TEST.

SECTION II: PROBLEM SOLVING

Time: 30 Minutes
20 Questions

DIRECTIONS

In this section solve each problem, using any available space on the page for scratchwork. Then indicate the *best* answer in the appropriate space on the answer sheet.

1. ¼ of ⅗ is what percent of ¾?
   (A) 15%   (B) 20%   (C) 33⅓%   (D) 75%   (E) 80%

2. A $75 lawn chair was sold for $60 at a special sale. By what percent was the price decreased?
   (A) 15%   (B) 20%   (C) 25%   (D) 60%   (E) 80%

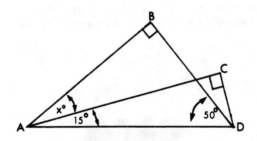

3. In the figure above, x =
   (A) 15   (B) 25   (C) 35   (D) 45   (E) 55

4. Acme Taxi lists the following rates on its door:

   $1.20 for first 1/6 mile
   $ .90 for each additional 1/6 mile
   $9.00 per hour for waiting time

   At these rates, a 3-mile taxi trip, including a 15-minute wait at the bank, will cost
   (A) $15.95   (D) $18.45
   (B) $16.50   (E) $18.75
   (C) $17.55

5. The average of four numbers is x. If the average of the first three numbers is e, what is the value of the fourth number?

(A) 3x − 4e   (D) (x + e)/4
(B) 3e − 4x   (E) 4x − 3e
(C) 4x − e

6. At an elementary school, 70% of the faculty members are women and 60% of the faculty members are married. If ⅔ of the men are single, what fraction of the women are married?

(A) ⁵⁄₇   (D) ⁷⁄₃₀
(B) ⁷⁄₁₀   (E) cannot be determined
(C) ⅓

7. The length of a rectangle is decreased by 15% and its width is increased by 40%. Does the area of the rectangle decrease or increase and by what percent?

(A) decreases by 19%   (D) increases by 19%
(B) decreases by 25%   (E) increases by 25%
(C) increases by 6%

8. In the figure above, the centers of 4 equal circles lie along the diameter of the large circle. If the circumference of the large circle is 64π, what is the area of the shaded region?

(A) 16π (B) 32π (C) 64π (D) 128π (E) 256π

9. If x is a positive even number, then each of the following is odd except

(A) (x + 3)(x + 5)   (D) $3x^2 + 4$
(B) $x^2 + 5$ (E) 5(x + 3)
(C) $x^2 + 6x + 9$

Questions 10–13 refer to the graphs.

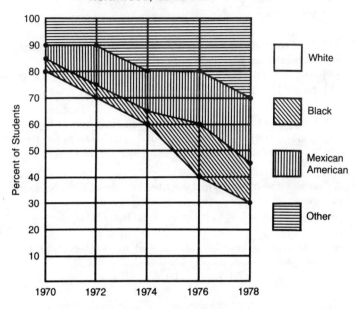

SCHOOL DISTRICT

**Student Enrollment Breakdown
Northwood, California**

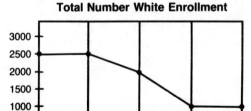

Total Number White Enrollment

10. Approximately how many black students were enrolled in 1974?
    (A) 500   (B) 300   (C) 224   (D) 167   (E) 100

11. What was the total student enrollment in 1976?
    (A) 1000   (B) 2400   (C) 2500   (D) 4000
    (E) none of these

12. Which of the indicated groups showed the largest percent change in percent breakdown from 1970 to 1978?
    (A) white   (B) black   (C) Mexican American   (D) other
    (E) cannot be determined

13. What happened to the number of "other" students from 1974 to 1976?
    (A) same   (B) up by less than 100   (C) down by less than 100
    (D) up by more than 100   (E) down by more than 100

14. A square, with perimeter 16, is inscribed in a circle. What is the area of the circle?
    (A) 4π (B) 8π (C) 12π (D) 16π (E) 32π

15. How many two-digit numbers are there whose remainder when divided by 10 is 1, and whose remainder when divided by 6 is 5?
    (A) 3   (B) 4   (C) 5   (D) 6   (E) 7

16. Which is closest to 1?

    (A) $\dfrac{3}{3 + .03}$

    (B) $\dfrac{3}{(3 + .03)^2}$

    (C) $\dfrac{3}{3 + .3}$

    (D) $\dfrac{3}{3 + (.03)^2}$

    (E) $\dfrac{3}{(3 + .3)^2}$

17. $2000 is deposited in a savings account which pays 6% annual interest compounded semiannually. To the nearest dollar, how much is in the account at the end of the year?
    (A) $2060
    (B) $2120
    (C) $2122
    (D) $2247
    (E) $2258

Questions 18–20 refer to the graphs.

AVERAGE FAMILY'S EXPENSES

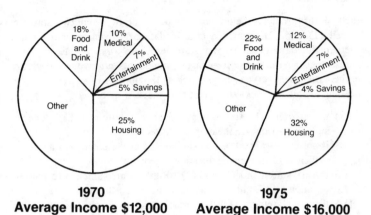

1970
Average Income $12,000

1975
Average Income $16,000

18. How much more money did the average family spend on medical expenses in 1975 than in 1970?
    (A) $500–$600 (B) $600–$700 (C) $700–$800 (D) $800–$900
    (E) $900–$1000

19. What was the percent increase from 1970 to 1975 in the percentage spent on food and drink?
    (A) 4%   (B) 18%   (C) 22%   (D) 40%   (E) 50%

20. What was the decrease in average savings from 1970 to 1975?
    (A) −$40   (B) $1   (C) $12   (D) $40
    (E) cannot be determined

STOP. IF YOU FINISH BEFORE TIME IS CALLED, CHECK YOUR WORK ON THIS SECTION ONLY. DO NOT WORK ON ANY OTHER SECTION IN THE TEST.

SECTION III: DATA SUFFICIENCY

Time: 30 Minutes
25 Questions

DIRECTIONS

Each of the problems below consists of a question and two statements, labeled (1) and (2), in which certain data are given. You must decide whether the data given in the statements are *sufficient* to answer the question. Using the data given in the statements *plus* your knowledge of mathematics and everyday facts (such as the number of days in July or the meaning of *counterclockwise*), you are to blacken space

- (A) if statement (1) ALONE is sufficient, but statement (2) alone is not sufficient to answer the question asked;
- (B) if statement (2) ALONE is sufficient, but statement (1) alone is not sufficient to answer the question asked;
- (C) if BOTH statements (1) and (2) TOGETHER are sufficient to answer the question asked, but NEITHER statement ALONE is sufficient;
- (D) if EACH statement ALONE is sufficient to answer the question asked;
- (E) if statements (1) and (2) TOGETHER are NOT sufficient to answer the question asked, and additional data specific to the problem are needed.

1. How many years old is Anne?
   (1) Next year, Anne will be half as old as her mother.
   (2) In five years, Anne will be twice as old as a decade ago.

2. What is the volume of a certain box?
   (1) One side of the box has an area of 16 square inches.
   (2) The box is cubical.

3. Given that $x = y + z$, where the three values are different positive integers, is x a prime number?
   (1) y and z are odd.
   (2) $z = 3y$

4. What is the distance from Chicago to Miami?
   (1) A 550 mph turbojet takes $3\frac{1}{4}$ hours for the flight.
   (2) The jet consumes 3 gallons of fuel per mile.

5. Is x greater than y?
   (1) $(x - y) > 0$
   (2) $x^2 < y^2$

248

6. What was the interest rate on a savings account?
   (1) The saver collected $42 simple interest over several months.
   (2) There was $1680 in the account initially.

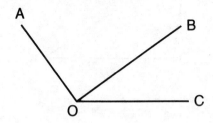

7. How many degrees is angle AOB?
   (1) Angle BOC = 35.
   (2) AO is perpendicular to OB.

8. Is a tick longer in duration than a tock?
   (1) There are 48 tocks each day.
   (2) A tick is longer than a minute.

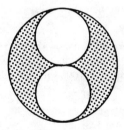

9. The centers of the 3 circles lie on one line (the circles intersect as shown). What is the area of the shaded part of the figure?
   (1) Each of the small circles has a diameter of 5.
   (2) The large circle has a radius of 5.

10. What is the value of m?
    (1) $4m - 5 = 7$
    (2) $m^2 + 9 = 6m$

11. How much ethylene glycol antifreeze must be mixed with water to fill a car radiator?
    (1) The radiator has a capacity of 3 gallons.
    (2) The solution must be 40% water.

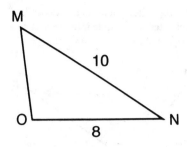

12. What is the perimeter of triangle MNO?
    (1) The area of triangle MNO is 24.
    (2) Angle MON equals 90°.

13. If a is to b as b is to c, is c positive?
    (1) c = 2a
    (2) $b^2 = 32$

14. What is sum of 5 numbers?
    (1) The average of the numbers is zero.
    (2) Only one of the numbers is positive.

15. How long would it take Billy to mow the lawn?
    (1) The lawn is rectangular, 60 feet by 130 feet.
    (2) Billy's rate of mowing is 1000 square yards an hour.

16. Is the number N an integer?
    (1) The factors of N are 3, 5, and 7.
    (2) N cannot be divided evenly by 2.

17. What is the orientation of a line in the xy plane?
    (1) The line passes through the point (5,a).
    (2) a = −3

18. Is angle A less than 90°?
    (1) Angle A is supplementary to a 30° angle.
    (2) Angle A is obtuse.

19. Which is greater, a or b?
    (1) 3a − b + 2c = 0
    (2) a + 4b − 4 = c

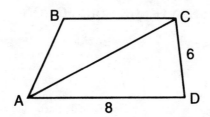

20. In the trapezoid ABCD, what is the area of triangle ABC?
    (1) AC = 10
    (2) BC = 7

21. A blip, a blap, and a blup are three linear measurements. Which is longer, a blip or a blap?
    (1) A blip equals 3 blups.
    (2) There are 2 blups in one blap.

22. What is the volume of the rectangular solid?
    (1) Its height is 4 inches and its width is 3 inches.
    (2) Its depth is between 5 and 6 inches.

23. How much did Earl earn during June in which he worked less than 4 weeks?
    (1) He received $6.35 an hour.
    (2) He worked forty hours each week.

24. Which is more expensive, a peach or a plum?
    (1) A dozen plums costs $1.79.
    (2) Peaches are 69¢ a pound.

25. Students took a test and received either A's, B's, C's, D's, or F's. If 30% of the class got A's or B's, and 50% got C's or D's, how many students got F's?
    (1) 10 students received B's.
    (2) There were a total of 40 students in the class.

STOP. IF YOU FINISH BEFORE TIME IS CALLED, CHECK YOUR WORK ON THIS SECTION ONLY. DO NOT WORK ON ANY OTHER SECTION IN THE TEST.

SECTION IV: SENTENCE CORRECTION

Time: 30 Minutes
25 Questions

DIRECTIONS

Some part of each sentence below is underlined; sometimes the whole sentence is underlined. Five choices for rephrasing the underlined part follow each sentence; the first choice (A) repeats the original, and the other four are different. If choice (A) seems better than the alternatives, choose answer (A); if not, choose one of the others.

For each sentence, consider the requirements of standard written English. Your choice should be a correct and effective expression, not awkward or ambiguous. Focus on grammar, word choice, sentence construction, and punctuation. If a choice changes the meaning of the original sentence, do not select it.

1. The vice president of the local bank spoke <u>for a half an hour and told his colleague that he, his colleague, must consider finding a new job.</u>
   - (A) for a half an hour and told his colleague that he, his colleague, must consider finding a new job
   - (B) for a half hour and told his colleague that he must consider to find a new job
   - (C) for half an hour and told his colleague that the colleague must get employed by a new bank
   - (D) for half an hour telling his colleague that he must find a new job
   - (E) for a half hour and told his colleague to consider finding a new job

2. <u>Secretly determined to break up the drug dealer's ring, the undercover agent with the local pushers joined forces.</u>
   - (A) Secretly determined to break up the drug dealer's ring, the undercover agent with the local pushers joined forces.
   - (B) Secretly determined to break up the drug dealer's ring, the undercover agent joined forces with the local pushers.
   - (C) The undercover agent secretly joined forces with the local pushers in order to destroy their ring.
   - (D) The undercover agent joined forces with the local pushers and secretly determined to destroy their ring.
   - (E) Secretly determined to destroy the rings, the local pushers and the undercover agent joined forces.

252

3. That she neglected the children, that the house remained dirty and cluttered, and poor personal hygiene were reasons for firing the house-keeper.
   (A) That she neglected the children, that the house remained dirty and cluttered, and poor personal hygiene were reasons for firing the housekeeper.
   (B) That she neglected the children, house dirt and clutter, and poor personal hygiene were reasons for firing the housekeeper.
   (C) That she neglected the children, dirty and cluttered house, and not good personal hygiene were reasons for firing the housekeeper.
   (D) Neglect of the children, poor housecleaning, and that she had poor personal hygiene were reasons for firing the housekeeper.
   (E) The housekeeper's neglect of the children, poor housecleaning, and lack of good personal hygiene were reasons for her firing.

4. Neither Barbara nor her friends is invited to pledge the local sorority.
   (A) is invited to pledge the local sorority
   (B) are invited to pledge the local sorority
   (C) is pledging the local sorority
   (D) are pledging the local sorority
   (E) will pledge

5. In studying diabetes, many doctors have concluded that early detection of the disease can permit control through diet.
   (A) In studying diabetes, many doctors have concluded
   (B) Many doctors, by studying diabetes, have concluded
   (C) Many doctors studying diabetes have concluded
   (D) Diabetes studies have led many doctors to conclude
   (E) The conclusion of those doctors who have studied diabetes is

6. The statement that the consequences of smoking marijuana are no greater than drinking alcohol is an argument often given for legalizing the use of marijuana.
   (A) that the consequences of smoking marijuana are no greater than drinking alcohol
   (B) that the consequences of marijuana are no greater than the consequences of alcohol
   (C) that the consequences of drinking alcohol are as great as the consequences of smoking marijuana
   (D) that the consequences of smoking marijuana are no greater than those of drinking alcohol
   (E) that the consequences of smoking marijuana are as great as drinking alcohol are great

7. As the shrill, piercing sound of the sirens <u>approached, several of my neighbors' dogs start</u> to howl.
   - (A) approached, several of my neighbors' dogs start
   - (B) approached, several of my neighbors' dogs started
   - (C) approach, several of my neighbors' dogs starts
   - (D) approach, several of my neighbors' dogs start
   - (E) approach, several dogs of my neighbor started

8. After reconsidering my original judgments, I feel obliged to reread <u>the book I maligned and which initially seemed so inconsequential</u>.
   - (A) the book I maligned and which initially seemed so inconsequential
   - (B) the book in which I maligned what first seemed so inconsequential
   - (C) the maligned book which I initially deemed inconsequential
   - (D) the book I malign initially and inconsequentially
   - (E) the book I will malign because of its initial inconsequentiality

9. <u>On arriving at Los Angeles International Airport, his friends met him and took him immediately to his speaking engagement.</u>
   - (A) On arriving at Los Angeles International Airport, his friends met him and took him immediately to his speaking engagement.
   - (B) Arriving at Los Angeles International Airport, his friends who met him immediately took him to his speaking engagement.
   - (C) When he arrived at Los Angeles International Airport, his friends met him and took him immediately to his speaking engagement.
   - (D) When he arrived at Los Angeles International Airport, he was taken immediately to his speaking engagement.
   - (E) After arriving at Los Angeles International Airport, he was immediately taken to his speaking engagement.

10. Among the members of the legal profession there are <u>many who try to keep their clients out of court</u> and save their clients' money.
   - (A) many who try to keep their clients out of court
   - (B) ones who try to keep their clients out of court
   - (C) they who try to keep their clients out of court
   - (D) many of whom try to keep their clients out of court
   - (E) a few who try to keep their clients out of court

11. <u>Whatever he aspired to achieve, they</u> were thwarted by his jealous older brothers.
   - (A) Whatever he aspired to achieve, they
   - (B) Whatever he had any aspirations to, they
   - (C) Whatever aspirations he had
   - (D) Whatever be his aspirations, they
   - (E) Many of his aspirations and goals

12. Neither the scientists nor the ecologists knows how to deal with the lethal effects of nuclear power plant explosions.
    (A) Neither the scientists nor the ecologists knows
    (B) Neither the scientists nor the ecologists know
    (C) Neither the scientists or the ecologists know
    (D) Neither the scientists together with the ecologists knows
    (E) Not the scientists or the ecologists know

13. The job application did not state to whom to be sent the personal references.
    (A) to whom to be sent the personal references
    (B) to who the personal references should be sent
    (C) to whom to send the personal references
    (D) to whom the personal references will be sent
    (E) to whom to send the personal references to

14. I'll never forget the tranquil desert resort where having golfed, while I vacationed, in winter, when I was younger.
    (A) where having golfed, while I vacationed, in winter, when I was younger
    (B) where I golfed, while having had vacationed in winter when I was younger
    (C) where I golfed while wintering, when I was younger
    (D) where I having had golf, while I vacationed in winter when I was younger
    (E) where I golfed while I vacationed in winter when I was younger

15. We who graduated from high school in the United States in the early 60's were caught in the middle of the crisis in education created by the Soviet Union's "Sputnik" success.
    (A) We who graduated from high school in the United States in the early 60's were
    (B) We, who graduated from high school in the United States in the early 60's, were
    (C) We who then graduated high school in the United States in the early 60's were
    (D) Those of us who then graduated from high school in the United States in the early 60's were
    (E) We high school graduates who were in the United States in the early 60's were

16. I will not object to <u>him joining the fraternity</u> if he is willing to accept its social and academic obligations.

   (A) I will not object to him joining the fraternity
   (B) I do not object to his joining the fraternity
   (C) I will make no objection to him joining the fraternity
   (D) I do not object to him joining the fraternity
   (E) I will not object to his joining the fraternity

17. After battling hypertension for years, Marvin Murphy was relieved by the results of <u>his doctor's annual physical examination, which</u> indicated his blood pressure was normal.

   (A) his doctor's annual physical examination, which
   (B) his annual physical examination, that
   (C) his annual physical examination, which
   (D) an annual physical examination by his doctor, which
   (E) his doctor's annual physical examination that

18. <u>If you would have witnessed</u> the fire roaring down through the canyon, you would have been terrified.

   (A) If you would have witnessed   (D) If you had witnessed
   (B) If you witnessed   (E) When you witnessed
   (C) If you could witness

19. When the Republican Party was the minority party, <u>its ability to win a presidential election was determined by the number of Democratic and independent voters it attracts.</u>

   (A) its ability to win a presidential election was determined by the number of Democratic and independent voters it attracts
   (B) its ability to win a presidential election is determined by the number of Democratic and independent voters it attracts
   (C) its ability to win a presidential election has been determined by the number of Democratic and independent voters it attracts
   (D) the number of Democratic and independent voters it attracts determines its ability to win a presidential election
   (E) the number of Democratic and independent voters it attracted determined its ability to win a presidential election

20. The boundaries of the Pleasant Valley School District <u>have and will continue to include</u> the small cities of Millerton, Cedarville, Granite, and Homersfield.

   (A) have and will continue to include
   (B) have included and will continue to include
   (C) has included and will continue to include
   (D) has and will continue to include
   (E) include and will include

21. Irregardless of her physical beauty, the judges did not vote for her to represent their state in the Miss America Pageant.
    (A) Irregardless of her physical beauty
    (B) In spite of her physical beauty
    (C) While her physical beauty was superb
    (D) No matter how extraordinary her physical appearance
    (E) Regardless how beautiful her physical appearance

22. Painting is a multifaceted, versatile, and a field in which a great deal of artistic diversity is possible.
    (A) multifaceted, versatile, and a field in which a great deal of artistic diversity is possible
    (B) field in which a lot of multifaceted, versatile artistry is possible
    (C) multifaceted field with versatility and diversity also possible
    (D) multifaceted, versatile, and artistically diversified field
    (E) field of multifaceted versatility and diversified artistry

23. One question haunted the swindled, penniless investor: What should his fortune have been if he had not been lured into that last, fateful investment?
    (A) What should his fortune have been if he had not been lured into that last, fateful investment
    (B) What will his fortune have been if he were not lured into that last, fateful investment
    (C) What would his fortune have been if he had not been lured into that last, fateful investment
    (D) What could his fortune have been had not he been lured into that last, fateful investment
    (E) What would his fortune be if he had only resisted the lure of that last fateful investment

24. The desert canyon, which in spring had appeared lush with scrub oak and blooming cacti, but grew brown and sere as the hot August winds continued.
    (A) canyon, which in spring had appeared lush with scrub oak and blooming cacti, but grew
    (B) canyon had appeared lush with scrub oak and blooming cacti and grew
    (C) canyon which in spring had appeared lush with scrub oak and blooming cacti grows
    (D) canyon in the spring appeared lush with scrub oak and blooming cacti, but has grown
    (E) canyon, which in spring had appeared lush with scrub oak and blooming cacti, grew

25. At first meeting with the lawyer, the lawyer seemed indecisive.
    (A) At first meeting with the lawyer, the lawyer seemed indecisive.
    (B) At first meeting, the lawyer seemed indecisive.
    (C) At first meeting the lawyer seems indecisive.
    (D) At first meeting, he seemed an indecisive lawyer.
    (E) At first meeting the lawyer, he seems indecisive.

STOP. IF YOU FINISH BEFORE TIME IS CALLED, CHECK YOUR WORK ON THIS SECTION ONLY. DO NOT WORK ON ANY OTHER SECTION IN THE TEST.

SECTION V: PROBLEM SOLVING

Time: 30 Minutes
20 Questions

DIRECTIONS

In this section solve each problem, using any available space on the page for scratchwork. Then indicate the *best* answer in the appropriate space on the answer sheet.

1. How many different three-person committees can be formed from six people?
   (A) 2   (B) 18   (C) 20   (D) 36   (E) 108

2. In ten years, David will be four times as old as Aaron. Twenty years ago, David was twice as old as Ellen. If David is seven years older than Ellen, how old is Aaron?
   (A) 1–5   (B) 6–10   (C) 11–15   (D) 16–20
   (E) 21–25

3. Dividing by ⅜ and then multiplying by ⅚ is the same as dividing by what number?
   (A) 3⅕   (B) ¹⁶⁄₅   (C) ²⁰⁄₉   (D) ⁹⁄₂₀   (E) ⁵⁄₁₆

4. What percent of 60 is 80?
   (A) 133⅓   (B) 75   (C) 60   (D) 33⅓   (E) 25

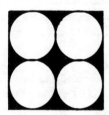

5. In the figure above, 4 equal circles are drawn within a square whose perimeter is 32. What is the area of the shaded region?
   (A) $32 - 16\pi$ (D) $32\pi - 32$
   (B) $64 - 16\pi$ (E) $64\pi - 64$
   (C) $64 - 32\pi$

259

Questions 6–8 refer to the graph.

U.S. Indian Head Nickels
Average Retail Cost

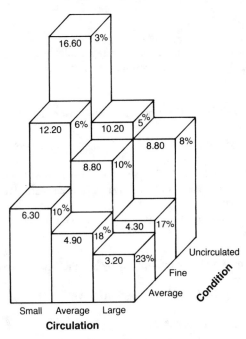

Percentages indicate percent of total coins
available for sale.

Other numbers indicate average price of
each coin.

6. Which of the following coin classifications represented the most coins?
   (A) large circulation   (B) average circulation   (C) average
   condition   (D) fine condition   (E) none of these

7. If 10,000 uncirculated coins were available for sale, what would be the
   average cost per coin?
   (A) $9.01–$9.50   (B) $9.51–$10.00   (C) $10.01–$10.50
   (D) $10.51–$11.00   (E) $11.01–$11.50

8. If 20,000 total coins are available for sale, how many of them would be from coins of average circulation?
   (A) 3500–5000   (B) 5001–6500   (C) 6501–8000
   (D) 8001–9500   (E) 9501–11,000

9. A coat is offered at a 20% discount. What is the original price of the coat if the sale price is $18.40?
   (A) $14.72   (B) $22.08   (C) $23.00   (D) $24.60
   (E) $36.80

Questions 10–11 refer to the graph.

MR. PHOTO

Number of Photos Printed Week of December 3, 1979

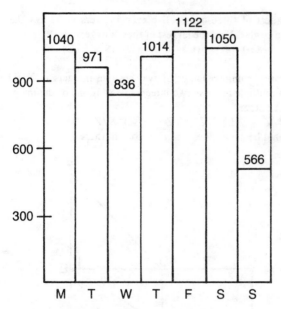

Cost of Printing (Supplies and Labor) = 5 cents per print

10. What was the average daily number of photos printed for the given week?
    (A) 851–900   (B) 901–950   (C) 951–1000
    (D) none of these   (E) cannot be determined

11. How much profit was made per unit on Friday, if sales amounted to $213.18?
    (A) 19 cents   (B) 17 cents   (C) 14 cents
    (D) 12 cents   (E) 2 cents

12. Felix earned 30% more per month than Oscar. If Felix's salary is decreased 10% and Oscar's salary is increased 10%, then Felix would be earning what percent more than Oscar?
    (A) 10%   (B) 9.09%   (C) 7%   (D) 6.36%
    (E) cannot be determined

13. How much water must be added to 10 gallons of 10% brine solution to decrease the concentration to 7%?
    (A) 0–1.5 gal   (B) 1.5–3 gal   (C) 3–4.5 gal
    (D) 4.5–6 gal   (E) 6+ gal

14. The smallest of three consecutive even integers is 40 less than three times the largest. Find the largest of these integers.
    (A) 14   (B) 17   (C) 18   (D) 19   (E) 20

15. The greatest common factor of two positive integers is X. The least common multiple of these two integers is Y. If one of the integers is Z, what is the other?
    (A) XY/Z   (B) XZ + YZ   (C) X/Z + Y
    (D) cannot be determined   (E) none of these

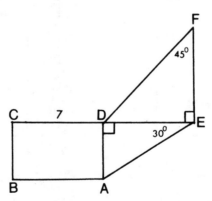

16. In the figure above, rectangle ABCD has perimeter 22; the length of DC is 7. What is the area of △DEF?
    (A) 12   (B) 8√3   (C) 24   (D) 32   (E) 64

17. Dan can do a job alone in 15 hours. Fred, working alone, can do the same job in just 10 hours. If Dan works alone for 9 hours and then stops, how many hours will it take Fred, working alone, to complete the job?
    (A) 4   (B) 5   (C) 6   (D) 12   (E) 12.5

18. In a circle, a 10-inch chord is drawn at a distance of 12 inches from the center. What is the radius of the circle?
    (A) $2\sqrt{61}$ inches   (D) 13 inches
    (B) 26 inches   (E) $2\sqrt{11}$ inches
    (C) $5\sqrt{3}$ inches

19. On a trip covering 360 miles, a motorist travels the first 150 miles at 30 miles per hour and the remainder of the distance at 35 miles per hour. What is the average speed, in miles per hour, for the entire trip?
    (A) 28   (B) $32\frac{1}{2}$ (C) $32\frac{8}{11}$ (D) $46\frac{4}{11}$ (E) 65

20. If $\dfrac{x^2 + 5x + 6}{x^2 - 4} = \dfrac{3}{2}$, then the value of x is

    (A) -12 (B) $-2\frac{2}{5}$ (C) -2 (D) 2   (E) 12

STOP: IF YOU FINISH BEFORE TIME IS CALLED, CHECK YOUR WORK ON THIS SECTION ONLY. DO NOT WORK ON ANY OTHER SECTION IN THE TEST.

SECTION VI: READING COMPREHENSION

Time: 30 Minutes
25 Questions

DIRECTIONS

Each passage in this group is followed by questions based on its content. After reading a passage, choose the best answer to each question and blacken the corresponding space on the answer sheet. Answer all questions following a passage of the basis of what is *stated* or *implied* in that passage. You may refer back to the passage.

Your brain is an organ. An organ is a whole part of an organism. You are an organism; so is an amoeba. An amoeba is a relatively simple organism; you are very complex because there are so many sorts of connections among your many sorts of parts. Organisms with brains have purposes; they can want things. An organ which helps an organism get what it wants has a function; it plays a part. An organism getting what it wants is a system "in being." Systems have purposes; organs have functions. Organs are also simple and complex. Thus a whole complex organ is made up of organic or interconnected parts. Your brain is the most complex organ in the universe. Indeed, Professor C. Judson Herrick once said that if the universe as we know it had but one human brain in it, that brain would be more complex than all the rest of the universe because of its almost infinite capacity for making interconnections among its millions of constituent parts.

It isn't as easy as you might think to define the term "part." We shall make a more thorough attempt later; for the moment it must be enough to say that we measure the importance of a part by the number of connections it has with other parts. Thus, a "principal part" is a part with many connections. That is why the brain, like the heart, is called a principal part of the body.

The brain, being a complex part, has many functions. We are concerned only with those that involve consciousness. For us the principal function of the brain is consciousness; and in dealing with the principal parts of the brain we deal only with the organs of consciousness. We want you to think of your mind as your private view of the working of three complex parts of your central nervous system that reach out into your body. We will call the complete set of sense organs one part; the organ or organs of emotion (which psychologists sometimes call "affection") a second part; and the organ of reason or logic that "sees" relations a third part. Now the logical or rational organ that sees relations or ratios is so called because its principal part is the language-using part of the brain; "logical" is made from the Greek word for "word." This language-using part will almost certainly be functioning whenever you are aware of a sensation or an emotion. Thus conscious states are never simple but always complexes of these primary brain functions: sensation, affection, and reflection (a somewhat more emphatic term for reason or logic). And any given moment of experience can, upon reflection, be more or less accurately resolved into these component parts.

We may now return to our key words "art," "philosophy," and "science" and to a demonstration of the utility of our psychological defining technique. It is a fair assumption that each of these terms has a place in your vocabulary. It is a possibility that you have never taken stock of the numerous ways you use them. Let us assume for the moment that they have senses which could be used to sort out the characteristic behavior of the developed mind, or that we might sort intelligent men and women into three groups insofar as their activity is predominantly artistic, philosophical, or scientific. Now, if it is true that conscious mental behavior is made up of three components and only three, then it follows that these three components must be present in various degrees in the three different sorts of persons or activities, which we may define by component analysis.

If we further assume that one type of mental behavior is essential to each sort and that one type is either irrelevant or least relevant, do we not discover after a little thought that to the artist sensation is the essential? He works in the world of seeing, or the world of hearing, or the world of muscular rhythm, or the world of tasting, smelling, etc. The sensation is essential to the production of whatever affective state he may seek to "express." Although his work may withstand the most exacting logical analysis, he does not characteristically make that analysis himself either before or after the creative act. As Walt Disney said of *Fantasia,* "We just make the picture and the professors tell us how we do it."

The philosopher, as such, is primarily concerned with value. To be a philosopher, he must "prize" something. He then makes use of whatever logical capacity he may possess to rationalize (that is, to make comfortable to reason) his essential prizing. Prizing is basically affective. Desire is emotion; without feeling, there is no value.

The scientist is concerned primarily with law and order. He is nothing if not logical. His logic operates directly or indirectly upon the data of sensation, and emotion is as irrelevant to his activity as sensation is to the activity of the philosopher. A judge as such is a political scientist; his personal emotions are irrelevant to his judgment. As mercy seasons justice, judges become philosophers. Thus we have a neat, logical method of distinguishing among the three sorts of complex mental behavior, as shown in tabular form.

Behavior:	Artistic	Philosophical	Scientific
Essential component:	Sensation	Affection	Logic
Relevant component:	Affection	Logic	Sensation
Irrelevant component:	Logic	Sensation	Affection

1. The author's argument relies on his talent for reducing complex processes to groups of
   (A) nonentities
   (B) behavioral mechanisms
   (C) simple processes
   (D) three
   (E) examples

2. According to the passage, you are quite different from an amoeba in your
   (A) beliefs
   (B) size
   (C) quantity of cells
   (D) complexity
   (E) purpose

3. The three complex parts of your central nervous system correspond to
   (A) sensation, emotion, and reason
   (B) the cerebral cortex
   (C) heart, lungs, mind
   (D) head, trunk, legs
   (E) words

4. According to the passage, one thing an artist does *not* do is
   (A) argue with professors
   (B) analyze his work in advance
   (C) create a logical structure
   (D) make films
   (E) confuse sensation with a way of perceiving

5. According to the author's definition of "principal part," a principal part of the body is the
   (A) cerebral cortex
   (B) index finger
   (C) lungs
   (D) right leg
   (E) aorta

6. The word which best describes the author's perspective on human behavior is
   (A) psychological
   (B) political
   (C) pedagogical
   (D) sociological
   (E) mystical

7. According to the author, an artist is no longer wholly an artist when he
   (A) constructs his work based upon an elaborate logical theory
   (B) relies predominantly upon sensation
   (C) consults with scientists and philosophers
   (D) delights in patterns of line and color
   (E) thrills at the colors of a sunset

8. According to the passage, an act of creation is essentially an act of
   (A) submission   (D) logic
   (B) anger   (E) sensation
   (C) emotion

9. When the author says that a judge's "personal emotions are irrelevant to
   his judgment," he is probably thinking that a fair judgment is also
   (A) illogical   (D) impartial
   (B) non-sensation   (E) legal
   (C) impractical

Let us describe with care and in some detail just what goes on when
one human being communicates with another. We must begin by
defining two fundamental concepts which we may call "complementary
structure" and "complementary experience." "Complementary structure" is for us a purely physical term. It is exemplified by the audible
response, say, of a tuning fork to a whistle, or of any other physical
object to another physical object which is producing a sound of the same
pitch. The vocal apparatus of an utterer and the auditory apparatus of
an interpreter must first of all be complementary in structure if one is to
communicate with the other through the medium of sound. Similarly,
an interpreter of visual symbols must be visually complementary to the
writer or printer of the symbols, and an interpreter of Braille must have
a tactile structure complementary to an utterer in Braille.

Most of us do not realize the extent of our deficiencies, particularly in
speaking and listening, and it is surely the proper business of any
thoroughgoing approach to the problems of communication to recom-
mend the measurement of one's capacity to hear as well as his capacity
to see. In this study, however, focused as it is upon the psychology of
meaning, adequate complementary structure between utterer and interpreter is assumed.

What is more important for us here is the second fundamental
concept—the concept of complementary experience. It is based upon
the kind of psychological behavior called conditioned response. If you
make a marked increase in the amount of light falling upon the normal
eye, you observe an immediate adjustment of the iris to reduce the size

of the pupil. This is called an unconditioned response, and the increased light is called an unconditioned stimulus. Now, if you make numerous trials taking care to sound a buzzer whenever the light is increased, the iris can be "taught," that is to say, conditioned, to reduce the pupil at the sound of the buzzer alone. This learned response is called a conditioned response and the sound of the buzzer, a conditioned stimulus.

Now symbols are our most important conditioned stimuli, and successful communication depends upon complementary conditioning, or, as we have already called it, complementary experience. It is one of the curious facts of life that we pay so little heed to this most fundamental of all psychological phenomena. Just as we find ourselves shouting at listeners who do not speak our language, so by a similar irrational impulse we assume that those with whom we attempt to communicate are equipped with complementary sets of conditioned responses to our own common stock of symbols.

It is easy to see the stupidity of expecting one who does not speak English to converse with you in English. It is not so easy to realize that one who does speak English may not have been conditioned to operate with the same set of senses for the familiar terms common to your vocabulary and his.

Let us first make a somewhat oversimplified structure analysis of a complementary pair of communicants. In addition to the similar bodily structure which we have already suggested, such as comparable eyes and ears, we must remember that the necessary similarity includes all those complex mechanisms of the brain that produce the conscious states we have called sensations, affects, and relations.

Let us consider a hypothetical pair of communicants, utterer and interpreter, from the operation point of view. We shall assume that our utterer has six hats: red, blue, yellow, black, gray, and white. If the rods and cones (the tiny end organs packed together on what corresponds to the sensitive films in the stereoscopic or double-lens camera) of the retinae of his eyes are not defective, he will be able to see that the six hats differ even though they are of the same shape and material. If we reduce the light so that he can barely see, the white and the yellow will seem to be the same. But as the light grows stronger he will be able to see that the red, blue, and yellow affect him differently from the black, gray, and white. He now has sufficient experience (remember, this is all grossly oversimplified) to conceive of color and shade. But he can also distinguish the red hat from the blue and yellow hats, the yellow from the blue and red, and so forth. He is thus ready for the concepts red, blue, and yellow if, for example, we provide him with a red feather, a blue feather, and a yellow feather. Indeed, he may have the human impulse to decorate the hat with the corresponding feather. And if the feathers seem to have more in common with the white hat than the other hats have in common with the white hat, he can see that his concept of shade will determine the difference between the two reds, the two blues, or the two yellows, and he will have need of the concepts of light and dark. And as we increase the number of shades he will require relation concepts like those expressed in the suffixes -er and -est. By repeating the conventional symbols "hat" and "red" with the red hat, he conditions the sound of the words to the sight of the hat. If he sees that the relation of each feather to its hat is similar to the other two, he has need of a relation concept like the one expressed by the preposition "in," and he is thus prepared to say to himself "light red feather in dark red hat." Now in the dark he is not able to tell one hat or one feather from another; but in the middle of a moonless night he is able to think "red feather in red hat" simply by uttering the appropriate symbols to himself. And with his human impulse to try new combinations, he can even think "yellow feather in blue hat" without ever having seen them thus combined.

10. Applying information in the passage, we may conclude that one reason for the one-time popularity of the 1950s song "Blue Suede Shoes" may be
   (A) Elvis Presley's vocal talent
   (B) the nonexistence of even one pair of blue suede shoes
   (C) the public's mastery of the difference between hats and feathers
   (D) the emergence of the phonograph as a complementary structure
   (E) the record-buying public's complementary sets of conditioned responses for the words "blue," "suede," and "shoes"

11. If a communicator uses vocal apparatus to speak, the complementary structure(s) to this apparatus is (are)
   (A) eyes to read lips
   (B) ears to hear
   (C) vocal apparatus to talk back
   (D) eyes to interpret paralingual gestures
   (E) hands to signal

12. The best title for this passage is
   (A) You and Your Object
   (B) Looking at Hats
   (C) Communication
   (D) People, Places, and Things
   (E) A Structure Analysis of a Complementary Pair of Communicants

13. One criticism that could be made about the author's "hats" example is
    that it is
    (A) pointless
    (B) irrelevant
    (C) too hypothetical
    (D) loaded with esoteric jargon
    (E) not reasonable

14. According to the passage, the acquisition of symbols not only allows us
    to communicate, it also allows us to
    (A) refute
    (B) imagine
    (C) stay in touch
    (D) see in the dark
    (E) choose an appropriate hat

15. Applying information from the passage, we may conclude that a blind
    person standing before a painting cannot appreciate its color because
    (A) he is quite naturally not interested
    (B) he has never painted
    (C) he has never painted in color
    (D) he lacks an adequate complementary structure
    (E) he is not an aficionado of art

16. Applying information from the passage, we may conclude that a child
    who begins feeling hungry five minutes before the school lunch bell rings
    each day may be demonstrating
    (A) a lack of proper diet   (D) a lack of appetite
    (B) a conditioned response   (E) a conditioned appetite
    (C) a complementary structure

17. Applying information from the passage, decide which of the following
    pairs of communicants might be conditioned differently toward the term
    "free enterprise."
    (A) a New Yorker and a Californian
    (B) a capitalist and a communist
    (C) a tenth grader and an eleventh grader
    (D) a speaker and a listener
    (E) a writer and a reader

    For hundreds of years grammarians have been telling us there are
eight sorts of words, but that bit of information has contributed very
little to the clarity of our thought. This is partly because so many words
occur in our natural language simply out of custom and not because

they are necessary to the thinking process in which they are employed. What we here require is a classification of language symbols not according to the way they are used in the sentence but according to the sort of thought they represent. "Gold standard" and "standard of gold" are different grammatically, although their semantic function may be the same. But the function of "gold" and the function of "standard" are vastly different. Gold as gold may be said to exist only in the mind insofar as it is something that is yellow, heavy, and precious. We feel, nevertheless, very certain about the "existence" of some external stimulus with which the conscious event originates. "Standard," on the other hand, stands for something going on in our heads that may be connected with concrete external realities only after due consideration, and we might add (somewhat paradoxically) that although gold is an exceedingly durable substance, from our point of view, it is decidedly not one of "the external verities," whatever they are.

Let us attempt a classification of symbols that aid all kinds of semantic navigation, whether our thoughts are moving upon the face of the good earth or zooming into the stratosphere of the imagination. Let us sort symbols according to the apparent relation between the thoughts they symbolize and the demonstrable contacts with "external reality" which have in part determined those thoughts. Demonstrable contact with reality is, of course, simply a synonym for what we have called elsewhere the process of corroboration. We have excellent precedent for founding our present enterprise upon a rock.

We must ask you to select your own rock—one that you can see, touch, heft, and name. Now watch us and do as we do, think as we think. We see one rock; it is an egg-shaped boulder from a river bed, smooth and hard; it seems to weigh about a pound. We shall name it "Pete," with a capital P. Now, the symbol Pete symbolizes our thought of this particular egg-shaped, smooth, hard, sixteen-ounce boulder. We give it a proper name because it is the very own name of that boulder and only that boulder. It does not stand for anything that that boulder has in common with anything else, but only for the respect in which that boulder differs from everything else; that is, the respect of being its peculiar, particular, especial self.

Now remember that the boulder can be its peculiar, particular, especial self only in respect to its being so egg-shaped, so smooth, so hard, so heavy only in our central nervous system. Its egg-shapedness derives from our experience with eggs—peacock eggs, as a matter of fact—a little matter you wouldn't understand if you don't know your peacock eggs, or rather our peacock eggs, which, of course, you can never know. (Indeed, some question the existence of peacock eggs.)

We are trying to express the idea that a proper name is the name of a very, very special sort; but with a little careful thought you will see that it is the name of a sort and not a thing; for if Pete can exist as Pete only in the central nervous system, the symbol "Pete" must stand for a class of Petrine events in experience. It is for this reason that the most proper of proper names is in fact a generalization and may be defined as the name of a group of interpretations assumed to be caused in part by the same external stimulus.

Operationally, a proper name may also be viewed as the name of an undefined operation, and/or the structures that perform it as identified by the utterer during one or more of its stages. That is, the name "Pete" stands not for the class of all Pete experiences but for the total Pete operation, Pete being Pete in time and space as connected with any or all specific Pete experiences.

Now when we call your attention to Pete, introducing him, as it were, and the symbol Pete becomes an instrument of communication as well as of reference, the symbol takes on a subtly new and different significance. That is, when we use Pete to refer to our reification (reification means thing-making) it has the shape, texture, and weight with which we endow it. Your reification may differ materially if one or the other of us is color-blind, or has no fondness for peacock eggs, or is paralyzed so as to be unable to estimate by sensory means the heft of the boulder.

Now if we operate with the word in full consciousness of these things, knowing that your Pete is not our Pete when we use that word to refer to Pete, it is performing a different function from the proper name as we have just defined it, for we must assume that at least some of our responses must be adequately similar, that Pete affects us in some respects in the same way. We might distinguish the two by calling the one a private proper name and the other a public one.

We would therefore define a public symbol as one referring to a public object, and then define a public object as the sum of the responses to an external stimulus that appear to be common to two or more interpreters. In this sense Tom might be said to use a public name because he assumed that Dick and Harry had enjoyed common responses to the stimulus for which it stood. To us, for example, the Rock of Gibralter is a public name whose meaning for us is based entirely upon hearsay and projection (photographic representation).

18. We may conclude from the passage that the difference between grammar and semantics is a difference between
    (A) classification and language
    (B) synonymous terms
    (C) arbitrary structures and actual meaning
    (D) "gold standard" and "standard of gold"
    (E) words and ideas

19. According to the passage, the "eight sorts of words" that grammarians tell us about are valuable only for tasks like
    (A) establishing connections between mind and brain
    (B) analyzing the thinking process
    (C) diagraming sentences
    (D) making economic and financial decisions
    (E) inventing figures of speech

20. If you are not a native American speaker and I am, our respective reifications of "egg" will probably
    (A) be incomprehensible to a third speaker
    (B) never refer to rocks
    (C) not exist
    (D) differ
    (E) correspond with an objective external reality

21. The author's discussion is germane to understanding which of the following phenomena?
    (A) geological identification
    (B) distinctive points of view
    (C) the individual pursuit of a particular vocation
    (D) vocabulary-building
    (E) spelling systems

22. Applying information from the passage, we may conclude that one public symbol which many Americans have never touched is
    (A) the Rock of Gibraltar   (D) the sound of a sunset
    (B) the Empire State Building   (E) Burt Reynolds
    (C) the American flag

23. An example of a private symbol, as implied by the passage, is
    (A) the nose on your face
    (B) a baby's first word
    (C) Paul Bunyan
    (D) the pledge of allegiance to the flag
    (E) this test

24. Applying information from the passage, we may suppose that *your* name
    (A) homogenizes you
    (B) particularizes you
    (C) obliterates you
    (D) corresponds to your size and weight
    (E) could not be the same as that of a rock

25. Which of the following statements is consistent with the author's idea that a name represents a group of assumed interpretations?
    (A) External reality is a mirage.
    (B) The world view of any individual is the result of a discourse structure.
    (C) You don't look like a Mary.
    (D) Peacocks don't lay eggs.
    (E) Time and space are abstractions.

STOP. IF YOU FINISH BEFORE TIME IS CALLED, CHECK YOUR WORK ON THIS SECTION ONLY. DO NOT WORK ON ANY OTHER SECTION IN THE TEST.

SECTION VII: PROBLEM SOLVING

Time: 30 Minutes
20 Questions

DIRECTIONS

In this section solve each problem, using any available space on the page for scratchwork. Then indicate the *best* answer in the appropriate space on the answer sheet.

1. If ax + by = c, then b =

   (A) $\dfrac{c}{y} - ax$ (D) $\dfrac{c - ax}{y}$

   (B) $c - ax - y$ (E) $\dfrac{ax - c}{y}$

   (C) $\dfrac{c}{ax} - y$

2. N is a positive integer. When N + 1 is divided by 5, the remainder is 4. What is the remainder when N is divided by 5?
   (A) 6   (B) 5   (C) 4   (D) 3   (E) 2

3. Mary spent 2/5 of her money on new clothes and then deposited 1/2 of what remained into her savings account. If she then had $21 left, how much did she have at the start?
   (A) $30   (B) $35   (C) $70   (D) $105   (E) $210

Station-to-Station and Credit Card	Person-to-Person	Each Additional Minute		
		8:00 A.M. to 5:00 P.M. Mon.–Fri.	5:00 P.M. to 11:00 P.M. Mon.–Sat.	11:00 P.M. to 8:00 A.M. Sun.–Fri.
first three minutes	first three minutes			
$2.75	$4.35	$ .46	$ .30	$ .19

4. Listed above are the rates for operator-assisted telephone calls from San Diego to New York City. On a Friday at 4:17 P.M., Mr. Talbot made a

275

person-to-person phone call from San Diego to New York City. When he received his monthly phone bill, Mr. Talbot noted that this call cost $14.09. To the nearest minute, for how long did this call last?
(A) 21   (B) 24   (C) 27   (D) 30   (E) 35

5. A right circular cylinder has a diameter of 20, as shown in the figure above. If its height is 100, then its total surface area is approximately
(A) 600   (D) 6600
(B) 3000   (E) 30,000
(C) 6000

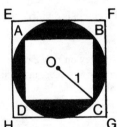

6. Square ABCD is inscribed in circle O which is inscribed in larger square EFGH, as shown in the diagram above. If the radius of circle O is 1, then the shaded area is approximately what percent of the area of square EFGH?
(A) 3%   (B) 4%   (C) 25%   (D) 50%   (E) 75%

7. A salesman receives a salary of $150 per week and earns a commission of 15% on all sales he makes. How many dollars worth of sales does he need to make in order to bring his total weekly income to $600?
(A) $3000   (D) $4150
(B) $3150   (E) $5000
(C) $4000

Questions 8–12 refer to the graphs.

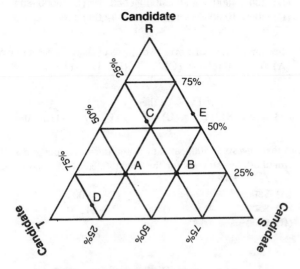

The above graph shows the distribution of votes among three candidates in five different cities in a statewide election.

The graph below shows the total votes cast for these three candidates in these five cities.

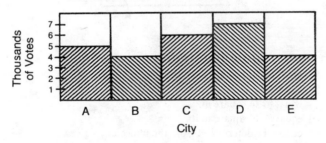

8. What city cast the most votes for candidate R?
   (A) A   (B) B   (C) C   (D) D   (E) E

9. How many cities cast more votes for candidate S than candidate T?
   (A) 0   (B) 1   (C) 2   (D) 3   (E) 4

10. Which cities cast the same number of votes for candidate R?
    (A) A and B   (B) B and C   (C) C and D
    (D) cannot be determined   (E) all cities were different

11. About how many votes did candidate T receive total in the five cities?
    (A) 2000–4000   (B) 4000–6000   (C) 6000–8000
    (D) 8000–10,000   (E) 10,000–12,000

12. How many cities cast over two-thirds of their votes for one candidate?
    (A) 0   (B) 1   (C) 2   (D) 3   (E) 4

13. If $x^2 + y^2 = 14$ and $xy = 3$, then $(x - y)^2 =$
    (A) 8   (B) 11   (C) 14   (D) 17   (E) 20

14. A man invests $1500, part at 8% and the remainder at 5%. If his interest from both investments for the year totaled $102, what is the amount he invested at 8%?
    (A) $500   (D) $900
    (B) $600   (E) $1200
    (C) $800

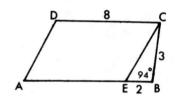

15. The area of parallelogram AECD is
    (A) greater than 24 square units
    (B) less than 24 square units
    (C) equal to 24 square units
    (D) equal to 40 square units
    (E) cannot be determined from the information given

16. If $1/3 + 1/2 + 1/x = 4$, then $x =$
    (A) 18/5   (B) 19/6   (C) 24/11   (D) 6/19   (E) 5/18

17. Gasoline varies in cost from $0.96 to $1.12 per gallon. If a car's mileage varies from 16 to 24 miles per gallon, what is the difference between the most and least that the gasoline for a 480 mile trip will cost?
    (A) $5.12   (B) $7.04   (C) $11.52   (D) $14.40
    (E) $52.80

Questions 18–20 refer to the graph.

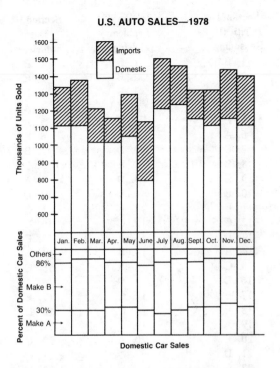

U.S. AUTO SALES—1978

18. Approximately how many cars of make B were sold in July?
    (A) 732,000   (B) 800,000   (C) 900,000
    (D) 1,049,200   (E) 1,290,000

19. During which month(s) did imports outsell domestics?
    (A) August   (B) June   (C) four months   (D) no months
    (E) none of these

20. What were the average monthly domestic sales (in millions) for the given year?
    (A) .6–1.8 (B) .8–1.0 (C) 1.0–1.2 (D) 1.2–1.4 (E) 1.4–1.6

STOP. IF YOU FINISH BEFORE TIME IS CALLED, CHECK YOUR WORK ON THIS SECTION ONLY. DO NOT WORK ON ANY OTHER SECTION IN THE TEST.

SCORING PRACTICE TEST 3

ANSWER KEY FOR PRACTICE TEST 3

Section I Critical Reasoning	Section II Problem Solving	Section III Data Sufficiency
1. E	1. B	1. B
2. B	2. B	2. C
3. C	3. B	3. D
4. B	4. E	4. A
5. E	5. E	5. A
6. A	6. A	6. E
7. E	7. D	7. B
8. B	8. E	8. E
9. E	9. D	9. A
10. E	10. D	10. D
11. E	11. C	11. C
12. C	12. C	12. D
13. D	13. E	13. E
14. B	14. B	14. A
15. C	15. A	15. C
16. D	16. D	16. A
17. E	17. C	17. E
18. E	18. C	18. D
19. A	19. C	19. E
20. E	20. A	20. C
21. D		21. C
22. C		22. E
23. D		23. E
24. D		24. E
25. D		25. B

ANSWER KEY FOR PRACTICE TEST 3

Section IV Sentence Correction	Section V Problem Solving	Section VI Reading Comprehension	Section VII Problem Solving
1. E	1. C	1. D	1. D
2. B	2. A	2. D	2. D
3. E	3. D	3. A	3. C
4. B	4. A	4. B	4. B
5. C	5. B	5. C	5. D
6. D	6. C	6. A	6. C
7. B	7. D	7. A	7. A
8. A	8. C	8. E	8. C
9. C	9. C	9. D	9. C
10. A	10. B	10. E	10. E
11. C	11. C	11. B	11. E
12. B	12. D	12. C	12. B
13. C	13. C	13. C	13. A
14. E	14. C	14. B	14. D
15. A	15. A	15. D	15. B
16. E	16. C	16. B	16. D
17. D	17. A	17. B	17. D
18. D	18. D	18. C	18. A
19. E	19. C	19. C	19. D
20. B	20. E	20. D	20. C
21. B		21. B	
22. D		22. A	
23. C		23. B	
24. E		24. B	
25. B		25. C	

HOW TO SCORE YOUR EXAM

1. Add the total number of correct responses for each section.
2. Add the total number of incorrect responses (only those attempted or marked in) for each section.
3. The total number of incorrect responses should be divided by 4, giving the adjustment factor.
4. Subtract this adjustment factor from the total number of correct responses to obtain a raw score.
5. This score is then scaled from 200 to 800.

Example:
A. If the total number of correct answers was 100 out of a possible 205.
B. And 60 problems were attempted but missed.
C. Dividing the 60 by 4 gives an adjustment factor of 15.
D. Subtracting this adjustment factor of 15 from the original 100 correct gives a raw score of 85.
E. This raw score is then scaled to a range of 200 to 800.

ANALYZING YOUR TEST RESULTS

The charts on the following pages should be used to carefully analyze your results and spot your strengths and weaknesses. The complete process of analyzing each subject area and each individual problem should be completed for each Practice Test. These results should then be reexamined for trends in types of errors (repeated errors) or poor results in specific subject areas. THIS REEXAMINATION AND ANALYSIS IS OF TREMENDOUS IMPORTANCE TO YOU IN ASSURING MAXIMUM TEST PREPARATION BENEFIT.

PRACTICE TEST 3: ANALYSIS SHEET

	Possible	Completed	Right	Wrong
Section I: Critical Reasoning	25			
Section II: Problem Solving	20			
Section III: Data Sufficiency	25			
Section IV: Sentence Correction	25			
Section V: Problem Solving	20			
Section VI: Reading Comprehension	25			
Section VII: Problem Solving	20			
OVERALL TOTALS	160			

WHY??????????????????????????????????

ANALYSIS—TALLY SHEET FOR PROBLEMS MISSED

One of the most important parts of test preparation is analyzing WHY! you missed a problem so that you can reduce the number of mistakes. Now that you have taken the practice test and corrected your answers, carefully tally your mistakes by marking them in the proper column.

	REASON FOR MISTAKE			
	Total Missed	Simple Mistake	Misread Problem	Lack of Knowledge
Section I: Critical Reasoning				
Section II: Problem Solving				
Section III: Data Sufficiency				
Section IV: Sentence Correction				
Section V: Problem Solving				
Section VI: Reading Comprehension				
Section VII: Problem Solving				
OVERALL TOTALS				

Reviewing the above data should help you determine WHY you are missing certain problems. Now that you have pinpointed the type of error, take the next practice test focusing on avoiding your most common type.

COMPLETE ANSWERS AND EXPLANATIONS FOR
PRACTICE TEST 3

SECTION I: CRITICAL REASONING

1. (E) This choice raises the question relevant to establishing the mural as art in Aristotelian terms.

2. (B) The first speaker puts forth a "perfect" view of friendship (idealistic), and the second questions the endurance of friendship (cynicism).

3. (C) Answering (A) or (D) requires the unsupported assumption that the 1933 minimum wage was too low and unfair to the workers. The statement describes a circumstance in the past which is obviously much different from present circumstances, thus suggesting choice (C).

4. (B) The conclusion that highway deaths will be reduced with the advent of automatic restraints is necessarily based upon the assumption that such restraints reduce highway deaths. None of the other choices focuses on the conclusion; (E) is an assumption which could motivate the passage as a whole, rather than just the conclusion.

5. (E) Choices (C) and (D) do not address the comparison between journalists and bank employees; and (A) and (B) use the comparison in statements irrelevant to the points in the passage. (E) criticizes the term that links bad journalists with bad bank employees—embezzlement—by pointing out that bank embezzlement does not so directly affect the customers of a bank in the same way as biased or false journalism affects the customers (readers) of a newspaper.

6. (A) *Heart and soul* is a metaphor, employing terms normally associated with another subject, humans, to refer to a nonhuman entity, business.

7. (E) This choice is related most fully to the subject matter of the original statement.

8. (B) This suggests that exterior forces, such as advertising, influence consumer choices and undercuts the contention that consumers know what they want. Each of the other choices is either irrelevant or strengthens rather than weakens the argument.

9. (E) Choices (A), (C), and (D) are irrelevant to the argument, and (B) actually strengthens the argument. (E) suggests that the evidence from one year cannot reliably predict a long-term trend.

10. (E) This is implied in the final sentence. Each of the other choices requires assumptions or beliefs extraneous to the passage.

11. (E) I and III. Neither consumers nor legal loopholes are mentioned in the statement.

12. (C) Voltaire's statement shows the irony that the descriptive word used (*common*) may not, in reality, be so. Likewise, the adjective describing the shrimp (*jumbo*) indicates that the shrimp are large; this may not be the case.

13. (D) Making *only* the first word of sentence 1 does not solve all of the logical problems in the passage but does strengthen the passage by indicating that customers with green necklaces must have bought them from the competition.

14. (B) The author does not realize that customers not wearing green necklaces may have bought other items from the competition.

15. (C) The passage establishes that the survivors were caught in a life and death "survival" situation. While (B) may be a possible choice, answer (C) logically follows the sense of their dilemma, clouded by uncertainty and the possibility of death.

16. (D) The letter fails to note that the decision concerns *officers,* and Smith and Krunkle have been merely nominated to be officers and are not yet such. The other choices are either not stated in the letter or are not essential to the argument.

17. (E) Answers (B), (C), and (D) are only partial descriptions and, although may be correct, are not as complete a description of possible future action as answer (E). Nothing in the letter would imply the action stated in (A).

18. (E) Flamo Lighters claim to be convenient ("in your pocket wherever you go"), have longevity ("ten-year guarantee"), winter-proof ("all-weather"), and dependable ("always reliable, always dependable"). They do not profess to be all-purpose, however.

19. (A) What is graceful and pleasing to the eye is "in the eye of the beholder," something quite subjective. While (B), (C), and (D) are possibly subjective statements, they would not be if their basic assumptions were proven—that is, that reporters do have a commitment, that poverty is a terrible affliction, and that the records are open to question; (A) is the best answer because it is the most identifiably subjective. In addition, only choices (A) and (E) use a clear *comparison.*

20. (E) The cost of a product may not be relevant to its quality. The amount we pay for Japanese televisions has only remote bearing on the quality of American goods in general.

21. (D) *Doubtful* and *open to question* mean nearly the same thing.

22. (C) All race-car lovers enjoy classical music. Since there are no backgammon players who enjoy classical music, then none of the backgammon players are race-car lovers. (D) is false because statement 3 does not necessarily exclude those who don't enjoy classical music from enjoying fine wine.

23. (D) This passage implies that the lie detector is sometimes worthless. If the lie detector can be fooled in certain instances, then in those instances it is worthless.

24. (D) The argument is "It has been *proven* that the 'lie detector' can be fooled." The best choice is the one which provides such proof—(D). (A) and (B) are too general, and (C) weakens the argument.

25. (D) Only this choice both represents a *strong* point *and* is not contradictory. (A), (C), and (E) contradict the argument, and (B) is not a relatively strong point.

SECTION II: PROBLEM SOLVING

1. **(B)** First, note that $\frac{1}{4}$ of $\frac{3}{5} = \frac{3}{20}$. We then have: $\frac{3}{20}$ is what percent of $\frac{3}{4}$?

$$\frac{\text{is number}}{\text{of number}} = \frac{\text{percent}}{100}$$

$$\frac{3/20}{3/4} = \frac{P}{100}$$

Cross multiplying gives

$$\frac{3}{4}P = \frac{3}{\cancel{20}}(\cancel{100})$$

$$\frac{3}{4}P = 15$$

$$P = \frac{4}{\cancel{3}}(\cancel{15})$$

$$P = 20$$

Thus, **(B)** 20% is the correct answer.

2. **(B)** Percent change is found by using the formula

$$\text{percent decrease or increase} = \frac{\text{change}}{\text{starting point}}$$

The change was $75 - 60 = 15$. The starting point was 75. Thus, $\frac{15}{75} = \frac{1}{5} = 20\%$.

3. **(B)** In $\triangle ABD$, the sum of $\angle A$, $\angle B$, and $\angle BDA$ is $180°$. If $\angle B = 90°$ and $\angle BDA = 50°$, then $\angle A = 40\%$. Since $\angle A = x° + 15°$, we have

$$40° = x° + 15°$$
$$25° = x°$$

Therefore $\quad x = 25$

4. **(E)** At $9.00 per hour, a 15-minute ($\frac{1}{4}$ hour) wait will cost $2.25. The first $\frac{1}{6}$ mile will cost $1.20. The remaining $\frac{17}{6}$ ($3 - \frac{1}{6} = 2\frac{5}{6} = \frac{17}{6}$) miles will cost $17(.90) = \$15.30$. The total bill will be the sum: $2.25 + $1.20 + $15.30 = $18.75.

5. (E) Let the four numbers be a, b, c, and d. Since the average of the four is x, we have

$$\frac{a + b + c + d}{4} = x$$

or $\qquad$ $a + b + c + d = 4x*$

Since the average of the first three numbers is e, we have

$$\frac{a + b + c}{3} = e$$

or $\qquad$ $a + b + c = 3e$

Then substituting for $a + b + c$ in equation *, we have

$$3e + d = 4x$$

Thus $\qquad$ $d = 4x - 3e$

6. (A) Suppose there are 100 faculty members at the school. If 70% are women, then 30% are men. We then have 70 women and 30 men. If ⅔ of the men are single, then ⅓ of 30 = 10 men are married. 60% or 60 teachers are married. If 10 are men, then 50 are women. Therefore, the fraction of women who are married is ⁵⁰⁄₇₀ or ⁵⁄₇.

7. (D) Let 85%L represent a 15% decrease in length. Then 140%W represents a 40% increase in width. The new rectangle will have

$$\text{area} = (\text{new length})(\text{new width})$$

$$= (85\%L)(140\%W)$$

$$= \frac{\overset{17}{\cancel{85}}}{\underset{20}{\cancel{100}}}L = \frac{\overset{7}{\cancel{140}}}{\underset{5}{\cancel{100}}}W$$

$$= \frac{119}{100}LW$$

$$= 119\%LW$$

The old rectangle has area 100%LW. Thus, the new rectangle has area *19% greater* than the original 100%.

8. (E) The circumference of the large circle is 64π.

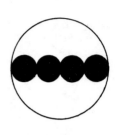

Since circumference = $2\pi r$
$$64\pi = 2\pi r$$
$$32 = r$$
Radius of large circle = 32
Diameter of *2* small circles = 32
So diameter of *1* small circle = 16
Radius of small circle = 8
Area of small circle = πr^2
$$= \pi \times 8^2$$
$$= 64\pi$$

So area of *4* small circles = 4 (area of 1 small circle)
$$= 4(64\pi)$$
$$= 256\pi$$

9. (D) Let us examine each choice.

(A): $(x + 3)(x + 5)$ Since x is even, both $x + 3$ and $x + 5$ are odd; then (odd)(odd) = odd.

(B): $x^2 + 5$ Since x is even, x^2 is even, and $x^2 + 5$ is odd.

(C): $x^2 + 6x + 9$ Since x is even, x^2 is even and $6x$ is even; then (even) + (even) + (odd) = odd.

(D): $3x^2 + 4$ Since x is even, $3x^2$ is even; then (even) + (even) = *even.*

(E): $5(x + 3)$ Since x is even, $x + 3$ is odd; then (odd)(odd) = odd.

10. (D) In 1974, there were 60% white and 5% black students. Thus there were 12 times as many whites as blacks. Since there were 2000 whites in 1974, there were 2000/12, or 167 blacks.

11. (C) In 1976, there were 1000 white students. This was 40% of the total. Thus, the total must have been 2500.

12. (C) Whites declined from 80% to 30%, (50/80), a 62.5% decrease. Blacks increased from 5% to 15%, (10/5), a 200% increase. Mexican Americans increased from 5% to 25%, (20/5), a 400% increase. Others increased from 10% to 30%, (20/10), a 200% increase.

13. (E) In 1974 there were 20% other and 60% white. Thus there were three times as many whites as others. Since there were 2000 whites, there

were 666 other. In 1976, 40% white and 20% other. Twice as many whites as other. Thus 500 other. Therefore, a decrease of 166.

14. **(B)** In square ABCD, each side is 4, since the perimeter is 16. Then by the Pythagorean theorem, $d = 4\sqrt{2}$.

$$4^2 + 4^2 = d^2$$
$$16 + 16 = d^2$$
$$32 = d^2$$
$$\sqrt{32} = d$$

Simplifying
$$d = \sqrt{32}$$
$$= \sqrt{16 \times 2}$$
$$= \sqrt{16} \times \sqrt{2}$$
$$= 4\sqrt{2}$$

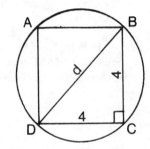

The radius is
$$r = \frac{d}{2}$$
$$= \frac{4\sqrt{2}}{2}$$
$$= 2\sqrt{2}$$

The area of the circle
$$= \pi r^2$$
$$= \pi(2\sqrt{2})^2$$
$$= \pi \times 4 \times 2$$
$$= 8\pi$$

Thus, **(B)** is correct. If you recognized $\triangle$DBC as a 45°–45°–90° triangle with side ratios $1 : 1 : \sqrt{2}$, you could quickly find d by $4 : 4 : 4\sqrt{2}$.

15. **(A)** The two-digit numbers whose remainder is 1 when divided by 10 are: 11, 21, 31, 41, 51, 61, 71, 81, and 91. When divided by 6, the remainder is 5 for the numbers 11, 41, and 71. Therefore, 3 numbers satisfy the conditions of the problem.

16. **(D)** Note that choices (B) and (E) are approximately equal to $\frac{3}{3}^2$ or $\frac{1}{3}$. For the remaining choices, the fraction closest to 1 will be the fraction whose denominator has the *least* value added to 3. Choice (D) has the smallest value, .0009, added to 3. Note: $(.03)^2 = .0009$.

17. (C) A 6% annual interest rate, compounded semiannually (every half year) is the same as a 3% semiannual interest rate. At the end of first half of year: Interest on $2000 at 3% = $2000 × .03 = $60. New balance at end of first half year = $2000 + $60 = $2060. At the end of first full year: Interest on $2060 at 3% = $2060 × .03 = $61.80 ≃ $62. New balance at end of first full year = $2060 + $62 = $2122.

18. (C) In 1970, 10% of $12,000, or $1200, was spent on medical. In 1975, 12% of $16,000, or $1920, was spent on medical. Thus, an increase of $720.

19. (C) There was an increase from 18% to 22%. That is a 4% increase. Therefore a 4% increase from 18% is a 22% increase in the percent spent on food and drink.

20. (A) In 1970, 5% of $12,000, or $600, was put in savings. In 1975, 4% of $16,000, or $640, was put in savings. This was an increase, not a decrease. Thus −$40 is the proper answer.

SECTION III: DATA SUFFICIENCY

1. (B) The first statement translates to the equation $A + 1 = \frac{1}{2}(M + 1)$ which has two unknowns and cannot be solved for A. But the second statement means $A + 5 = 2(A - 10)$ and we can solve for Anne's age, 25 years.

2. (C) If the box is cubical, then each side is square. An edge of the box would be the square root of the side, or 4 inches. The volume equals the edge cubed, or 64 cubic inches.

3. (D) No, x is not prime. From the first statement we know that x is even, or divisible by two. From the second statement we deduce that $x = y + 3y = 4y$, so 4 is a factor of x.

4. (A) Distance equals rate times time. Statement (1) tells us the rate and time. Multiplying 550 by $3\frac{1}{4}$ yields a distance of 1788 miles.

5. (A) Inequality (1) informs us that x exceeds y, whether positive, zero, or negative. Inequality (2) does not tell us so much, for the sign of the numbers is masked by the squaring.

6. (E) Simple interest equals principal times rate times time. We are not told the length of time the money was in the account.

7. (B) Since AO is perpendicular to OB, AOB is a right angle.

8. (E) The first statement implies that a tock equals 30 minutes, but the duration of a tick is indefinite.

9. (A) The shaded part equals the area of the large circle minus the areas of the two small circles. For any circle, $A = \pi r^2$ and we can ascertain the radii of the circles from statement (1) alone. The small circles are of equal size, with radii of $2\frac{1}{2}$. Because the small circles are equal, their diameter is the radius of the large circle. Shaded area $= 25\pi - 2(25/4)\pi = (25/2)\pi$.

10. (D) To solve the first expression, we add 5 to both sides and divide by 4. The second expression is solved by collecting terms on the left, $m^2 - 6m + 9 = 0$, and factoring, $(m - 3)^2 = 0$. From either expression, $m = 3$.

11. (C) The radiator requires 60% antifreeze in its 3 gallons, or 1.8 gallons antifreeze.

12. (D) Since statement (1) tells the area of triangle MNO is 24, its height must be 6. Note that side MO will be the height as 6-8-10 is a Pythagorean triple. Thus we can find the perimeter. Using statement (2) we know MON is a right triangle and can use the Pythagorean theorem to find the third side.

13. (E) The first statement reveals only that c and a have the same sign. From the initial proportion and the second statement, $ac = b^2 = 32$, but the sign of c is indeterminate.

14. (A) Because the average is the sum divided by 5, the sum must be the average times 5. Therefore the sum is zero.

15. (C) The lawn is 20 yards by 43.3 yards, or 867 square yards. It would take Billy 0.87 hour or 52 minutes to mow the lawn.

16. (A) The product of the factors is 105. N must be an integer that is an odd multiple of 105. The very mention of factors in (1) implies that N is an integer.

17. (E) Combining both statements, all we know is that the line passes through the point $(5, -3)$, and the orientation is unspecified.

18. (D) No, angle A exceeds 90°. The first statement informs us that A + 30° = 180°, from which we could find A = 150°. The second statement's "obtuse" means exceeds 90°.

19. (E) Since there are 3 unknowns and only 2 equations, we cannot solve for a and b.

20. (C) In the trapezoid, BC is evidently parallel to AD. The first statement reveals that triangle ACD is a 6-8-10 right triangle, with angle ADC = 90°. Because BC is parallel to AD, angle BCD must also equal 90°. Consider triangle ABC with base BC. The altitude to vertex A equals CD, because CD is perpendicular to BC. Then the area = ½bh = ½(BC)(CD) = ½ × 7 × 6 = 21.

21. (C) Since 1 blip = 3 blups (from statement 1) and 1 blap = 2 blups (from statement 2), then a blip is larger than a blap.

22. (E) To find the volume of a rectangular solid, you need exact measurements for depth, width, and height. You do not have an exact amount for the depth.

23. (E) It is uncertain as to exactly how many days Earl worked.

24. (E) The first statement enables us to find the cost of one plum. But without the weight of one peach, we cannot use (2) to find the cost of a peach.

25. (B) Since a total of 80% received A's, B's, C's, and D's, then 20% received F's. 20% of 40 (the total given in statement 2) = 8 students. The first statement does not help because we don't know how many students received A's.

SECTION IV: SENTENCE CORRECTION

1. (E) Choice (E) best simplifies the awkward wording of the original sentence. Choices (C) and (D) change the meaning slightly by eliminating the notion of *consider*, and choice (B) is not idiomatic.

2. (B) Choice (B) corrects the poor structure of the original wording. Choices (C), (D), and (E) change the meaning of the original expression slightly, (C) and (D) suggesting that the ring belongs to the *pushers* not to the *drug dealer* and (E) implying that the *pushers* were determined to destroy the ring.

3. (E) Choice (E) best expresses the parallel form called for in this sentence (*neglect, housecleaning, lack*—all nouns). The other choices contain the same "unparallel" structure of the original wording.

4. (B) Choice (B) contains the correct form *are* for the *neither . . . nor* construction. The verb in this case should be plural to match *friends*, which is the closer of the two subjects to the verb. Choice (D) correctly uses *are* but changes the meaning of the original.

5. (C) All choices are grammatically correct; however, choice (C) is the most direct expression of the original wording. Choices (D) and (E) change the meaning of the original, and choice (B) is awkward.

6. (D) Choice (D) correctly states the comparison by adding *those*. The alternative wordings do not clearly express the comparison. Choice (B) is wordy and imprecise, and (C) changes the meaning of the original sentence.

7. (B) Choice (B) corrects the verb agreement problem in the original wording. The verbs must both be past tense or both be present tense. No other choice uses proper tense without introducing a subject-verb agreement error.

8. (A) The original is better than any of the alternatives. All other choices are less direct, create ambiguities, or change the meaning of the original.

9. (C) Choice (C) clarifies the ambiguous wording of the original sentence. It is clear in (C) who is arriving and who is doing the meeting.

10. (A) The original wording is the best expression of this idea. Choice (E) changes the meaning slightly. The other choices are either stylistically awkward or ungrammatical.

11. (C) Choice (C) best expresses the idea without changing the intent of the sentence as (E) does. The original and choices (B) and (D) are awkward.

12. (B) Choice (B) correctly supplies the plural *know,* which agrees with *ecologists.* The subject closest to the verb determines the number of the verb in this case. Choice (B) also retains the necessary *neither . . . nor.*

13. (C) Choice (C) best corrects the awkward wording in the original sentence. Choice (D), although grammatically correct, changes the meaning of the original.

14. (E) Choice (E) corrects the "disjointed" wording of the original sentence.

15. (A) Of the choices given, the original is the best phrasing. The commas in choice (B) change the meaning of the original by making the phrase nonrestrictive. In (C), *graduated high school* is not acceptable standard written English. Choice (D) is awkward and (E) changes the meaning of the sentence.

16. (E) Choice (E) correctly states *his joining.* The possessive *his* is called for here before the *ing* verb form *joining.* Choice (D), while grammatically correct, slightly alters the meaning of the original sentence.

17. (D) Choice (D) clarifies whose physical examination is in question— Marvin's or the doctor's. Choice (C) is straightforward and concise, also leaving no doubt as to whose examination it is; however, the *doctor* is not mentioned, and because one cannot assume that all physical examinations are administered by a doctor, this information must be included.

18. (D) Choice (D) supplies the correct verb form *had witnessed* called for by the original sentence.

19. (E) Choice (E) is the most direct, concise wording of the original sentence. The verbs in these answer choices are the problem areas. Choice (B), for example, is incorrect because of the present tense *is* and *attracts.*

20. (B) Choice (B) corrects the verb problem in the original sentence. *Have and will continue to include* is better expressed as *have included and will continue to include.*

21. (B) Choice (B) eliminates the *irregardless* of the original wording. *Irregardless* is incorrect in standard written English. Choices (C) and (D) change the original meaning slightly and are therefore wrong. Choice (E) is not idiomatic.

22. (D) Choice (D) provides the parallel structure needed in this sentence for the three ideas stated in a series. The other choices are structurally wrong or alter the original meaning.

23. (C) Choice (C) supplies the correct verb for this sentence, *would*. The other choices either introduce additional errors or change the original meaning.

24. (E) Choice (E) eliminates the *but* in the original wording and supplies the correct punctuation for the *which* clause, needing commas to set it off from the rest of this sentence.

25. (B) Choice (B) is correct because it is both concise and clear. The other choices are ambiguous or unnecessarily change the past tense of the original to the present tense. Choice (D) is a less direct, more wordy way to express what choice (B) does more concisely.

SECTION V: PROBLEM SOLVING

1. **(C)** The following are the possible combinations: 123, 124, 125, 126, 134, 135, 136, 145, 146, 156, 234, 235, 236, 245, 246, 256, 345, 346, 356, 456. Thus there are 20 combinations. Using the formula,

$$\binom{6}{3} = \frac{6}{3!\,(3!)} = \frac{6 \times 5 \times 4 \times 3 \times 2 \times 1}{3 \times 2 \times 1 \times 3 \times 2 \times 1} = 20$$

The formula is $\binom{n}{r} = \dfrac{n!}{r!\,(n-r)!}$

2. **(A)** The solution to this problem can be seen through the following grid. The sequence of the solution is indicated by the arrows.

	20 years ago	now	in 10 years
David	4x − 30	4x − 10	4x
Ellen	2x − 15	2x + 5	
Aaron		x − 10	x

$$4x - 10 = (2x + 5) + 7$$
$$4x - 10 = 2x + 12$$
$$2x = 22$$
$$x = 11$$

Therefore Aaron is now x − 10 = 1

3. **(D)** Dividing by a number is the same as multiplying by its inverse, and vice versa. Thus multiplying by 5/6 is the same as dividing by 6/5. Thus the answer is (3/8)(6/5) = 18/40 = 9/20.

4. **(A)** One method: $\dfrac{\text{is number}}{\text{of number}} = \dfrac{\text{percent}}{100}$

$$\frac{80}{60} = \frac{x}{100}$$

Cross multiplying gives $\quad 60x = 8000$

Divide by 60 $\quad x = \dfrac{8000}{60}$

Then $\quad x = 133\tfrac{1}{3}\%$

Another method is making an equation by replacing "what percent" with x/100, "of" by times (·) and "is" by equals (=) giving the equation

301

$$\frac{x}{100} \cdot 60 = 80$$

Simplifying gives $\qquad (3/5)x = 80$

Multiplying by $\frac{5}{3}$ $\qquad \left(\frac{5}{3}\right)(3/5)x = 80\left(\frac{5}{3}\right)$

$$x = \frac{400}{3}$$

Then $\qquad x = 133\frac{1}{3}$

5. **(B)** Since the perimeter of the square is 32, each side of the square is 8.

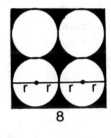

Area of square $\quad = 8^2 = 64$

Note that $\qquad 4r = 8$ or $r = 2$

Area of *1* circle $\quad = \pi r^2$

$\qquad\qquad\qquad = \pi \times 2^2$

$\qquad\qquad\qquad = 4\pi$

Area of *4* circles $\quad = 4$ (area of 1 circle)

$\qquad\qquad\qquad = 4 (4\pi)$

$\qquad\qquad\qquad = 16\pi$

Then shaded area $\; = $ (area of square) $-$ (area of 4 circles)

$\qquad\qquad\qquad = 64 - 16\pi$

6. **(C)** Adding the percentages, the large circulation coins represent (23%, 17%, 8%), 48%, while the average condition coins represent (23%, 18%, 10%), 51%.

7. **(D)** The number of coins is irrelevant. Since 3%, 5%, and 8% add to 16%, we have the following:

   16.60 × 3% plus 10.20 × 5% plus 8.80 × 8% = 1.712, and 1.712/.16 = 10.70 which is the average price.

8. **(C)** There are (5%, 10%, 18%), 33% in this category. Thus 33% of 20,000 is 6600.

9. **(C)** Since the sale price is 20% off the regular price, if x is the original price, .80x = $18.40. Therefore x = $23.00.

10. (B) Add the seven figures at the tops of the columns and divide by 7. The average is 942.7.

11. (C) On Friday, 1122 prints were made. Thus, 213.18/1122 = .19, but each print costs 5 cents to produce. Thus the profit is 14 cents.

12. (D) Since Felix earns 30% more than Oscar, let x = Oscar's salary and 1.3x = Felix's salary. If Felix's salary is reduced by 10%, he is now earning 1.3x − .13x = 1.17x. If Oscar's salary is increased 10% he is now earning 1x + .1x = 1.1x. Felix is now earning (.07x/1.1x) = 6.36% more than Oscar.

13. (C) Set up an equation for the amount of salt.

   10% of 10   plus   0% of x   equals   7% of (10 + x)
   1.0 + 0 = .7 + .07x, or .3 = .07x, .3/.07 = x

   Solving for x, we get x = 4²⁄₇

14. (C) Set the three consecutive even integers equal to x, x + 2, and x + 4. The equation: x = 3(x + 4) − 40, x = 3x + 12 − 40, −2x = −28. Thus x = 14. But that is the smallest of the three integers. Thus 18 is the largest.

15. (A) The product of the LCM and GCF of two numbers is the same as the product of the two original numbers. Thus, the answer is XY/Z.

16. (C) Since the perimeter of rectangle ABCD is 22 and DC = 7, we have

$$22 = 2(AD) + 2(7)$$
$$22 = 2(AD) + 14$$
$$8 = 2(AD)$$
$$4 = AD$$

Next note that $\triangle ADE$ is a 30°-60°-90° triangle with side ratios $1 : \sqrt{3} : 2$. Since the side across from 30° is 4, the side across from 60° is $4\sqrt{3}$. Thus $DE = 4\sqrt{3}$. Also note that $\triangle DEF$ is a 45°-45°-90° triangle with side ratios $1 : 1 : \sqrt{2}$. Since $DE = 4\sqrt{3}$, then $EF = 4\sqrt{3}$. Then the area of DEF

$$= \tfrac{1}{2}(EF)\,(DE)$$
$$= \tfrac{1}{2}(4\sqrt{3})\,(4\sqrt{3})$$
$$= \tfrac{1}{2} \times 16 \times 3$$
$$= 24$$

17. (A) Since it takes Dan 15 hours to complete the job, then in 9 hours he will be able to do only $9/15$, or $3/5$, of the job. This leaves $2/5$ of the job to be finished by Fred. Since Fred takes 10 hours to do the *whole* job by himself, to do only $2/5$ of the job, it would take Fred $2/5 \times 10 = 4$ hours.

18. (D) From the figure and using the Pythagorean theorem, we find the radius is 13 inches.

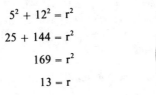

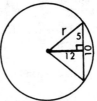

$$5^2 + 12^2 = r^2$$

$$25 + 144 = r^2$$

$$169 = r^2$$

$$13 = r$$

   Alternate method: If you recognized the 5-12-13 right triangle, you could quickly find r to be 13.

19. (C) Average speed is (total distance)/(total time). The total distance is 360 miles. Time for the first 150 miles is $150/30 = 5$ hours. The time for the remaining 210 miles is $210/35 = 6$ hours. Thus average speed is $360/(5 + 6) = 360/11 = 32\,8/11$ mph.

20. (E) Factoring both numerator and denominator of the left side gives

$$\frac{\overset{1}{(\cancel{x+2})}(x + 3)}{\underset{1}{(\cancel{x+2})}(x - 2)} = \frac{3}{2}$$

Thus

$$\frac{x + 3}{x - 2} = \frac{3}{2}$$

Cross multiplying gives

$$2(x + 3) = 3(x - 2)$$

$$2x + 6 = 3x - 6$$

$$6 = x - 6$$

$$12 = x$$

SECTION VI: READING COMPREHENSION

1. **(D)** Throughout, the author elaborates his distinction between sensation, affection, and reflection insofar as these respectively correspond with art, philosophy, and science. His reliance on threes is especially evident in the three-part chart which concludes the passage. (E) is too general to be the best answer.

2. **(D)** In the first paragraph the author says, "An amoeba is a relatively simple organism; you are very complex. . . ."; he elaborates this particular point at some length. Although the other choices may be true, they are not mentioned in the passage.

3. **(A)** The author defines the central nervous system as the brain plus all its tributary branches and says in the third paragraph that the brain's organs of consciousness deal with *sensation, affection,* and *reflection.* (A) most closely matches these terms.

4. **(B)** Throughout the passage the point is made several times that the artist works through sensation rather than through logic (which is the stuff of *analysis*). At one point we are told that the artist does not characteristically analyze his work "either before or after the creative act." An artist may create a logical structure, (C), but not deliberately.

5. **(C)** A principal part is a part with many connections to other parts. The choice which interconnects with the most complexity is the lungs. Notice that all principal parts are *large organs,* like the heart and the brain.

6. **(A)** The author is exclusively concerned with the workings of the mind.

7. **(A)** Choices (B), (D), and (E) connect the artist with sensation; this is consistent with the author's view of what an artist *is.* What artist is *not* is logical, so (A) is correct.

8. **(E)** Emotion, (C), is the essential component of a philosopher's behavior, and logic, (D), is the essential component of a scientist's behavior. (A) and (B) are irrelevant to the passage.

9. **(D)** Although (E) is true relative to a legal decision, it does not relate to the question, which seeks a term denoting the opposite of judgment by emotion. That term is "impartiality."

10. **(E)** This question requires you to apply the argument of the passage to a specific situation. Since a song would tend to be less popular if its lyrics are incomprehensible to the record-buying public, we may apply the inverse idea, supported by the passage, that the popularity of a song relies on the

audience's shared appreciation (shared conditioned response) of the song's lyrics.

11. (B) The first paragraph tells us that "the vocal apparatus of an utterer and the *auditory apparatus of an interpreter* must first of all be complementary in structure if one is to communicate with the other through the medium of sound." (A) is a possibility, but is not best because its application is too narrow.

12. (C) Choices (A) and (D) are vague and almost irrelevant. (B) and (E) refer only to the last part of the passage.

13. (C) This answer might be arrived at by considering that the "hats" example *is* reasonable, relevant, pointed, and simply written; therefore, all choices except (C) are eliminated. But it may also be argued that the example does not describe a "real" situation.

14. (B) This is the passage's final point, that one can think "yellow feather in blue hat," without seeing or having seen the items together.

15. (D) We are told in the passage that "an interpreter of visual symbols must be visually complementary to the writer or printer of the symbols"; that is, he/she must be able to *see*. This point is consistent with the general thrust of the passage, that communicants must be complementary individuals.

16. (B) The bell conditions the child's response, just as the buzzer conditions the eye's response in the example in the passage. That is, after many days of associating the bell with lunch, he has been "taught" to feel hungry in anticipation of the bell.

17. (B) A capitalist and a communist differ most strikingly in their respective understanding of "free enterprise." In other words, the social context of each "conditions" him differently. Such is not necessarily true for any of the other choices.

18. (C) The author begins by discussing the contributions of grammarians, saying that they have "contributed very little to the clarity of our thought." He then goes on to discuss at length how words (like "Pete") come to mean what they do. In short, he dismisses the mere "structures" of grammar and writes about the "meaning" which is the province of semantics.

19. (C) It is implied in the first paragraph that the grammarians' classifications deal only with "the way they [language symbols] are used in the sentence." (C) is most closely related to this idea.

20. (D) According to the passage, reification means "thing-making." And the passage's central point is that each of us conceives things in a

different way. This would be especially true between two speakers from different countries, whose perception *and* vocabulary differ.

21. (B) In the first paragraph the author sets out to tell us about the "sort of thought" that language represents and goes on (with his "rock" example) to show that the way we think about an object depends on the qualities with which each of us "endows it." That is, upon each individual's distinctive point of view.

22. (A) This is stated explicitly in the passage, in the final paragraph.

23. (B) A symbol, as defined by the passage, is a word or name. This restriction eliminates (D) and (E). (C) is the name of a legendary character of American folklore; therefore, Paul Bunyan might be called a "public" symbol. Of the choices remaining, (B) is best, because it refers to a word which is normally not well understood by those outside the baby's "private" family circle.

24. (B) The third paragraph tells us that a name stands for an object's "peculiar, *particular*, especial self."

25. (C) Only (C) declares an *assumption* about a *name*, an assumption based upon the speaker's opinion (interpretation) of what a "Mary" looks like.

SECTION VII: PROBLEM SOLVING

1. (D)
$$ax + by = c$$
$$\underline{-ax \qquad\qquad -ax}$$
$$by = c - ax$$
$$\frac{by}{y} = \frac{c - ax}{y}$$
$$b = \frac{c - ax}{y}$$

2. (D) When $N + 1$ is divided by 5, the remainder is 4. When N (which is one less than $N + 1$) is divided by 5, the remainder should be 3 (which is one less than 4).

3. (C) Having spent 2/5 of her money on clothes, Mary has 3/5 of her money left. Then 1/2 of 3/5, or 3/10, is placed in her savings account. She has now spent $2/5 + 3/10 = 7/10$ of her money. Thus, she has 3/10 remaining. If m is the money she started with, and she has only $21 left, we have the equation

$$(3/10)m = 21$$
$$m = 21(10/3)$$
$$m = 70$$

4. (B)

Mr. Talbot's charge for the call	$14.09
Cost of first *3* minutes of a person-to-person call	−$ 4.35
Cost of additional minutes	$ 9.74

$$\frac{\text{Cost of additional minutes}}{\text{Cost of each additional minute}} \quad \frac{\$\ 9.74}{\$\ .46} \simeq 21 \text{ minutes}$$

Total length of call = first 3 minutes + additional minutes
$$= 3 + 21 = 24 \text{ minutes}$$

5. (D) To find the total surface area of a right circular cylinder, you must not only find the area of the "barrel" portion but also the area of the top and bottom circles. The area of the "barrel" portion equals the circumference of either the top or bottom circle times the height. $C = \pi d \simeq 3 \times 20 = 60$. Thus the area of the "barrel" $= C \times h = 60 \times 100 = 6000$. Now to find *total* surface area, add the areas of both top and bottom circles, or $2 \times \pi r^2 \simeq 2 \times 3 \times 10^2 = 600$. Therefore the total surface area $= 6000 + 600 = 6600$.

6. (C) The area of any square equals one-half the product of its diagonals. Thus, the area of square ABCD = $\frac{1}{2}(2)(2)$ = 2. The area of circle O equals $\pi r^2 \simeq 3 \times 1 = 3$. The shaded area = the area of circle O minus the area of square ABCD, or $3 - 2 = 1$. Notice that to find the area of square EFGH, you may move the radius as follows:

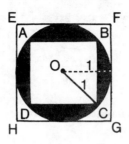

Thus the sides of square EFGH are each 2, so its area is $2 \times 2 = 4$. Therefore the shaded area is approximately 1 out of 4, or 25% of square EFGH. You may also have simply eliminated answer choices (A), (B), (D), and (E) by inspection. Every choice except (C) is ridiculous. Be aware that this type of elimination by inspection is possible only if the diagram is drawn close to scale and if the answer choices are far enough apart to allow approximating.

7. (A) The desired weekly income is $600. $600 − $150 (weekly salary) = $450 (amount to be made up from commission). Let x = number of dollars in sales for one week. Since the salesman earns 15% on all sales, this gives the equation

$$.15x = 450$$

$$x = 450/.15$$

$$x = 3000$$

Therefore the salesman must make sales totaling $3000.

8. (C) City E cast 60% of its 4000 votes (2400) for candidate R. City C cast 55% of its 6000 votes (3300) for candidate R.

9. (C) City B and city E are closer to the 100% point of candidate S than candidate T.

10. (E) Cities A and B cast the same percentage of votes for candidate R but different numbers of votes.

11. **(E)** For city D, 75% of 7000 = 5250. For city A, 50% of 5000 = 2500. For city B, 25% of 4000 = 1000. For city C, 25% of 6000 = 1500. Therefore 5250 plus 2500 plus 1000 plus 1500 equals 10,250.

12. **(B)** Only city D cast *more* than two-thirds for one candidate.

13. **(A)** Note that $(x - y)^2 = x^2 - 2xy + y^2$
$$= \underbrace{x^2 + y^2} - \underbrace{2xy}$$
$$= \quad 14 \quad - \quad 2(3)$$
$$= 14 - 6$$
$$= 8$$

14. **(D)** Let e = amount invested at 8%. 1500 − e = amount invested at 5%. This gives the equation

$$.08e + .05(1500 - e) = 102$$

Multiplying by 100 gives
$$8e + 5(1500 - e) = 10,200$$
$$8e + 7500 - 5e = 10,200$$
$$3e + 7500 = 10,200$$
$$3e = 2700$$
$$e = 900$$

15. **(B)** Notice that in triangle BCE the angle at B equals 94°. Therefore any perpendicular dropped from C to line AB must be less than 3 (see diagram below). Since the area of a parallelogram = base × height, then the area of parallelogram AECD = 8 × (a height less than 3) = an area less than 24.

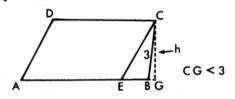

16. **(D)** Multiplying the equation $1/3 + 1/2 + 1/x = 4$ by the common denominator 6x, we get $6x/3 + 6x/2 + 6x/x = 4(6x)$. Reducing, we get

$$2x + 3x + 6 = 24x$$
$$5x + 6 = 24x$$
$$6 = 19x$$
$$6/19 = x$$

17. (D) The most the trip would cost is when gas cost $1.12 and the mileage was 16 mph. Thus $1.12 × (480/16) = $33.60
The least would be $0.96 × (480/24) = $19.20
The difference is thus $14.40.

18. (A) From the bottom graph we see that Make B amounted to about 60% of the total domestic sales in July. Thus, 60% of 1,220,000 is about 732,000.

19. (D) If you thought the answer was June, look again at the graph. The bottom of the graph is cut off, so the domestic portion of the column appears shorter than it really is.

20. (C) From the upper graph, we see that all the columns except one are more than 1,000,000, and all the columns except two are less than 1,200,000. Thus, the average is between 1.0 and 1.2 million. Taking the time to add up all the months' totals and divide by 12 is not a good use of time.

FINAL PREPARATION: "The Final Touches"

1. Make sure that you are familiar with the testing center location and nearby parking facilities.
2. The last week of preparation should be spent primarily on reviewing strategies, techniques, and directions for each area.
3. Don't *cram* the night before the exam. It's a waste of time!
4. Remember to bring the proper materials to the test—identification, admission ticket, three or four sharpened Number 2 pencils, a watch, and a good eraser.
5. Start off crisply, working the ones you know first, and then coming back and trying the others.
6. If you can eliminate one or more of the choices, make an educated guess.
7. Mark in reading passages, underline key words, write out information, make notations on diagrams, take advantage of being permitted to write in the test booklet.
8. Make sure that you are answering "what is being asked" and that your answer is reasonable.
9. Using the SUCCESSFUL OVERALL APPROACH (p. 7) is the key to getting the ones right that you should get right—resulting in a good score on the GMAT.